CONVIVIAL TOOLBOX

GENERATIVE RESEARCH
FOR THE FRONT END OF DESIGN

ELIZABETH B.-N. SANDERS & PIETER JAN STAPPERS

B/S

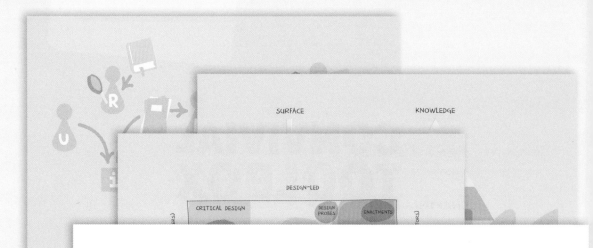

CONTENTS

PREFACE

WHAT PEOPLE NEED

This book is dedicated to the memory of Ivan Illich, the radical Austrian philosopher and critic of the institutions of contemporary Western culture, who so succinctly described, in *Tools for Conviviality*, the most basic and underserved need of people.

People need not only to obtain things, they need above all the freedom to make things among which they can live, to give shape to them according to their own tastes, and to put them to use in caring for and about others (Illich, 1975, page 11).

Illich goes on to introduce a concept that he calls 'convivial tools'. To understand what he means by convivial tools , it is necessary to consider his definition of tools. He uses the word 'tools' to refer to *"all rationally designed devices including hardware, machines, procedures, productive institutions such as factories that produce tangible commodities like corn flakes or electric currents, and productive systems for intangible commodities such as those which produce 'education', 'health', 'knowledge' or 'decisions'"*. Tools are the man-made consequences of design and development processes. Illich defines convivial tools by contrasting them to industrial tools (Illich, 1975, *page 20*).

Convivial tools are those which give each person who uses them the greatest opportunity to enrich the environment with the fruits of his or her vision. Industrial tools deny this possibility to those who use them and they allow their designers to determine the meaning and expectations of others. Most tools today cannot be used in a convivial fashion (Illich, 1975, page 21).

Tools for Conviviality was first published in the United States in 1975 (and in Great Britain in 1973), at a time when Illich's insights and implications for the future fell on deaf ears. And so now almost 40 years later, the situation in industrialized parts of the world is at least as bad as Illich imagined it would be. Our tangible and intangible commodities have been tuned and tweaked over those years with increasingly sophisticated industrial tools that promote efficiency and productivity over happiness and creativity. New technologies for automation have taken time and steps as well as worker pride out of the production processes for goods and services. The consumptive mindset has been passed on from generation to generation, growing stronger and more powerful in each transfer. This is particularly true in the United States. In part, the design profession is to blame. As designers, we have become masters at creating and disseminating what Illich describes as *"useful things for useless people"* (Illich, 1975, page 34). It is time to acknowledge that people want to be useful and creative and not just spend their time shopping, buying and consuming.

In introducing the concept of convivial tools, we are not necessarily talking about people making their own products (i.e., end-use fabrication) although that might be an example. The concept of convivial tools is much broader than that. We can interpret and envision convivial tools at many different levels of abstraction to include, for example:
> end-user fabrication of products
> platforms for the creative expression of individuals
> the means for achieving community goals
> methods, tools and techniques for exploring what conviviality might look like and feel like
> scaffolds for collective creativity

Imagine what we will learn about convivial tools over the next 50 years!

WHAT NEEDS TO HAPPEN?

It is time to balance industrial tools with convivial tools. We need to learn how to balance consumptive behavior and lifestyles with more creative behavior and convivial lifestyles. The situation today is looking positive as there are a number of small points of light at the end of the tunnel.

> There is the growing realization that we can't continue living the way we have been living because we simply don't have the resources. The internet has helped us to see first-hand that the distribution of resources is not at all equally distributed, making the need to conserve all the more important, e.g., www.worldbank.org.

> The recession, difficult as it is for many people, is actually helping us to see more clearly what we really need. And it is helping us to realize how good it feels to give to others.

> There is a resurgence in interest in and emphasis on creativity at all levels: in learning, at work and at play (Pink, 2006; Florida, 2002).

> People have dreams for how they want to live and what is most important in life. And we now are beginning to see that people are choosing experiences over stuff (Pine and Gilmore, 1999).

> New information and communication technologies are connecting people to each other and facilitating collective thinking and doing. Social networks, in particular, bring the promise of facilitating more convivial ways of living.

We need to begin to explore what convivial tools will become. How can we make and use them? How can new technology support conviviality? And how can we evaluate the application of new technologies by new human-centered standards for convivial living? For example, can we measure whether the new technologies support people in their needs to:

> Be and feel creative?
> Make a contribution?
> Give shape to the things among which they can live?
> Put these things to use in caring for and about others?

WHAT IS THE BOOK ABOUT?

This book is about generative design research, an approach to bring the people we serve through design directly into the design process in order to ensure that we can meet their needs and dreams for the future. Generative design research gives people a language with which they can imagine and express their ideas and dreams for future experience. These ideas and dreams can, in turn, inform and inspire other stake-holders in the design and development process.

This book is about a future that provides for and supports the use of convivial tools. Until now, only experts such as designers, engineers and business people have been involved in making industrial tools for people. Such industrial tools include consumer products, computer systems, banking and retail services, etc. But the team of experts approach will not work for the making of convivial tools. Convivial tools must be made with the people, not only for the people who are being served through design. By co-creating with the people served through design, we can ensure that the tools we design are convivial.

AN IMPORTANT DISCLAIMER

There is one thing that we need to make clear from the beginning. The key idea on which the book is based is that all people are creative. By this we mean that all people have ideas and can contribute to design processes that aim to improve their lives as well as the lives of others. It is a key idea but it is also a controversial hypothesis and we are well aware that not everyone believes it to be true.

We will not spend time trying to convince you that everybody is creative. We will show how they can be creative in design. We will take their creativity as a given and describe how you can best involve people in the creative process starting in the front end of design. To the extent that you can already see or can come to believe that all people are creative, you will be able to maximize the potential of generative design thinking.

If you don't already believe that all people are creative, the best way to see this for yourself is to get hands-on learning experience. If you never come to see and believe that all people are creative, you can still use the tools, techniques and methods described here to inspire your own creative process.

WHO IS THE BOOK WRITTEN FOR?

This book is for people who work (or who aim to work) in the front end of the design process to innovate in human-centered ways or to facilitate cultural transformation. It is for people who want to change how we live and work and play for the better. It is for people who seek a better balance of industrial and convivial ways of living. The book is also for people who are trying to understand people in deep ways as might be the situation for applied social scientists.

In thinking about who the book is for, the categories don't follow the traditional academic disciplines. The categories are better described as mindsets. Let us explain. In many years of teaching and sharing the ideas about generative design research, we have seen four distinct mindsets emerge with regard to the key idea that all people are creative and can be involved in the ideation, design and development of new products and services that will affect their futures.

> Intuitives
> Learners
> Skeptics
> Converts

The **intuitives** already know that all people are creative. They don't need to be convinced that co-designing has value. They may, in fact, have been operating all along with a co-designing mindset without knowing there was a name for it. They are excited to find that this worldview is finally being given a formal description, which can help them to share their thinking with others.

Others are **learners**. They will come to understand the hows and whys of co-designing after a number of hands-on experiences. They may, through experience, come to see co-designing as their own mindset or they may choose to only pull out the tools and methods to support to their dominant worldview or to differentiate themselves in the marketplace.

The **skeptics** are those who do not believe that all people are creative. It is likely that they were rigorously trained to think of themselves as the experts in their domain. They are not open to co-designing with the people they consider to be less knowledgeable or less creative than they are. Or they may be those who have witnessed a failure of participatory processes before, such as in an ineffective focus group or a commercial co-creation scam that lead nowhere.

The last category includes the **converts**. These are skeptics who, for one reason or another are put into a learning situation about co-designing, and question it the entire time, only to become extremely strong advocates and sometimes even evangelists at the end. It is impossible to distinguish the convert from the skeptic during the learning experience. The converts are a small group of people who might turn out to play a very important role in the evolution of human-centered innovation.

The distribution of intuitives, learners and skeptics varies greatly between different parts of the world, and across gender and generational lines. For example, you will find more intuitives among young women living in Scandinavia than you will find among American males over the age of 50 (who are more likely to be skeptics).

Would you consider yourself to be an intuitive, a learner or a skeptic? How you use the material presented in this book will probably be different in each case. As an intuitive, you may benefit most from the frameworks that provide some order and guidance to the process. As a learner, you will want to carefully consider both the theory and the practice of generative design research. And even if you consider yourself to be a skeptic, you may find the tools and techniques to be useful. You might find that you are actually a convert once you have the opportunity to learn by doing.

HOW DID WE PLAN FOR THE BOOK TO BE USED?

We have assumed that the primary users of the book will be university **students** at the advanced undergraduate and the graduate levels. And we have planned for the book to be used in a number of different academic departments such as design, psychology, marketing, engineering, business, communications, education, etc. The material that we cover is relevant to any discipline that aims to understand or improve the human condition. The book is particularly well-suited for academic programs that are exploring and offering interdisciplinary and transdisciplinary learning experiences. In that latter respect it may appeal to the **academic researcher in design**, in that it tries to bring together descriptions of state of the art methods, their underlying principles, and relation to practice, which in inter- and transdisciplinary areas is needed to connect the fields involved.

We also see this book as a preliminary text for the **research practitioner** working in industry who is looking to learn about new ways to approach the understanding of people in order to innovate at the front end of the design and development process. It can also be useful for **practicing designers** who find themselves becoming more and more interested in doing the research that can inform and inspire their own design process.

The book contains practical tips that at first sight are relevant for practice, not academic research. But with the increasing interest in and use of qualitative and situated research approaches, seeming 'practicalities' (such as do you conduct a session in the offices of the client, in the university, in a hired place, or in users' homes?) are of importance, and should be included in the discourse.

And lastly, the book can also be used as a source of practical ideas and inspiration for those who are **already experienced** in the principles and practices of co-designing or human-centered innovation. For example, the frameworks for analysis and communication may offer new ways to think about these activities. The tips may come in handy during fieldwork. And the contributions from our colleagues around the world may provide inspiration for new ways of working.

Keep in mind that the book is intended to be a primer, i.e., it presents the most basic elements for understanding and conducting generative design research. It describes how this approach works and how to get started. It is not a recipe book that spells out in detail how to execute well-defined methods and procedures. For that, the state of the art is still developing too quickly, and also the methods cannot be mindlessly executed. The book presents a toolbox of generative research methods, tools and techniques that can be used to inform and inspire futures that will support community and conviviality.

The book is a convivial toolbox. It assumes that the people who will use the toolbox are creative.

HOW IS THE BOOK STRUCTURED AND WHY?
Because the audiences that we are addressing are varied, we have organized the book to offer options in how it is used. There are four main parts.

> *Underlying principles.* The first part introduces the basic components of generative design research and provides a broad theoretical background for support and grounding.

> *Getting a sense of scale.* The second part consists of four cases, ranging from a very small project that was executed by a group of students over a few days to a very large, global project that involves many different team members working together over several months of time. The cases were selected to show the range of applications of generative design research, give a sense of scale and complexity, and illustrate how the many different aspects and stages discussed in part 3 fit together in practice. The two smaller cases describe real projects. The two larger cases are hypothetical cases that have been formed by combining bits and pieces of many different client-sponsored projects that the first author participated in over many years as the project manager in design research firms. Client-sponsored work is generally proprietary so we have taken the hypothetical case approach to introduce you to many different types of experiences that have actually taken place.

> *The mechanism.* The third part is the how-to section that describes how to plan, gather, document, analyze and communicate the data from the generative design research process. There are no explicit recipes for successful generative design research in the how-to chapters because there are many options from which to choose. Instead of recipes, we offer frameworks for the reader to use in considering the most relevant options based on the objectives, time frame, skills, etc. at hand.

> *Samples from the field.* Throughout the book are 50 contributions from a diverse range of people in the field. These provide examples and instantiations of tools, highlight specific aspects of theory or practice, or relate experience and practical tips. They also show how the techniques are used in different places and across disciplines.

Students will probably want to read all the parts in order. Research practitioners may be most interested in reading the cases, followed by the how-to section. Practicing designers will likely want to read all the contributions first to see if this is the way they would like to work in the future. Educators may want to link the principles of the first part to the tips of the later parts to further the fundamental understanding in their students. Experienced co-design researchers may find the frameworks for action that appear throughout the how-to section are the most useful in giving them new ways to expand their repertoire.

ACKNOWLEDGEMENTS

We have been very fortunate to have had interest in and support from people all over the world as we were writing the book. There are over 50 people who wrote either a one page or a two page contribution. This has added tremendously to the diversity of voices to share their experiences with innovation through co-creation with generative design research. The contributions can be found at the ends of the chapters so as not to interrupt the flow of the reading. The people who wrote the contributions are our current or past colleagues, students, clients and co-workers who are now engaged in doing or using generative design research. The list of potential contributors grew as the book was being written and broadened to represent more parts of the world. And although some parts of the world are more advanced in their interest in and acceptance of generative design research, it is clear now that the phenomenon is universal.

The book has benefitted from many co-creators. Six reviewers took the time to read and critique the book in the first draft format over the winter of 2009-2010, and eight more reviewed the second draft over the summer of 2010. Reviewers came from various parts of North America and Europe, from academia and practice, and included design (research) educators and students. Several became contributors when they identified a hole in the draft version of the book that they were able to fill. The reviewers were Kanter van Deursen, Lois Frankel, Marzieh Ghanimifard, Carol Gill, Mercè Graell, Peter Jones, Sanne Kistemaker, Christine de Lille, Samad Khatabi, Susan Melsop, Carolien Postma, Daan Roks, Helma van Rijn, and Froukje Sleeswijk Visser. We are incredibly grateful for their support!

We also want to thank the graphic designers who worked with us: Corrie van der Lelie who came up with several visual solutions in the working drafts, and Karin Langeveld, who gave the final book its clear yet playful form. The dialogue with them helped us improve the content by *making* the final message.

Any remaining errors, of course, are ours.

Contributor

Catey Corl

User Experience Consultant

Nationwide Financial

Columbus, Ohio USA

catey.corl@gmail.com

Catey's contribution was written when
she was working as the Director of
Design Research
SonicRim
Columbus, Ohio USA.

DESIGN STUDENT TO DESIGN RESEARCHER: FROM 'EXPERT' TO 'TRANSLATOR'

A degree in visual communication design left me equally prepared and unprepared for the skills that I would need in my future role as a design researcher, as the diagram below shows. The true challenge came not from acquiring the needed practical research skills, but from the change in perspective that practicing design research required.

In design school, we were taught to be 'experts': to use our creativity to come up with great ideas or turn everyday ideas into something compelling. Shifting to the participatory design mindset meant learning to be the facilitator and translator of ideas rather than the creator.

It was no longer about being the 'expert' and coming up with the ideas, but instead about using creativity to find new ways to help everyday people share their ideas and experiences, and then using design thinking to translate those stories into frameworks that inspire new design directions.

how well did my degree in visual communication design prepare me for a career in design research?

PRACTICAL SKILLS DESIGN SCHOOL **DID** PREPARE ME FOR

PRACTICAL SKILLS DESIGN SCHOOL **DID NOT** PREPARE ME FOR

FLEXIBILITY

willingness to iterate
on ideas

doing whatever it takes
to get things done

CREATIVITY

using design thinking
to solve problems

exploring new research
tools and methods

brainstorming ideas

synthesis, building frameworks

planning fun activities
& workshops

COLLABORATION

working on projects in a team
environment

engaging multiple perspectives
(cross-disciplinary)

thinking & working up on the wall

VISUAL THINKING

storytelling, speaking in examples

speaking in pictures
rather than words

using diagrams to represent
complex ideas & information

PROJECT MANAGEMENT

managing budgets

coordination &
scheduling resources

client & vendor
communication

BUSINESS STRATEGY

understanding current
business practices

making business strategy
recommendations

PRODUCTIVITY SOFTWARE

entering & analyzing data in
Excel or similar

building findings, diagrams, &
presentations in PPT

STRUCTURED, LINEAR THINKING

creating charts & graphs

crafting succinct observations

calculating percentages
& stats

thorough analysis

bullet points!

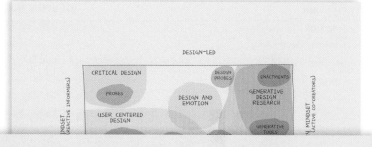

PART1 BASICS

INTRODUCTION TO PART ONE

This book is about generative design research, an approach to bring the people we serve through design directly into the design process in order to ensure that we can meet their needs and dreams for the future. Generative design research gives people a language with which they can imagine and express their ideas and dreams for future experience. These ideas and dreams can, in turn, inform and inspire other stakeholders in the design development process.

Part One introduces the basic components of generative design research and provides a broad theoretical background to ground the discussion. Here we introduce the key idea of the book, i.e., the view that all people are able to bring creative contributions to design processes. We also describe a number of related theories and observations from social and cognitive science because the way generative tools and techniques are structured and conducted is based on an understanding of how people think, feel and act. After the theoretical grounding, we will introduce the basic building blocks of generative design research.

The chapters in Part One can be used as a stand-alone resource. For example, if you want to understand the why behind the tools and techniques of generative design research, these beginning chapters provide a framework for understanding, adapting, and further developing them. On the other hand, if you are looking primarily for how-to information, you may want to skip over Part One initially, and focus on Part Three. But you will want to return to it later since the first three chapters contain explanations underlying the practical information. The explanations in Part One will be called upon regularly in Part Three where we provide information on how to plan and execute generative design research. These explanations will help you to generalize from localized tips to broader applications as you explore further.

CHAPTER 1
INTRODUCTION

OVERVIEW OF CHAPTER ONE

In this first chapter we will describe generative design research by connecting it to theoretical and practical precedents, and situating it in current practice. We will position generative design research with regard to business and marketplace contexts as well as within recent developments/trends in design and design research. We will explain the emergence of the design research landscape, and the place of generative design research tools and techniques within it. We will also describe how the roles of the different stakeholders in the design development process have changed over time. We will conclude Chapter One by describing three perspectives on how co-creation and generative design research can be used.

WHO IS CREATIVE?

Everyone is creative. In fact, people are particularly creative with regard to experiences that they are passionate about such as living, playing, learning and working. But many people do not engage in creative activities in their everyday lives. They see creativity as something that is meant for children, not adults. Or they believe that only certain people such as artists, musicians or designers are capable of being truly creative. Since many adults in our society don't engage in creative activities regularly, they may not see themselves as being creative.

But people today want to be creative and to engage in creative ways of living. This hypothesis comes from the many years the first author has spent with people in their homes, workplaces and schools in her role as a generative design researcher. The single most consistent aspiration that people express for their own futures is the need to be and to feel creative. They communicate this whether they are at home or at school or at work. People want control over how they live, where they live and what kinds of products and services will best support them in doing so. The dream people have to engage in creative ways of living is not only pervasive, it has been gaining ground quickly in the past decade.

WHY ARE PEOPLE EXPRESSING A NEED FOR CREATIVITY NOW?

Why is the need for creativity so consistently expressed today? It is an antidote to consumerism. We have been living in a consumer-driven culture for some time now. Starting in the 1950's, consumerism has grown, leading to conspicuous consumption which has been growing ever since. People are seen as customers and consumers who live in the marketplace. Businesses are interested in people only in so far as they shop, purchase and then own and use the products or services that are designed, produced and sold to them. Design as a profession has traditionally been focused on serving industrial production for the marketplace. So design students have been trained to design stuff such as products and packages and communications that help people to consume goods and services.

Conspicuous consumption has resulted in many nonsustainable products and practices. In fact, many consumers are not even aware of or are confused about the negative environmental impacts of their behavior. Consumerism has also led to a preoccupation in the business sector with innovation at all costs. In fact, even innovation is not enough. It is 'radical innovation' (Verganti, 2009) that companies seek in order to stay ahead of the competition.

Fortunately, a countermovement to this pattern has recently become evident. The recession has made

it abruptly and abundantly clear that continuous conspicuous consumption can no longer be maintained. And at the same time we see that many people are seeking ways to be socially and environmentally responsible. This is true for individuals as well as for large, established corporations.

People will always be consumers of products, services and experiences. But what they need now is a balance between the consumptive activities and the ability to engage in creative activities. They need to be able to choose for themselves when to be consumers and when to be creators. They need opportunities to make better choices, including choices about how to live not only choices about how to spend and consume.

BUSINESS AND DESIGN ARE CHANGING

Manifestations of change can be seen at the intersection of design and business. One of these is the recent interest and enthusiasm in what is called 'design thinking' (Martin, 2009). Design thinking is already of such interest that business schools at universities around the world are attempting to revamp their curricula to meet the needs of business students who do not want to play the 'business as usual' game.

Another major sign of change is the practice of co-creation at all stages of the design development process (Sanders and Simons, 2009). Co-creation can be seen at all points along the process. The applications of the concept range from co-creation at the front end of the design process where the potential for sustainable innovation lies to co-creation at the tail end of the design development process where the potential for brand loyalty lies. We will talk more about the relationship between co-creation and its position in the design process later in this chapter.

Yet another manifestation of change at the intersection of business and design is the rise of creative activity seeking by everyday people. The growth of the

DIY (do-it-yourself) industry and the resurgence of crafting at all levels (e.g., Stewart, 2009 and Sedaris, 2010) is a strong indicator that people are seeking ways to express their creativity. The rise of social networks and other means of online sharing have contributed widely to this phenomenon. www.etsy.com is a good example. The rise of creative activity seeking by everyday people may be a reaction against the overemphasis on consumption over the past 50 years. Or perhaps it is a seeking for the 'convivial tools' that Illich (1975) described over thirty years ago?

The changes in the business marketplace are impacting the disciplines of design and design research. The shifting foundations of the design disciplines are described in the chart below (see Figure#1.1) which shows that we are in the midst of a transformation. Design has been, until recently, primarily concerned with the making of 'stuff'. The traditional fields of design education are characterized by the type of 'stuff' that designers learn to make (e.g., industrial designers make products, architects make buildings, etc.). Prototypes made during the traditional design process represent objects such as possible products, spaces or buildings. The languages that designers learn in school are specialized for the creating of such objects. For example, traditional design embodiments for making stuff include sketches, drawings, prototypes, and models of objects, often in isolation.

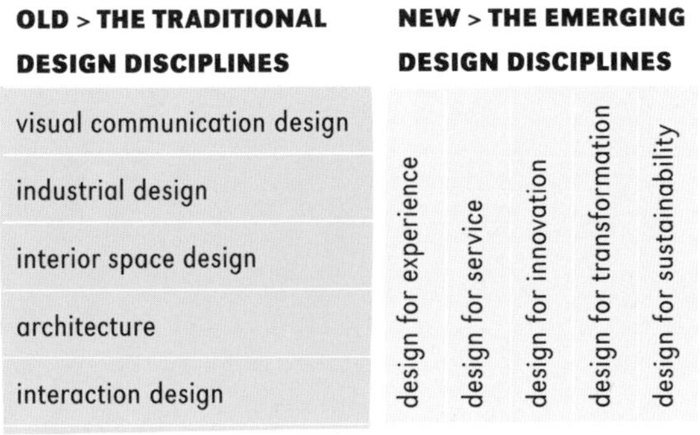

OLD > THE TRADITIONAL DESIGN DISCIPLINES	NEW > THE EMERGING DESIGN DISCIPLINES				
visual communication design	design for experience	design for service	design for innovation	design for transformation	design for sustainability
industrial design					
interior space design					
architecture					
interaction design					

Figure#1.1: The disciplines of design are transforming from a focus on the objects of design (old) to a focus on the purpose of designing (new).

Design practice is now moving from a preoccupation with the making of stuff to a focus on making stuff for people in the context of their lives. The emerging design domains on the right side of the chart are focused on the purpose of designing, e.g., design for the purpose of serving or healing or transforming. Thus, in these new design domains, there is the need for alternative forms of conceptualization and embodiment beyond 'stuff'. Some of the alternative embodiments for describing and enacting experience that are being explored today include stories, future scenarios, narratives, performance art, documentaries and timelines of experience. In addition, personas (hypothetical yet representative people) are frequently used to ensure that people are a focal point in the design process.

The new and emerging design domains are bigger and more ambitious than the traditional disciplines. The emerging design disciplines require the collaboration of people from many different backgrounds, including both designers and nondesigners.

THE LANDSCAPE OF DESIGN RESEARCH

In the past two decades the study of people as users of products, services and environments has grown both in industry and in practice. We will refer to this area of study as 'design research'. In other words, it is research to inform and inspire the design and development process. The emerging landscape of design research approaches and methods is shown in Figure#1.2 as a map.

Why make a map? Making a map is a way to hold a domain still for long enough to be able to see the relationships between the various approaches, methods, and tools. Maps are good for visualizing relationships, finding dense and empty spots, and spotting opportunities. Maps can be useful for showing complexity and change. For example, the underlying landscape of the map may be relatively permanent, changing only as

major forces affect it. But the tools and methods shift and change somewhat like trends. And the people who inhabit the landscape may come and go. As in the real world, some people like to stay put and others like to travel. So maps are good for layering complexity and for revealing change as it occurs.

The map of design research is defined and described by two intersecting dimensions. One is defined by approach and the other is defined by mindset. Approaches to design research have come from a research-led perspective (shown at the bottom of the map) and from a design-led perspective (shown at the top of the map). The research-led perspective has the longest history and has been driven by applied psychologists, anthropologists, sociologists, and engineers. The design-led perspective, on the other hand, has come into view more recently.

There are two opposing mindsets evident in the practice of design research today. The left side of the map describes a culture characterized by an expert mindset. Design researchers here are involved with designing for people. These design researchers consider themselves to be the experts, and they see and refer to people as 'subjects', 'users', 'consumers', etc. The right side of the map describes a culture characterized by a participatory mindset. Design researchers on this side work with people. They see the people as the true experts in domains of experience such as living, learning, working, etc. Design researchers who have a participatory mindset value people as co-creators in the design process and are happy to include people in the design process to the point of sharing control with them. It can be difficult for many people to move from the left to the right side of the map (or vice versa), as this shift entails a significant cultural change.

The largest and most developed of the areas on the map is the user-centered design zone. People in this zone work to help make new product and services better meet the needs of 'users'. They use research-led

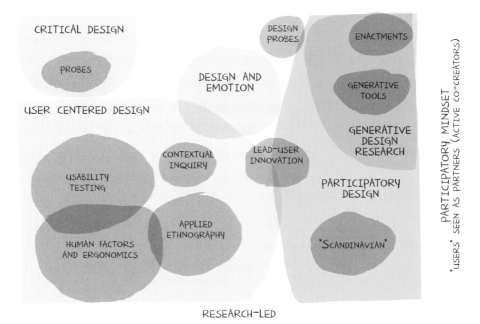
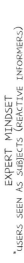

Figure#1.2: The emerging landscape of design research approaches and methods.

approaches with an expert mindset to collect, analyze, and interpret data in order to develop specifications or principles to guide or inform the design develop-ment of product and services. They also apply their tools and methods in the evaluation of concepts and prototypes. The three large areas of activity in the user-centered zone come from the applied social and behavioral sciences and/or from engineering: human factors/ergonomics, applied ethnography, and usability testing. There are also two smaller bubbles within the user-centered territory: contextual inquiry and lead-user innovation. (More information about the map can be found in Sanders, 2006).

The participatory design zone spreads across both the research-led and design-led approaches on the right side of the map. Participatory design is an approach to design that attempts to actively involve the people who are being served through design in the process to help ensure that the designed product/service meets their needs. Participatory design attempts to involve those who will become the 'users' throughout the

design development process to the extent that this is possible. A key characteristic of the participatory design zone is the use of physical artifacts as thinking tools throughout the process, common among the methods emanating from the research-led Scandina-vian tradition.

The design and emotion bubble emerged in 1999 with the first Design and Emotion Conference in Delft, the Netherlands. It represents the coming together of research-led and design-led approaches to design research. Today Design and Emotion is a global phenomenon, with practitioners as well as academics from all over the world contributing to its develop-ment.

The critical design bubble (in the top left corner) is design-led, with the designer playing the role of the expert. The emergence of this bubble came about as a reaction to the large user-centered zone, with its pervasive focus on usability and utility. Critical design evaluates the status quo and relies on design experts to make things that provoke our understanding of the current values people hold. Critical design "makes us think" (Dunne and Raby, 2001). Cultural probes is a methodology in the critical design bubble (Gaver, Dunne and Pacenti, 1999). Probes are ambiguous stimuli that designers send to people who then respond to them, providing insights for the design process. Probes (in their original form) were intended to be a method for providing design inspiration rather than a tool to be used for understanding the experiences of others.

The generative design bubble (in the top right corner) is design-led and fueled by a participatory mindset. Generative design empowers everyday people to generate and promote alternatives to the current situation. The motto of this book, "all people are creative", belongs here. The name 'generative tools' refers to the creation of a shared design language that designers/researchers and other stakeholders use to communicate visually and directly with each other. The design language is generative in the sense that with it, people can express an infinite number of ideas through a limited set of stimulus items. Thus, the generative tools approach is a way to explore ideas, dreams, and insights of the people who will be served through design. Both critical design and generative design aim to generate and promote alternatives to the current situation. But they operate from opposing mindsets. Many of the new tools and methods that have emerged in the last five years are design-led and sit along the top of the map, spanning the range from the critical design bubble to the generative design research bubble. Some examples include design probes (e.g., Mattelmäki, 2006) and various forms of enactment (e.g., Burns et al., 1995; Buchenau and Fulton Suri, 2000; Ouslasvirta et al., 2003; Simsarian, 2003; Diaz et al., 2009).

Why are the emerging design disciplines shown in Figure#1.1 not included on this map? For example, why are design for service, design for experience and design for sustainability not included as zones on the design research map? It is best to think of the emerging design disciplines as journeys that are taken across the map since they will rely on more than one location on the map. The emerging design disciplines are focused on purpose as opposed to approach or method, and so they can be addressed with either the expert or the participatory mindset. For example, the emerging discipline that is called 'service design' has adopted many of the tools, techniques and methods from participatory design and from generative design research. Time will tell as to whether service designers are practicing with a participatory mindset or whether they are using the tools and methods with an expert mindset.

POSITIONING THIS BOOK ON THE DESIGN RESEARCH MAP

In this book we will be focused on the upper right corner of the design research landscape, i.e., the generative design research territory, where the design-led approach and the participatory mindset intersect at their most extreme positions as shown in Figure#1.3. We will describe the contexts and conditions for which generative design research is most useful and relevant. We will give many examples, some from our own work and some from contributors, to make the learning experience more concrete.

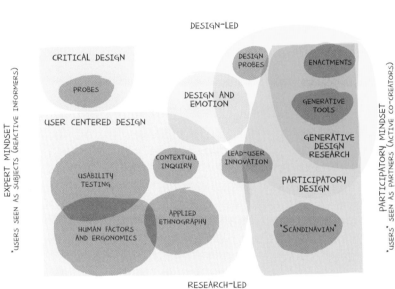

Figure#1.3: The yellow zone shows where the book is focused on the landscape of design research and practice.

We will describe the generative design research territory in relation to the other parts of the design research map but we will not describe the whole map. For that exercise we would need to write another book. We will not cover the user-centered design territory but we will talk about how preliminary exploration with traditional user-centered design methods and tools is highly recommended as a precursor to the creation and development of generative toolkits. And we will talk about how generative design research can be used to identify relevant ideas and opportunities to be further investigated and evaluated with user-centered design thinking, tools and methods.

We will not cover the entire participatory design territory in detail but we will talk about how generative design thinking and the Scandinavian approach to participatory design research are now learning from and being inspired by one another. We will not cover the design and emotion territory but we will talk about how generative tools can be used to extend the vocabulary of the people (e.g., researchers, designers and everyday people) who focus their efforts in that territory.

THE DESIGN PROCESS IS CHANGING

The shape of the design development process has changed in response to the shifting foundations in the design research landscape. A very large front end has been growing and gaining in importance over the last ten years, as is shown in Figure#1.4.

FUZZY FRONT END   GAP   TRADITIONAL DESIGN DEVELOPMENT PROCESS

Figure#1.4: The shape of the design development process has changed in response to the shifting foundations in the design research landscape.

The large front end is often referred to as the 'fuzzy front end' because of its messy and chaotic nature. It is made up of the many activities that take place in order to inform and inspire the exploration of open-ended questions and to determine what are the most relevant problems to be solved. In the fuzzy front end, there is no clear path on how to proceed and there may be many divergent paths to explore before any patterns can be discerned. In the fuzzy front end it is often not known whether the deliverable of the design process will be a product, a service, an interface, or something else. The goal of this exploration is to define the fundamental problems and opportunities and to determine what could be (or should not be) designed.

Another change in the design process is that designers are being increasingly called upon to join, and sometimes to lead, teams that are tasked with very large challenges. The types of challenges that designers are facing today are often referred to as 'wicked problems'. *"Wicked problem are difficult or impossible to solve because of incomplete, contradictory, and changing requirements that are often difficult to recognize. Moreover, because of complex interdependencies, the effort to solve one aspect of a wicked problem may reveal or create other problems"* (Rittel and Webber, 1973).

Design is not just about visualization and the application of individual creativity anymore. The problems that designers are being invited to help identify and to solve cannot be addressed by individuals, no matter how smart or creative they are. The situation is far too complex. We face significant challenges in that the problems we face are wicked and the new landscapes of design are fuzzy. But we can address the challenges of wicked problems and fuzzy pathways through collective forms of creativity and generative design thinking.

Who are the real experts when we talk about designing and innovating for future experience? We will argue that it is the people we are attempting to serve through the design process. With this shift in mindset, we can invite future 'users' into the front end of the design process and move toward designing with them, not just for them. A participatory mindset can break down the disciplinary and/or cultural boundaries. Add to that the tools that can put everyone on the same playing field and support a shared language, and you have a design space that supports the exploration of new ideas, even in wicked problem situations.

PEOPLE'S ROLES IN THE DESIGN PROCESS ARE CHANGING

The move from the traditional user-centered design process to a design process based on collective creativity (i.e., a co-design process) is having an impact on the roles of the players in the design process. Let's consider, for example, the roles of the user, the researcher and the designer.

Let's start with a warning, though: there are no satisfactory definitions of these terms. Although we think we have a clear image about who we refer to with a word such as 'user', the literature refers to this person as 'user', 'consumer', 'customer', 'insider', 'participant', 'co-creator', 'beneficiary', 'human', 'person', and sometimes 'victim'. Each word carries its nuances, is the standard term used by some disciplines, and has been criticized by others. The same holds for the roles of 'researcher' and 'designer'. We don't think that looking for the definitive term will help us much; but it helps to be alert for hidden assumptions in these words.

THE ROLE OF THE USER: EXPERT OF HIS/HER EXPERIENCES

In a caricature of the traditional user-centered design process (see Figure#1.5), the user is a passive object of study, and the researcher brings knowledge from theories and develops more knowledge through observation and interviews. The designer then passively receives this knowledge in the form of a report and adds an understanding of technology and the creative thinking needed to generate ideas, concepts, etc.

In a co-design process, on the other hand, the roles change: the person who will eventually be served through the design process is given the position of

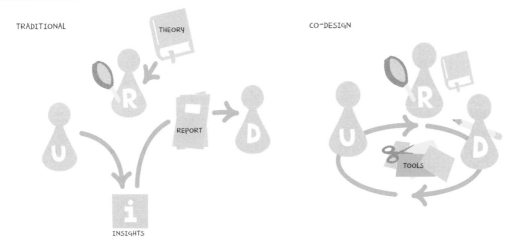

Figure#1.5: The roles of the researcher, designer and user change in the transition from the traditional design process to the co-design process.

'experts of their experience', and plays a large role in knowledge development, idea generation and concept development. In generating insights, the researcher supports the 'expert of his/her experience' by providing tools for ideation and expression. The designer and the researcher collaborate on the tools for ideation because design skills are very important in the development of the tools. (The designer and researcher may, in fact, be the same person). The designer continues to play a critical role in giving form to the ideas. (More on the changing roles of the key players in the co-design process is discussed in Sleeswijk Visser et al., 2005).

Users can become part of the design team as 'expert of their experiences' (Sleeswijk Visser et al., 2005), but in order for them to take on this role, they must be given appropriate tools for expressing themselves. Over the past decade, research groups within a number of academic institutions, practitioners in design research consultancies and design research groups within industrial institutes, have all explored co- designing tools and techniques and the processes by which they can be applied. The interest in tools and techniques for co-designing has been growing rapidly.

THE ROLE OF THE RESEARCHER: FROM TRANSLATOR TO FACILITATOR
In the traditional design process, the researcher served as a translator between the "users" and the designer. In co-designing, the researcher (who may be a designer) takes on the role of a facilitator. When we acknowledge that different levels of everyday creativity exist (as will be discussed in the Chapter 2), it becomes evident that we need to learn how to offer relevant experiences to facilitate people's expressions of creativity at all levels. In addition to bringing people into the design process in the ways most conducive to their ability to participate, researchers will need to bring in applicable domain theories in ways that can be addressed by the co-design team. For example, the social psychologist who becomes a design researcher doesn't just bring interviewing skills etc., but can also bring in background knowledge and theories about social interactions, indicating patterns and factors which can guide and/or inspire the design (e.g., Postma & Stappers, 2006).

THE ROLE OF THE PROFESSIONAL DESIGNER
What role is there for professional designers to play if future users are co-creating tangible visions of new products and/or services? Some people worry that the role of the designer will become obsolete in the near future. On the contrary, design skills will become even more important in the future as the new landscapes of design emerge. A user can never fully replace a designer as designers are trained and experienced in designing. This requires specific skills. The complete process can never be outsourced.

Designers will be in demand as the usefulness of design thinking is acknowledged in our drive to address the challenges of solving wicked problems and exploring fuzzy opportunities. Designers will be needed because they hold highly developed skills that are relevant at larger levels of scope and complexity. By selection and training, most designers are good at visual thinking, conducting creative processes, finding missing information, and being able to make necessary decisions in the absence of complete information. Designers are expert prototypers and natural facilitators of collective prototyping activities.

Designers will need to play a role on co-designing teams because they provide expert knowledge that the other stakeholders don't have. Designers professionally keep track of existing, new and emerging technologies, have an overview of production processes and business contexts. This knowledge will still be relevant throughout the design development process. Even in the design profession there is considerable specialization. The skills, knowledge and methods of the interior designer, the interaction designer, the graphic designer, etc. are quite different. These professions will not disappear overnight as 'users' become co-designers (Buxton, 2007). Expertise within a problem area will remain important even as new design practices emerge.

Designers will be integral to the creation and exploration of new tools and methods for generative design thinking. The onus is on designers to explore the potential of generative tools and to bring the languages of co-designing into their practice. Designers in the future will make the tools for non-designers to use to express themselves creatively.

COLLECTIVE CREATIVITY AND CO-CREATION

In review, we have described how the design process is changing, particularly in the front end where the challenges of solving wicked problems and exploring fuzzy opportunities are growing, making the necessity of collective creativity more and more important. We have also discussed how people's roles in the design process are changing, with the people formerly known as 'end-users' becoming acknowledged as co-creators and participants in the process because they are being recognized as the experts of their own experience.

Before moving ahead, we will define how we are using the words co-creation and co-design because you will see that the usage of these terms varies widely. We take co-creation to refer to any act of collective creativity, e.g., creativity that is shared by two or more people. Co-creation is a very broad term with applications ranging from the physical to the metaphysical and from the material to the spiritual, as can be seen by the output of search engines. By co-design we indicate collective creativity as it is applied across the whole span of a design development process. Thus, co-design is a specific instance of co-creation.

Co-design refers, for some people, to the collective creativity of collaborating designers. However, we use co-design in a broader sense to refer to the creativity of designers and people not trained in design working together in the design development process. Generative design research is an approach for co-designing and co-creating that is focused on the front end of the design development process.

HOW AND WHERE IS CO-CREATION TAKING PLACE?

The word 'co-creation' has been adopted across many different situations and it is often used in different ways, leading to a lack of clarity over what co-creation really is. For example, we can see:

> co-creation within communities
> co-creation inside companies and organizations, often referred to as 'internal co-creation'
> co-creation between companies and their business partners or other companies
> co-creation between companies and the people they serve, who are variously called customers, consumers, users or end-users

It is important to clarify up front where co-creation is taking place in order to avoid confusion in discussions about what works and what does not work.

The business community is talking a lot these days about 'co-creation' and the discussion here is usually framed by the 'value' that accrues from co-creation. It is the monetary value of co-creation that usually receives the most attention in business circles. But there are at least three types of value in co-creative activities and relationships: monetary, use/experience and societal. Co-creation that results in monetary value is fueled by the desire to make money in new ways, more efficient ways, or in ways that provide revenues over longer periods of time. Co-creation associated with monetary value may not require direct face-to-face contact between the company and its customers, for example, because the conversation can be mediated by new tools of information and communication. This can be seen in web-based surveys that ask consumers to select features of choice or the crowd-sourcing of large numbers of respondents to obtain ideas for new products or services.

The use/experience value of co-creation is fueled by companies' desires to transform consumers into users and so that the products and services they design, produce and sell will better meet people's wants and needs. One could argue that this is directly related to monetary value, but in this case the value extends beyond that of a mere monetary gain. The experience value of co-creation applies not only to products and services, but also to brands and branded environments.

The societal value of co-creation is fueled by aspirations for longer-term and more sustainable ways of living. It supports the exploration of open-ended questions such as "how can we improve the quality of life for people living with a chronic illness?" When working within this context one does not generally have pre-conceived notions of the outcome since determination of the form of the outcome is part of the challenge. Thus, the problem is likely to be a wicked one. Co-creation of this type usually involves the integration of experts and everyday people working closely together. Empathy between the co-creators is essential and so face-to-face communication works best. Although social networks can be used to help identify and locate the participants, the real work in this form of co-creation favors face-to-face interactions.

All three types of value in co-creation are important to understand and to develop, and are at times inextricably linked. In fact, they can work together. Societal value can provide use/experience value as well as financial reward in the long run.

In addition to the various purposes toward which co-creation can be applied, co-creation can also take place at any stage of the design development process. (See Figure#1.6). A quick tour of Google hits to the phrase 'where is co-creation?' reveals applications of co-creation at every stage of the design process as well as many applications of the concept in the spiritual realms.

The stages of the design development process include:
> pre-design: where research, problem definition and the highest opportunity for innovation takes place
> discovery: where opportunity identification and translation of the research to design occurs
> design: where continued exploration, design, and development take place
> making: where production, building and/or manufacturing take place
> marketing, sales and/or distribution: where implementation, roll-out and sales occur
> after sales: where product use and service experience happen

PRE–DESIGN   DISCOVER   DESIGN   MAKE   MARKET + SELL   AFTER SALES

Figure#1.6: Co-creation (shown by the orange dots) can take place at any point along the design development process.

An interesting pattern emerges when the types of value co-creation (i.e., monetary, use/experience, societal) are aligned with the different stages of the design process. Value co-creation with a focus on monetary objectives is more likely to take place later in the design development process, such as in marketing, sales and distribution. Value co-creation of the use/experience variety tends to take place during design. And societal value co-creation is most likely to occur in the very early front end of the design process, in pre-design and discovery as shown in Figure#1.7.

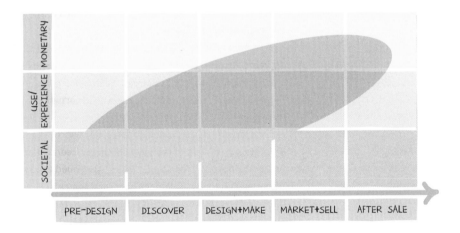

Figure#1.7: There is a relationship between the level of value in co-creation and the position along the design development process.

In fact, the earlier in the design development process that co-creation occurs, the greater and broader the likely impact. Societal value co-creation tends to start at the very early front end. Practicing co-creation in the fuzzy front end will most likely produce the largest benefit in terms of societal value. Although use/experience value and monetary value may follow, it may not become apparent until later on.

Again, in order to avoid confusion, it is important to clarify at the beginnings of conversations about co-creation for what purpose co-creation is being used and where in the design development process this is happening. So to clarify, the focus of this book is on the use/experience and societal levels of value in co-creation as practiced toward the front end of the design development process.

RELATED APPROACHES IN CO-CREATIVE DESIGN

Co-creative approaches to solving complex problems and identifying future opportunities are not without precedents, and did not emerge from any single direction. In fact, a number of related approaches are being practiced today. In this section we introduce some of these to show how similar approaches are being used by design academics, in design practice, in international development, and the social sciences.

PARTICIPATORY DESIGN

The practice of collective creativity in design has been around for nearly 40 years, going under the name 'participatory design'. Much of the activity in participatory design has been going on in Europe. Research projects on user participation in systems development date back to the 1970s. In Norway, Sweden and Denmark, the Collective Resource Approach was established to increase the value of industrial production by engaging workers in the development of new systems for the workplace. The approach combines the expertise of the systems designers/researchers and the situated expertise of the people whose work is to be impacted by the change. The approach, thus, built on the workers' own experiences and provided them with the resources to be able to act in their current situation (Bødker, 1996).

Participatory design practices have developed significantly since the early pioneering work. Participatory design today spans a wide spectrum of domains and makes use of a broad repertoire of methods, tools and techniques in both commercial, community oriented and research contexts.

POSITIVE DEVIANCE AND LEAD USER DESIGN

Both in movements for social change as well as in design, approaches have arisen that build on the principle that among the multitude of end-users, there are some who are more capable than others of using their first-hand knowledge for creating solutions. The task of the 'designer' in these approaches is to channel the contributions of these participants into the larger process. Positive Deviance started in nutrition, health and emancipation work in the 1970s (Pascale, Sternin, and Sternin, 2010). The lead user approach has been developed and advocated by von Hippel (2005) and has been applied successfully in software design and other technical domains.

ACTION RESEARCH

From the side of the social sciences, the paradigm of Action Research has been growing since the 1940s (Susman and Evered, 1978). As the name implies, it is framed within research, and involves researchers and practitioners actively exploring possible improvements to the practitioners' situation together. A key element of the approach is an iterative sequence of interventions in work practice, and learning from this by critical reflection (Avison et al., 1999). The interventions serve two purposes simultaneously: to improve the work situation, and to understand that situation better (Gilmore et al., 1986). Action Research provides a theoretical basis for the research methodology of much academic work in this area, which is stepping outside the laboratories into practice, and benefits from its participatory and holistic viewpoints.

CONTEXTMAPPING

Contextmapping started in design education in the early 2000s to bring recent developments in understanding the contexts of user-product interaction into mainstream design education. It is a procedure for conducting contextual research with users, where tacit knowledge is gained about the context of use of products (Sleeswijk Visser et al., 2005). It aims to inform and inspire design teams, where users and

stakeholders actively participate in the design process to ensure a good fit between the design and the use of a future product or service. The name 'contextmapping' illustrates two main elements about the information or understanding that the design team needs: the *context* of product use, defined as 'all factors which influence the interaction between user and product'. Generative tools, as described in this book, are used for gathering user insights The word 'mapping' was chosen to indicate the form of this information: a tool to help access the terrain of experience, which can take many forms depending on the needs of the traveler for whom the map is made (Stappers & Sleeswijk Visser, 2006). This emphasis on communication was based on the situation in large companies and design agencies, where the design team often does not meet the participating users, but needs to be informed through techniques such as personas, scenarios, and documentaries.

RAPID AND PARTICIPATORY RURAL APPRAISAL

In the area of international development, it has been seen that improvements in the life conditions of rural populations could not be imported by benevolent outsiders, but needed active involvement of the rural insiders (Chambers, 1994). Similar to participatory design, the approaches here focus on the emancipation of the role of the end-users, and a shift from informing 'outsiders' (i.e., designers) to giving control to 'insiders' (i.e., end-users).

EXPERIENCE DESIGN AND SERVICE DESIGN

The last few years have shown a number of new design approaches that look beyond the product as a physical thing. In experience design, the focus lies on creating meaning or affect in the user, as opposed to creating a physical artifact that fulfills a functional purpose. In service design, the emphasis is on creating complex systems that create value for people through both material and organizational means. In these emerging approaches, longer-term interactions between providers and customers are taken into account, and a thorough focus on the user, and methods of co-creation are widely advocated.

The list of related approaches described in this section shows two things. First, that co-creative approaches have come up from many areas in science and design, and that the same ideas have emerged from seemingly different domains. Second, that these approaches have until now developed quite separately within the fields involved. Typically, the publications about one of the fields make little or no reference to the others, and the jargon in which the subject matter is described is also different. But in each of the areas, there is a recognition that people such as 'end-users' hold expertise about their needs and dreams and that their contributions are essential for finding and implementing solutions to problems. There is also a recognition of the need for appropriate, and often new, methods for facilitating them in this process.

Clearly, with the dialogue between these methods coming out in the open (also through the findability of all the above terms in Wikipedia, for instance), we can expect this field of co-creative design to mature rapidly in the coming years.

CO-CREATION: IS IT A MINDSET, METHOD OR TOOL?
As we have discussed, the word 'co-creation' is being used today to describe an incredibly wide array of activities with many different goals. In fact, there appears to be somewhat of a gold rush in regard to applications of co-creation as can be seen in the increasing interest in it in the popular press. Is co-creation a new way to differentiate your company in the marketplace? Is it yet another method with an interesting collection of tools that can be called upon in the design process? Or is co-creation much larger than that? Is it a mindset (established set of attitudes held by someone), or a worldview (a philosophy of life or conception of the world) that changes how the entire design development process is seen and takes place? Co-creation can be any one or all three of these

perspectives, depending on how you view it and use it.

Co-creation as a mindset. This is the broadest and most long-range of the three perspectives and the one that has the most potential to have a positive impact on the lives of people. Co-creation practiced from a mindset perspective is best executed by either very experienced generative design research practitioners or by young, intuitive practitioners. It is most useful and effective toward the front end of the design development process.

Co-creation as a method. Here we see co-creation as a collection of tools and techniques that are often compared to other collections of methods (e.g., contextual inquiry or ethnographic fieldwork). The choice of methods may depend upon who is leading the project, what the budget and timing are, and other constraints. We see co-creation as a method being used mainly during the design exploration and design phases.

Co-creation as a tool or technique. This perspective describes the use of co-creation as just another option in the toolbox of all tools and techniques that can be used in the processes of design, development, marketing and/or distribution. For example, you often see participatory design listed on resumes of design researchers in a context similar to the one shown below.
*"My design research skills include: usability tests, personas, concept tests, task analysis, diary studies, contextual inquiry, **participatory design**, paper prototype evaluation, focus groups, cognitive walkthroughs, card sorting, eye-tracking, remote usability and surveys, ethnographic field studies and phone interviews."*

It is apparent from the context that the author of this list understands co-creation/participatory design to be a tool or technique that can be applied in specific situations. They are not viewing it as a mindset. Co-creation as a tool or technique is the perspective that has received the most attention in the popular press tp date as it is being used as a fast and low-cost way to drive interest in and attention to brands and/or new products and services in the marketplace.

Figure#1.8 shows the relationship between the three perspectives on co-creation and the point in the design development process at which the perspective is most useful.

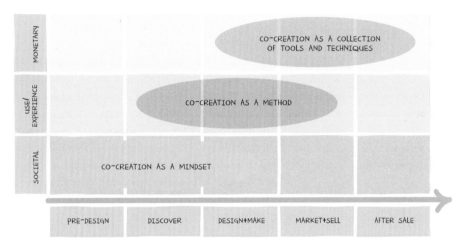

Figure#1.8: The three perspectives on co-creation are positioned by level of value co-creation and the place along the design development process.

Co-creation as a mindset is most useful in the front end. Co-creation as a method is useful in the design-focused phases of the process. Co-creation as a tool or technique is most useful at the tail end of the process. This is not to say that the three perspectives must be used only at those parts of the process, but that these are very good starting points.

WHERE THIS BOOK IS FOCUSED

In summary, because co-creation is such a broadly used term, it can be confusing when people use the word 'co-creation' from different perspectives. It is important to be clear up front about:

> who is involved in the co-creation (e.g., communities, companies, organizations, partners, people, etc.)?
> what perspective is leading the effort (e.g., co-creation as a mindset, method, tool or technique)?
> what is the value (e.g., monetary, use/experience, societal) that is of interest in co-creation?
> where in the design development process (e.g., front, middle or end) will the effort be taking place?
> how are the responsibilities distributed across all the players? For example, who can give suggestions, make interpretations, come up with ideas, etc.?

The focus in this book will be toward the front end of the design development process (to include pre-design, design exploration and design), with the co-creation as a mindset perspective and with an interest in all levels of value co-creation. The cases and contributions will describe a variety of examples showing:

> co-creation within communities
> co-creation inside companies and organizations
> co-creation between companies and their business partners
> co-creation between companies and the people they serve, who are variously called customers, consumers, users or end-users

In the next chapters we present some fundamental psychological mechanisms underpinning creativity in general, and co-creation in particular. In the chapter after that, we show how these mechanisms find their form in generative tools and techniques.

Contributor

Marlene Ivey

Associate Professor

NSCAD University

Halifax, Nova Scotia

Canada

mivey@nscad.ca

Marlene's title and organization at time of writing
the contribution was Senior Lecturer at Duncan
of Jordanstone College of Art & Design at the
University of Dundee in Scotland, UK.

References and source of photos

Ivey, M. & Sanders, E.B.-N. (2006) Designing
a Physical Environment for Co-experience and
Assessing Participant Use. *Wonderground,
Design Research Society International Conference
Proceedings 2006,* 1-4 November 2006 CEIADE
Portugal.

Ivey, M., Sanders, E.B.-N. et al., (2007) Giving Voice
to Equitable Collaboration in Participatory Design
Research. *Design, Discourse & Disaster, 7th
European Academy of Design Conference 2007,
11 - 13 April 2007* Turkey: Izmir University.

EQUITABLE COLLABORATION IN PARTICIPATORY DESIGN RESEARCH

Equitable collaboration is one of the three conditions required for participatory action research*. Participant involvement is conventionally embedded in the research as data, analysis or findings and participant contribution is anonymously acknowledged. However, the consequences for generative approaches to design research can be quite positive if the research aims to include participants with shared expertise and allows the research to evolve as an activity of equitable collaboration. The constituents of a relationship with integrity include consideration for the individual balanced with group dynamics, time/space for play, ownership, reflection, opportunity, empathy and meaningful acknowledgement. Engaging users as participants in developing design vision has been a distinctive characteristic of what has been described as the co-design era. Beyond, design research is open to recursive action where participants may evolve as research partners. Clarity contributes to integrity and borders on the ethical dimension. Not only do we need to be clear with our participants with regard to what we may publish, we need also to be clear about how we share intellectual property.

* Action research is a reflective process of progressive problem solving led by individuals working with others in teams or as part of a "community of practice" to improve the way they address issues and solve problems. www.wikipedia.com

COMBINING APPROACHES IN DESIGN RESEARCH

Approaches to design research relate and have points of convergence, evident in the makeup of interdisciplinary teams, and across the various phases of a typical design project.

Design research is an inherently creative activity, and should therefore be flexible, allowing appropriateness to be the determining factor in selecting best methods for information collection, guiding inspiration, and the testing of ideas. There will be points of convergence and relationship with the methods that are selected or created, both as a function of the makeup of interdisciplinary teams, and across the phases of a typical project.

In design research conducted with interdisciplinary teams, the multiple perspectives of team members merge to foster a complete understanding of users and context, ideally in a mutually informing way. This bears some resemblance to triangulation, or the use of multiple methods to challenge or verify information from one source alone. The quantitative approach of the social scientist may indeed be complementary to the qualitative approach promoted by the ethnographer, and both may have a positive influence on infusing appropriate levels of rigor and objectivity into the empathic approach of the designer in a participatory session.

Contributor

Bruce M. Hanington

Associate Professor and Program Chair in Industrial Design

Carnegie Mellon University

School of Design, MMCH 110

Pittsburgh, PA

15213-3890

hanington@cmu.edu

Approaches will also combine or relate across the phases of a design research project. Certainly design ethnography, contextual inquiry, and cultural probes may serve well as exploratory tools to inform the construction of generative kits for participatory research sessions, which may be used to uncover issues of emotion and design, and inform the development of products later destined to be tested for usability and human factors fit. In the efforts of design research to foster innovative products responsive to human needs and desires it is critical not to be rigidly bound by a particular approach in isolation, nor to an inventory of methods artificially constrained to a specific phase or purpose by traditional thinking.

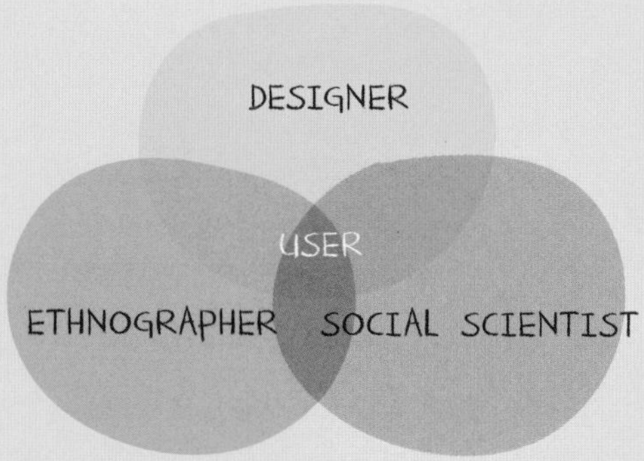

DESIGNER

USER

ETHNOGRAPHER   SOCIAL SCIENTIST

A complete understanding of users and contexts results from converging perspectives of multiple team members, for example, ethnography, social science and design.

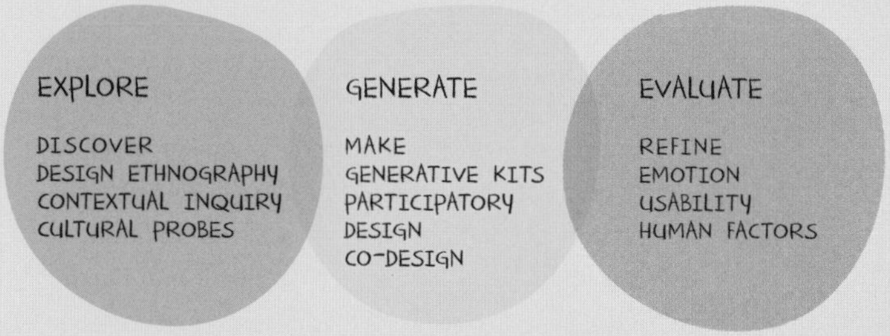

EXPLORE

DISCOVER
DESIGN ETHNOGRAPHY
CONTEXTUAL INQUIRY
CULTURAL PROBES

GENERATE

MAKE
GENERATIVE KITS
PARTICIPATORY
DESIGN
CO-DESIGN

EVALUATE

REFINE
EMOTION
USABILITY
HUMAN FACTORS

Approaches relate across phases of design research. Exploratory tools inform the construction of generative kits, which in turn present issues for design evaluation.

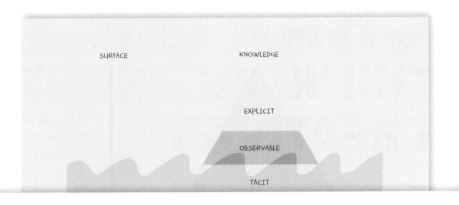

SURFACE   KNOWLEDGE

EXPLICIT

OBSERVABLE

TACIT

OVERVIEW OF CHAPTER TWO

OVERVIEW OF CHAPTER TWO

In the second chapter we will describe what you need to know about creativity to understand how generative design research works. It is possible to practice generative design research without having this level of understanding, but without it you will not be able to grow in your abilities as a generative design researcher. So if you choose not to read this chapter now, you will want to return to it after you have had one or two hands-on experiences.

You can think of this chapter as the grounding for Chapter Three (How it Works: Generative Tools and Techniques) as well as for Part Three of the book. The models, theories and principles that we present in Chapter Three apply to all parts of the generative design research process including what happens in planning the fieldwork, during generative sessions or interviews, in the analysis sessions, and during communication events.

We will start by describing what we mean when we talk about everyday creativity. We will discuss what creativity is all about, starting with the traditional perspective that creativity is something that happens "in the head." Then we will introduce larger and larger perspectives on creativity as the chapter progresses. We will end with a model of collective creativity that describes how people are creative together.

CHAPTER 2
THINKING ABOUT CREATIVITY

WHAT IS CREATIVITY?

There is no generally accepted definition of creativity. In fact, the definition of creativity has been debated for years. There are many theories
about what creativity is, how it works and who does or does not have it.
But there is not a lot of agreement. A quite general definition in the area
of problem solving is that an idea is regarded as creative if it is both new
and an appropriate solution to the problem. But design is not only about
problem solving. The Wikipedia entry on 'creativity' (viewed January
2011) gives a good overview of this lack of clarity.

On the other hand, there is agreement on the fact that creativity is being
increasingly recognized and discussed. A few of the books that have
really helped spark interest in the rise of creativity include:

> Richard Florida's (2002) book: *The Rise of the Creative Class: And
> How It's Transforming Work, Leisure and Everyday Life*. Florida uses
> economic data to show that regions with high concentrations of
> creative professionals tend have high levels of economic develop-
> ment. He then goes on to describe what can be done to attract the
> Creative Class.

> Daniel Pink's (2005) book: *A Whole New Mind: Why Right Brain-
> ers will Rule the World*. Pink describes the six "senses" that one
> should harvest to build a balanced mind: design, story, symphony,
> empathy, play and meaning.

> Roger Martin's (2009) book: *The Design of Business: Why Design Thinking is the Next Competitive Advantage.* Martin describes why organizations need to embrace design thinking in order to balance their overreliance on analytical thinking.

We will center our discussion with a much older but still much sited theory about creativity. According to Arthur Koestler (1964), every creative act involves bisociation, a process that brings together and combines previously unrelated ideas. Koestler's definition of creativity is broad enough to cover all types of creative acts, whether in art, science or humor. In *The Act of Creation* (1964) he writes: *"The logical pattern of the creative process is the same in all three cases; it consists in the discovery of hidden similarities. But the emotional climate is different in the three panels: the comic simile has a touch of aggressiveness; the scientist's reasoning by analogy is emotionally detached, i.e., neutral; the poetic image is sympathetic or admiring, inspired by a positive kind of emotion."*

EVERYDAY CREATIVITY

Many people think of creativity as a manifestation of genius that is possessed by rare individuals and often in the arts or the sciences. Within design, and especially in problem solving, creativity is often defined as the ability to produce novel and appropriate works (Sternberg and Lubart, 1995). But there are other types of creativity.

Margaret Boden (1990) makes a distinction between H-creative and P-creativity. H-Creative refers to historically creative. For example this would be someone who came up with an idea, concept or product that no one has ever thought of before. P-creative is Psychologically Creative, where someone borrows an idea from one domain and applies it to another. This type of creativity is not so unique, and it applies to everyone. Boden claims that people who have had creative ideas in the past are more likely to have them in the future and people who have new ideas frequently will continue to do so.

We will refer to P-creativity as 'everyday creativity'. A framework for everyday creativity has been developed based on many years of experience in observing and talking with people about their needs and dreams for living (Sanders, 2005). For everyday creative activities we can distinguish four levels, as shown in Figure#2.1.

LEVEL	MOTIVATED BY	PURPOSE	EXAMPLE
1 doing	productivity	"getting something done"	organizing my herbs and spices
2 adapting	appropriation	"making things my own" or "make it fit better"	embellishing a ready-made meal
3 making	asserting my ability or skill	"make with my own hands"	cooking with a recipe
4 creating	curiosity	"express my ability"	dreaming up a new dish

Figure#2.1: Four levels of everyday creativity are observed when talking with people about their needs and dreams for living.

The most basic level of creativity is **doing**. The motivation behind doing is to accomplish something through productive activity. For example, people have told us that they feel creative when they are productively engaged in everyday activities such as exercising or organizing their closets. Doing requires a minimal amount of interest. The skill requirements are low as well. Many of the goods and services offered to 'consumers' today can be said to satisfy the doing level of creativity. They come to the consumer readymade. For example, in the food preparation domain, a doing activity would be to buy or select a prepackaged microwave entrée and prepare it for a meal. Another cooking related example could be organizing one's herbs and spices.

The next level of creativity, **adapting**, is more advanced. The motivation behind adapting is to make something one's own by changing it in some way. People might do this to personalize an object so that it better fits their personality. Or they might adapt a product so that it better fits their functional needs. We can see adaptive creativity emerging whenever products, services, or environments don't exactly fit people's needs. Adapting requires more interest and a higher skill level than doing. It takes some confidence to go 'outside of the box.' Following our example in food preparation, an adapting activity might be to add an extra ingredient to a cake mix to make it special.

The third level of creativity is **making**. The motivation behind making is to use one's hands and mind to make or build something that did not exist before. There is usually some kind of guidance involved, e.g., a pattern, a recipe, or notes that describe what types of materials to use and how to put them together. Making requires a genuine interest in the domain as well as experience. People are likely to spend a lot of their time, energy, and money on their favorite making activities. Many hobbies fit in this level of creativity. A food-related example might be to create an entrée using a recipe.

The most advanced level of creativity is **creating**. The motivation behind creating is to express oneself creatively or to innovate. Truly creative efforts are fueled by passion and guided by a high level of experience. Creating differs from making in that creating relies on the use of raw materials and the absence of a predetermined pattern. For example, making is cooking with a recipe, whereas creating is making up the dish as you go.

All people are capable of reaching higher levels of creativity, but they need the passion and the experience to do so. Consequently, people differ in the level of creativity they attain in different domains. In fact, they may find themselves at all four levels of creativity simultaneously in different domains. They may attain the higher levels of creativity only in their hobbies or other domains for which they have high interest and/or passion.

The path from doing to adapting to making and finally to creating develops in the individual over time and through experience. Many people never reach the final level of creating as they are satisfied with the creativity they express at the making level, for example. In fact, people don't always progress through the levels in the same order. Although most of us will start with doing, some will continue to creating by way of first adapting, and then making. Others will get there by first making, then adapting. For example, in the domain of wardrobe and clothing, it is as though the act of making one's own clothes allows the maker to see new possibilities for clothing or outfits that they already own (Meyer, 2010). Others may leave out either adapting or making, but it is rare that people move straight from doing to creating.

It is important to offer relevant experiences to facilitate people's expressions of creativity at all levels. It takes different kinds of support at the different levels of creativity. For example, it is best to:
> lead people who are on the doing level of creativity,
> guide those who are at the adapting level,
> provide scaffolds that support and serve peoples' need for creative expression at the making level, and
> offer a clean slate for those capable of creating things from scratch.

What this means is that it will take more time and preparation for people at the doing and making levels of creativity to be able to express themselves creatively in that domain. We will introduce the path of expression framework later in the chapter to describe how you can prepare people to express themselves creatively.

Here are four principles for facilitating everyday creativity. They have proven to be very useful in establishing a common ground for the team that is embarking on generative design research.

In this chapter we will provide background information (in the form of theories, frameworks and models) to support these principles.

1. All people are creative.
2. All people have dreams.
3. People will fill in what is unseen and unsaid based on their own experience and imagination.
4. People project their needs onto ambiguous stimuli because they are driven to make meaning.

It will be helpful for you to reflect on these principles and discuss them with others you are collaborating with in conducting generative design research.

A FRAMEWORK FOR INDIVIDUAL CREATIVITY

Most of the research that has been published about creativity has been about individual creativity and the leading work has been done by cognitive psychologists. So most of the theories about creativity describe what happens in the mind of one person. But this is changing. It is recognized now that creativity is not just in the head. But we will start there to keep it simple.

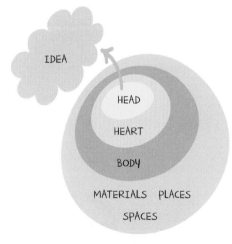

Figure#2.2 shows a framework for individual creativity that reveals the many layers of context around the 'in the head' perspective. It shows that individual creativity is not only in the head but in the heart as well: it involves emotion. And creativity takes place in the body. It is evoked through activity and motion. There is a timeframe for creativity and creativity can be greatly enhanced through preparation. And the last layer shows that creativity is in the environment as it is influenced by the places and spaces and through the props and materials that are available for use.

Figure#2.2: A framework for individual creativity

Generative design thinking acknowledges and makes use of all these layers of the creative context with a special emphasis on the environmental level in the form of tools and techniques and materials.

This framework is not another theory about creativity. It is a model for holding together the bits and pieces of many other theories and principles, particularly those that we felt were relevant to the workings of generative design research. We will describe later in the chapter how this framework for individual creativity expands into a model for collective creativity. But first we will discuss it layer by layer, starting with the more traditional view of creativity being something that happens in the mind of one person and describe some of what is known about ideas.

IDEAS: THE BASIC BUILDING BLOCKS OF CREATIVITY

We will start with the core, i.e., the innermost layer in the framework for individual creativity. This layer is focused on ideas in a person's head. Ideas are the basic building blocks of creativity. An idea can be represented by a word or words or it can be depicted in a picture. Take a look at the photograph in Figure#2.4.

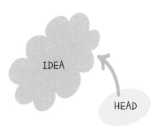

Figure#2.3: At the core of the framework for individual creativity is the idea in the head.

It shows Anneke Keller making a phone call, while reading the oil gauge of her car. You cannot be sure from the picture why she is making the call. She may be calling a colleague to postpone a meeting because her car won't run. Or she might be calling the garage to ask what she can do about the oil. If we consider the situation depicted in Figure#2.4, many different kinds of ideas come to mind. For example, "I see a woman standing beside a car making a phone call", 'woman', 'car', 'a green Volkswagen', 'standing' 'a phone number'. Other ideas may be more difficult to express, e.g., "the freedom given by being able to call" or "how the scene makes me think of something I did last week."

We'll try to keep the discussion focused here, and concentrate on the simpler examples when we talk about ideas. There are basically two ways of thinking about what we mean by an idea such as 'a phone number'.

Figure#2.4: There are many different ideas in this photograph of Anneke Keller making a phone call.

Ideas can be defined as they are in the dictionary. The classical way to think about what an idea is is to have a strict rule such as definitions we find in a dictionary. For example, "A phone number is a 9 or 10-digit sequence, consisting of a country code, an area code, and a local number." An example is '+31152785202'. It defines a telephone connection, either fixed or mobile. This definition helps us to see that '+31152785202' and '+31152783029' are both phone numbers, that 'abcdefghijk' is not a phone number, although it consists of 10 characters. The good thing about ideas as defined by a dictionary is that there is an explicit definition, which can be the same for everybody, and which can be relied upon not to change. The bad thing is that it doesn't explain a lot about how people deal with ideas.

Ideas can also be thought of as clouds of associations. Another way of thinking about ideas is that people carry clouds of associations that are connected to every idea they know. Some of these are close to the dictionary definition, but most of these associations have to do with their personal histories and how they have used or thought about the idea before. For example, when I think about the idea of a 'phone number', some of these could be:

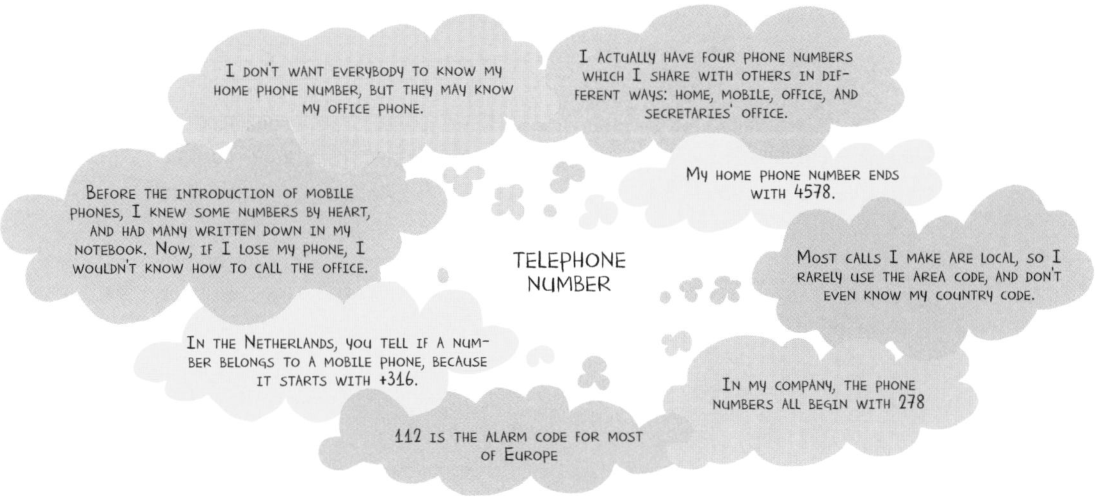

I DON'T WANT EVERYBODY TO KNOW MY HOME PHONE NUMBER, BUT THEY MAY KNOW MY OFFICE PHONE.

I ACTUALLY HAVE FOUR PHONE NUMBERS WHICH I SHARE WITH OTHERS IN DIFFERENT WAYS: HOME, MOBILE, OFFICE, AND SECRETARIES' OFFICE.

BEFORE THE INTRODUCTION OF MOBILE PHONES, I KNEW SOME NUMBERS BY HEART, AND HAD MANY WRITTEN DOWN IN MY NOTEBOOK. NOW, IF I LOSE MY PHONE, I WOULDN'T KNOW HOW TO CALL THE OFFICE.

MY HOME PHONE NUMBER ENDS WITH 4578.

TELEPHONE NUMBER

MOST CALLS I MAKE ARE LOCAL, SO I RARELY USE THE AREA CODE, AND DON'T EVEN KNOW MY COUNTRY CODE.

IN THE NETHERLANDS, YOU TELL IF A NUMBER BELONGS TO A MOBILE PHONE, BECAUSE IT STARTS WITH +316.

IN MY COMPANY, THE PHONE NUMBERS ALL BEGIN WITH 278

112 IS THE ALARM CODE FOR MOST OF EUROPE

Figure#2.5: Every idea is connected to clouds of associations that are related to the idea.

The clouds of associations in Figure#2.5 would be somewhat different for every individual. These clouds of associations can be larger or smaller, and can easily be triggered. Once one cloud is remembered or triggered, nearby clouds will be remembered as well. This phenomenon is known as priming or as "spreading activation in semantic memory" (Collins and Loftus, 1975). When people are asked to quickly write down as many associations as possible to a given word, some people will quickly jot down a long list, others stop after a few words. With a bit of practice, the lists get longer due to the spreading activation of the associations in the clouds.

When we speak about a 'phone number', what we really mean is most often connected to these clouds of associations, rather than to the dictionary-style definition. For example, if somebody asks you: "Can I have your phone number?" he or she doesn't just want a 10-digit sequence, but may implicitly be asking also "may I call you?"

Think of ambiguity as a tool. Ideas possess ambiguity. For example, many words are ambiguous in that they have more than one meaning. The sentence "I'll phone you to tell you the number of phone numbers on my phone" means roughly the same as "I'll call you to tell you how many contacts I have on my mobile" and uses three different forms of 'phone', and two different forms of 'number'. But unless it gets complicated, we usually have no problem in recognizing what was intended. This means that if we present people with a single word, they may react to a variety of the meanings that are carried with the idea that the word triggers. The context they are in is likely to change how they think of the idea. For example, "time" at work may not mean the same thing as "time" at home.

Ambiguity also holds for pictures. A picture of a clock, such as the one shown here, can bring out different meanings to people depending on their past experiences and the context they are in:
> "a clock, i.e., a time-indicating device"
> "a time: ten after ten"
> "something is due to start"
> "a deadline"
> "time pressure"
> "keeping track of time"
> "I forgot to go to the bank"

Figure#2.6: This picture of a clock is ambiguous: it can mean different things.

Traditionally in education there has been an emphasis on avoiding ambiguity. For example, the avoidance of ambiguity is stressed in the reporting of scientific research where reproducibility and precision are deemed key values. On the other hand, art, design and creativity thrive on ambiguity. Creating generative tools and applying generative techniques takes skill in working with and comfort in dealing with ambiguity. In fact, it has been established that creative people "tolerate ambiguity well" (Zenasni, Besançon, and Lubart, 2008). So it is perhaps not surprising that designers and design students tend to readily learn and apply generative design thinking. It may be more difficult for people who have been trained in the scientific (i.e., expert-driven) mindset to embrace generative design thinking and to not only tolerate but embrace ambiguity. Ambiguity is a resource to call upon and not a state to be avoided. (Gaver, Beaver, and Benford, 2003). You can use ambiguity as a resource for sparking creativity.

Incompleteness compels people to fill in. Incompleteness is one form of ambiguity. People are very good at filling in holes in an otherwise coherent whole. The act of 'filling-in' or 'closure' is, in fact, one of the core principles in how we understand comics and graphic novels as Scott McCloud clearly demonstrated in his classic book called *Understanding Comics: The Invisible Art* (McCloud, 1993). By the way, for any reader who is at this point somewhat uncomfortable with these discussions about ambiguity and incompleteness, a reading/looking at *Understanding Comics* is a highly recommended diversion.

Figure#2.7 shows a part of a storyboard about a communication product, in which the product is hidden in each picture by a white cloud. In this way, the reader is invited to think first of the story, and not yet respond to details of the envisaged product. In fact, a storyboard like this may help the reader to imagine what the product could do or what it might look like.

Leaving holes can be used to trigger people's imaginations. Similarly, an open-ended sentence can be a very inviting way to ask a question. Compare the following two ways of asking people to talk about what they do in their free time (See Figure#2.8). By having people complete the sentence, rather than provide an answer to a question, we are likely to learn much more about the person and also get a much wider variety of responses across people.

Figure#2.7: Leaving holes is a storytelling technique that can be used to trigger ideas in people's minds

AS A QUESTION TO ANSWER	AS AN OPEN-ENDED SENTENCE TO COMPLETE
What is your favorite pastime?	When I have nothing to do, I like to ... ...

Figure#2.8: Two ways to ask for input. The open-ended sentence on the right invites a much wider variety of responses than the closed-question format on the left

Creative thinking often works by having people make new connections between previously unconnected ideas. There are two theories about creative thinking that rely on that fact which are helpful to know about: bisociation (Koestler, 1964) and metaphor (Schön, 1963).

Use bisociation to make new connections. Ideas connect to other ideas in two ways: through either association or bisociation. Association links similar or related ideas as we described earlier in the discussion about how ideas can be thought of as clouds of associations. Koestler (1964) introduced the concept of bisociation wherein two apparently unconnected ideas are brought together, and a new connection is explored. *"I have coined the term 'bisociation' in order to make a distinction between the routine skills of thinking on a single 'plane', as it were, and the creative act, which, as I shall try to show, always operates on more than one plane."*

Koestler hypothesized that bisociation is the basic creative act and that this act is the same for art, science and humor. Koestler stated that *"every creative act involves bisociation, a process that brings together and combines previously unrelated ideas."* Koestler's evidence for bisociation came from a common pattern of intersecting conceptual planes of thought (See Figure#2.9) that he has described with many examples showing creative achievements in the arts, sciences and humor.

The principle of bisociation can be used to facilitate idea generation. For example, when brainstorming for extensions of a line of toothbrushes (think of this as the first plane of thought), seemingly unrelated ideas (e.g., swimming) and/or objects (e.g., peanut butter) can be used to set up the second plane of thought. Bisociations in the form of new ideas are very likely to emerge at the intersections of the two planes.

Use metaphor to make new connections. In metaphor, one idea is positioned against another and the fit between the two is explored. According to Schön (1963), this mechanism is the best explanation of how new ideas and solutions are found. He writes: *"I know what a drum is. I know about snare, bongo, bass, and oil drums. But when I found myself in a metal room with a thin metal wall that reverberated whenever it was jarred, it was a new*

Figure#2.9: Koestler explained bisociation as a new idea emerging from the spark as two concepts (each represented by a line in a plane) are brought together (picture after Koestler, 1964).

thought for me that the room was a kind of drum. (...) I am not mistaking a room for a drum (...) There is a change in my concept of 'this' (...the room), there is a change in what I have been calling the concept itself (...drum), and these changes are interdependent. (...) These concepts have been displaced to situations outside of their ordinary patterns of use and they have been transformed in the process" (pages 30-31).

After the event, both the notion of 'room' and 'drum' changed in the thinker's mind. In Schön's case, from then on, the ideas 'room' and 'drum' were connected as associations in his mind. In Schön's view, this is the way a designer, when asked to improve the quality of, say, a ship's cabin, might use a principle he knew from another domain, e.g., muffling a drum by placing a pillow inside it.

By exploring the connections in the use of metaphor, we learn about both ideas at the same time. In the example of choosing a way to spend next year's holiday, a mother's insight that "holiday is like another job to me" calls forth a consideration of comparing how the ideas of holiday and job are similar (e.g., a camping holiday calls for a lot of organizing and planning, preparing dinner under challenging conditions, etc.), but also different (you get paid for a job, but not for going on holiday). A metaphorical comparison is like the collision of two clouds of associations, not like the logical comparison of two dictionary definitions. It explains how two ideas are similar, not whether they are equal.

CREATIVITY AND EMOTION

The second layer in the framework for individual creativity looks beyond the head to the heart, i.e., to one's emotional state and its role in creative thinking and doing.

For many years, cognitive psychologists studied the mind while doing their best to ignore the effect of emotions because emotional states were harder to control and to quantify than were cognitive events. But more recent psychological research has shown that cognition and emotion cannot be separated. In fact, emotion drives cognition, which is shown in the framework by positioning the head within the larger context of the heart. Our emotional states have a large influence not only on how we feel but also on how we think and act, including our ability to be creative. For example, the link between creativity and positive affect (i.e., emotion) was firmly supported in a meta-analysis of 66 studies about creativity and affect (Baas et al., 2008). Alice Isen's (1999) work provides insight into how this works. Her research shows that:

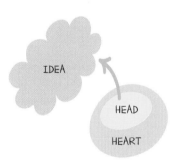

Figure#2.10: Emotions play a large role in creative thinking and doing

> Positive emotion increases the number of ideas available for association and/or bisociation,
> Positive emotion increase the breadth of ideas that are relevant to the problem,
> Positive emotion increases cognitive flexibility, making it more likely that the ideas will connect.

Michele and Robert Root-Bernstein (1999) believe that the role of emotion in creativity is fundamental. They write that *"creative thinking in all fields occurs preverbally, before logic or linguistics comes into play, manifesting itself through emotions, intuitions, images and bodily feelings. The resulting ideas can be translated into one or more formal systems of communication such as words, equations, pictures or music or dance only after they are sufficiently developed in their prelogical forms."*

Evoke emotions through the use of ambiguous materials but please be careful. If positive emotional states contribute toward creativity, it is important to facilitate this state of mind in generative sessions where creative thinking and doing is the goal. Giving people a chance to prepare themselves for the sessions helps, as does keeping the atmosphere casual and familiar.

This principle about evoking emotion applies also to the selection of triggers as we will see in the next chapter. But it is not possible to anticipate or to control the kinds of emotions that might emerge in using visual stimuli as triggers in generative design research. If there is any reason to expect extreme emotional responses from people in generative sessions, it is best to be prepared. For example, in a project using generative design research tools and techniques to inform and inspire the design of the new healthcare campus for American War Veterans in New Orleans, we anticipated and prepared for negative emotional responses to photographs because many of the

participants suffered from PTSD (Post Traumatic Stress Disorders) as a result of their military experiences. A clinical psychologist was present for all the generative sessions to manage the negative emotional memories that sometimes occurred.

People think of people and stories best. People are very good at thinking in terms of stories about people and the things they do and what happens to them. This is contrary to the view from higher education where we take great pride in being able to reason in abstract terms, and much of our academic education is directed at training people in abstract reasoning. But most people are not good at dealing with abstractions, as in mathematics and formal logic.

An illustration of this is Wason's (1966) selection task, shown in Figure#2.11. It describes how a simple logical problem, when defined in abstract terms, can be very difficult to solve. But if that same problem is formulated in terms of a story about an everyday situation, we can deal with it more easily.

This finding provides a counterweight to information processing theories which claim that when we encounter problems in the world, we translate them to their basic logical (symbolic) structure, apply logic, and then translate the conclusions back to the real world. Actually, people are not good at that. They're much better at reasoning in terms of story elements.

Our ability to deal with stories lies at the root of the value of narrative techniques in design, such as scenarios, storyboards, and personas. Stories are useful for joining together many different details into a whole. Such story elements provide rich pictures (literally or metaphorically) with which we can connect. When designing a new stroller for use in the city, the story about Mary and Jim Jones trying to enter the subway station with their two children aged 1 and

6 is more meaningful to the designer than are ergonomic specifications of the people involved. The ergonomic specifications will become relevant later in the process, however. Stories are very useful in generative design research because they are engaging and they invoke empathy and imagination. Stories can be true or imagined or even a combination of the two. So storytelling can be a very effective way of triggering ideas about the future.

All senses can be used as generative tools. All senses, but scents exceptionally so, are powerful means of eliciting emotion-laden memories and stories and they can be used as a component in generative toolkits. However, using scents as generative stimuli is best done by design researchers with some experience under their belts because the memories and emotions that come from smells may be so powerful and time-consuming that they derail the session's agenda (Khanna, 2008).

CREATIVITY IN MOTION
The third layer in the framework for individual creativity looks at the whole person in action. So here the head and the heart are in the body moving through time. The implications of this much larger layer for creativity are immense and are just now beginning to be explored.

Pretending and enactment can facilitate creativity. Design involves imagining and creating new life situations for people in circumstances that have never been experienced before. Or as Henrik Gedenryd (1998) succinctly stated, *"Design is an inquiry into the future situation of use."*

ABSTRACT RULE

The left half of each sign carries a letter, the right half a number, guaranteed!
The hypothesis is that if the letter is a vowel (a,e,i,o,u,y), the number must be an even number (2,4,6,...), or in mathematical notation: vowel => even.

Question: which of the four sticky notes *must* you lift to determine whether the hypothesis is true? You should lift as few as logically possible.

STORY RULE

Suppose you are a policeman inspecting a bar to see whether the law about 'no alcohol for minors' is upheld. The four displays show a guest and his drink.
The law says: "if a person is under 16 years of age, his or her drink must be non-alcoholic".

Question: for which of the four covered age/drink answers should you find out what is covered by the sticky note?

Figure#2.11: Solving the task using an abstract rule is more difficult than solving the same task with a story rule.

Over the years, designers have developed a range of expressions to help them imagine possible futures, and explore situations in them. These expressions include traditional design visualizations such as sketches, models, and prototypes. But with the larger scale and scope of design challenges we face today has come the need to explore alternative ways to visualize future situations of use. More recently, the complexities around computers, interactive technologies, and mobile services have strengthened the attention for techniques such as enacting, i.e., acting out envisaged interactions with props, rather than merely talking about the interaction. Enacting helps people to experience the time scales, the complexities, and the effect of body scale. By experiencing new or possible situations in a bodily way, (e.g., Burns et al., 1995; Buchenau and Fulton Suri, 2000; Oulasvirta et al., 2003; Buxton, 2007; Simsarian, 2003; Diaz et al., 2009) things may become apparent which were not evident under abstract consideration alone.

Enacting refers to the use of the body in the environment to express and experience ideas about future use situations. Early in the design process, enactment might take the form of pretending, with future "products" used as props to facilitate the pretending. Enactment can also be used later in the design process. For example, if we want to consider the experiential impact of a small-sized toilet space on a train or plane, experiencing it in a full-scale cardboard mockup helps us to form a judgment of it with far more understanding and empathy than we could get from a dimensioned drawing.

Creativity happens over time. It is not an instantaneous event. Graham Wallas introduced what may be the very first model of the creative process in his book *The Art of Thought* in 1926. He identified five stages in the process:

> **preparation** (preparatory work that focuses the individual's mind on the problem),
>
> **incubation** (where the problem is internalized into the unconscious mind and nothing appears externally to be happening),
>
> **intimation** (the creative person gets a "feeling" that a solution is on its way),
>
> **illumination** (where the creative idea bursts forth into conscious awareness) and
>
> **verification** (where the idea is consciously verified, elaborated, and then applied).

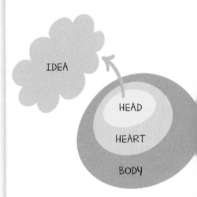

Figure#2.12: Individual creativity takes place in the body and over time

Figure#2.13: Enacting future scenarios of use can be facilitated with props.

Engaging in the creative process (from the perspective of Wallas' five stage model) may go something like this: We first immerse ourselves in all the data, then we let go of thinking in an incubation period, during which we don't consciously work on the problem, but let it simmer in the background. Often after a good night's sleep, fresh insights turn out to have formed and we try to explore, verify, and elaborate on them. The process of letting go of the problem can be difficult for people who need to feel in control, or who need every step to be rational and proven. To let go of thinking is a skill that typically takes practice before we can gain confidence with it.

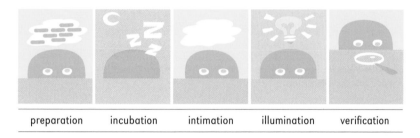

| preparation | incubation | intimation | illumination | verification |

Figure#2.14: Five stages in Wallas' model of the creative process

Incubation, a period of downtime, is often an important step in the creative process. It accounts for the observation that when puzzling about a problem, the solution can often hit us unexpectedly after a good night's sleep or in the shower. Famously, Archimedes was said to have come to his famous principle when having a bath, after agonizing about his assignment for a long time.

We cannot expect everyday people to be instantly creative. They will need some time to go through the stages in the creative process and they will need some space for incubation.

Priming and spreading activation are automatic but take time. Priming refers to the phenomenon that you are more likely to remember something if information related to it has been presented previously. Priming is thought to be caused by spreading activation in the network of associations (i.e., the clouds of associations that we discussed earlier in this chapter) in the mind. Priming can occur through associations between words or ideas. For example, a word can prime another word that is 'associated' with it but not necessarily related in meaning. For example, dog primes cat, since the ideas tend to be associated with each other. Pictures can prime and be primed as well.

Priming is automatic and is based on implicit memory events. This means that priming can occur even if the subject is not conscious of the priming stimulus. An example of this was done by Bargh et al., in 1996. Subjects were implicitly primed with words related to the stereotype of elderly people (example: Florida, forgetful, wrinkle). While the words did not explicitly mention speed or slowness, those who were primed with these words walked more slowly upon exiting the testing booth than those who were with neutral stimuli (see Kahneman, 2011, for a discussion of priming and other cognitive processes and the role they make play in intuitive decision making).

Understanding how priming and spreading activation work can help us to select and prepare tasks and materials to use in preparing people for creative sessions. Priming and spreading activation may be automatic, but they still take time.

There are four levels of knowledge.

Knowledge refers to thoughts and ideas that have already been experienced and have been stored in memory. We can distinguish four levels of knowledge: explicit, observable, tacit, and latent. The examples below relate to the photo of Anneke in Figure#2.4, discussed earlier.

Explicit knowledge can be stated in words, and is relatively easy to share with others; e.g., "Today I have three appointments on my agenda."

Observable knowledge refers to thoughts and ideas that can be obtained by watching how things happen or how people behave. People are generally not often aware of their own behavior that others can readily observe. For example, "She sometimes makes faces at people when she is on the phone."

Tacit knowledge refers to things we know but are not able to verbally communicate to others. For example, you probably know how to make a phone call when your hands are full of stuff but this would be difficult to explain to someone else.

Latent knowledge refers to thoughts and ideas that we haven't experienced yet, but on which we can form an opinion based on past experiences. Latent knowledge will be knowable in the future. It is not easy for people to express this type of knowledge. For example, "I'd like to be able to automatically postpone meetings when I have trouble with my car."

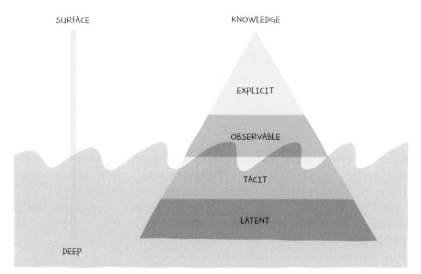

SURFACE   KNOWLEDGE

EXPLICIT

OBSERVABLE

TACIT

LATENT

DEEP

Figure#2.15: Some levels of knowledge are easier to access than others

In Figure#2.15 (after Sanders, 2002) these levels are shown as a pyramid, with two levels above water, and two below. The figure indicates two things: explicit and observable knowledge are only the tip of the iceberg of the things that people know. And it takes effort of looking beneath the water surface, to see what is happening on the tacit and latent levels. Generative design research tools and techniques will give you the means to see what is going on at the tacit and latent levels of what people know.

Layering the levels of knowledge. We want people to reflect on and express their needs and values in order to explore future scenarios of use. But needs and values are abstract qualities that people are not often used to talking about directly. They fall at the level of tacit and/or latent knowledge. If someone asks you "what are your needs and values for travel on a holiday?" it's difficult to give an answer right away. But given a specific holiday, it is not so difficult to explain why you did or did not like a certain part of it. We can best think about values by linking them to situations or occurrences, that is, to stories.

This observation lies at the basis of generative exercises such as the 'day in the life' exercise, which consists of three steps. First, someone is asked to describe the steps that occurred in one specific day. This forms the 'layer of facts'. When that has been completed, they are asked to explain which of these activities they enjoyed (the high points) and which they hated (the low points), forming a 'layer of valence'. In the third step, he or she is asked to indicate, for each high and low point along the story, why it was high or low. Their explanations about why reveal the layer of needs and values. Instead of asking people to attach valence and value to individual facts in isolation, we let them make these judgments within the context of a whole layer. Stepping up from stories about specific days to needs and values is a way of releasing tacit and latent knowledge.

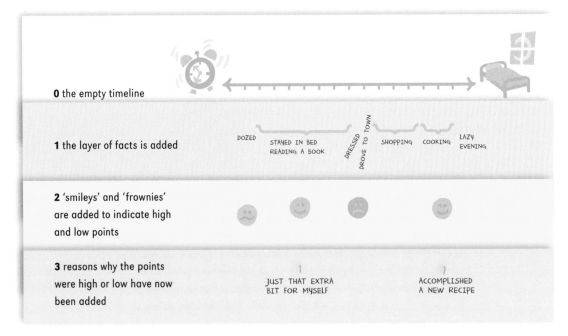

Figure#2.16: The day in the life exercise can be used to layer people from stories to a description of their needs and values

The strength of the layering approach is that it invites people to first create a complete story, then evaluate it, and then find reasons for their evaluations. If we had asked them for a single good or bad event and its reason, it would be difficult for them to answer. But now, when they are asked to evaluate events, they can compare the whole layer that they mapped out in the first step. And when they are asked for the reasons, they can review all the highs and lows that they evaluated before, again comparing the wholes. The day in the life exercise serve two purposes. First, it prepares people for the generative session by getting them to remember and reflect upon their day. Second, it provides the foundation for layering through the levels of knowledge.

SENSITIZING

Insight into the deeper layers of understanding requires that the participant has been thoroughly involved in the problem or situation for some time. Therefore, people who will be involved in creative sessions will need to be prepared for these sessions before they come. Ideally they will have a week or two for the preparation or immersion process that takes place in a familiar setting such as their home or place of work. We often give the participants diaries or workbooks to guide them in daily self-documentation of their thoughts, feelings and ideas about the experience being investigated. Or we may ask them to observe and document their daily lives through photographs or videos. By having them immerse themselves over a longer period, they can become more sensitive to their awakened memories and associations and have the opportunity to gather stories that illustrate things they find interesting or worthwhile. In the generative sessions, we are able to build on this awakened sensitivity and expressive ability.

THE PATH OF EXPRESSION

At the larger time-scale of method, we follow "the path of expression" which guides the time course of the creative process.

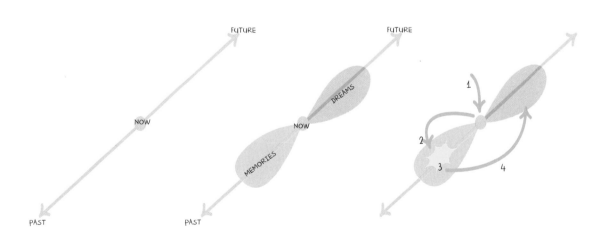

Figure#2.17: The experience of the moment (now) is connected to past and future through memories and dreams. The path of expression (right) shows how a person's awareness can be guided in steps by thinking first of the present, then of the past, then looking for underlying layers, in order to move toward the future.

The path of expression is based on a model for understanding experience that is shown in the middle of Figure#2.17. The model illustrates that the concept of experience is focused on the 'moment,' the center of the model marked as 'now'. The moment connects both backward to past experiences and forward to future experiences. Thus, people's memories of past experiences influence how they behave and feel in the moment. Similarly, people's dreams for future experience also influence their perception of the moment. To gain a rich understanding of people's experiences, we give them tools and techniques to explore their current situation as well as past experiences. And in order to invite people to explore future experience, it is vital to provide them with the space and the materials with which to imagine and to make things that they can use to show or to tell their ideas about future scenarios of use.

The path of expression is a process that can be used for exploring present, past, and future experience. It serves as a framework for planning the path that the participant will take in a generative design research session, culminating in their ability to imagine and communicate their hopes, dreams and fears for the future. This is how the path of expression method typically works. The numbers correspond to the numbers in Figure#2.17.

1. Participants are asked to observe, reflect on, and describe their current experiences in the immersion period before they come to a workshop session, e.g., through diaries and photo-taking as described above.
2. They are also asked to select, and reflect on, memories of previous experiences. Then during the session, they are invited to share their observations and past memories and discuss current events with each other.
3. This sharing of experiences helps them to access underlying needs and values, which serve as the basis for exploring their aspirations for future experience (step 4).

Utilizing the path of expression framework enables people to connect to what is meaningful from their past and present experiences, using that as a springboard for ideation about the future. The path of expression serves as a scaffold upon which to build the journey that the participant will take in a generative design session. Utilizing the path of expression framework also stimulates creativity on the part of our participants. It lets them avoid the pitfalls of becoming fixated on preconceived ideas or their first ideas about the future. In fact, we find that people are often pleasantly surprised and proud of how creative they are in generative design sessions.

CREATIVITY IN THE ENVIRONMENT

The fourth layer in the framework for individual creativity is described by the environment in which the action is taking place. This layer includes the physical environment with its places and spaces as well as all the stuff in the environment such as materials, supplies, props, and tools.

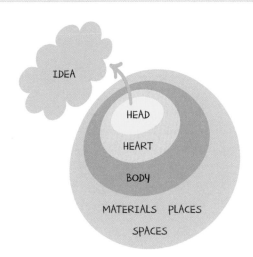

Figure#2.18: Individual creativity is influenced by environmental factors such as places, spaces and stuff.

Creativity is fostered by having a choice of spaces in which to explore. The design of spaces that facilitate creativity is a relatively new area of architecture and interior space design practice, but one that is being aggressively pursued today by progressive architecture firms and workplace furniture manufacturers. Some general principles about workplaces that foster creativity and innovation exist. The spaces and places for creativity should:

> have furniture that can easily be rearranged,
> have walls where material (especially visual material) can be posted for all to see and to act upon,
> accommodate a wide variety behaviors such as quiet reflection, relaxation, active collaboration, mess-making, etc.,
> provide both for individuals and for groups of varying size in working face-to-face,
> provide for many moods including playful, stimulating, and informal as well as formal, and
> be open to people both inside and outside of the organization.

It is very important to think ahead about the space in which generative sessions or analysis sessions are to be held. How well do they adhere to these design criteria for creative spaces and places? The contributions written by Arnold Wasserman (at the end of Chapter#10) show how these design criteria have been embodied in the form of charrette spaces in an innovation consultancy.

The materials present in the environment can also foster creativity. Generative design research has to lot to say about the nature and quality of the tools and other materials that can be used to support creative thinking and doing. The Make toolkits that we will describe in the next chapter are designed to facilitate, support and provoke creative thinking. These toolkits contain a collection of ambiguous (as well as unambiguous) elements, such as words and images for making something such as a collage or a map. These words and images have been selected to trigger associations in the area of experience that is studied. Some triggers are chosen to not be ambiguous so that the participants can start by choosing recognizable stimuli that relate directly to the area of experience. This can help people feel at ease in the creative session. Other triggers in a toolkit are chosen to be ambiguous, so they can evoke a range of associations and can be selected for many reasons. This has two advantages: first, by being ambiguous, it gives the person freedom to interpret the trigger from the perspective of his or her own experience. Second, when that person presents their collage or map to others, the ambiguity of the trigger invites them to explain their interpretation of it and reasons for choosing it.

The physical environment and the materials available there can help to stimulate creative thinking or innovative solutions. We will describe more about the materials for facilitating creativity in Chapter Three.

SOCIAL OR COLLECTIVE CREATIVITY

"Creativity does not happen inside a person's head but in the interaction between a person's thoughts and a socio-cultural context." (Csikszentmihalyi, 1996)

The framework for individual creativity explodes in scope and scale when we think about people coming together in creative ways. When people come together, the number of ideas and the breadth of the ideas that are brought to the table increase dramatically. This is especially true when people from different backgrounds come together. The diagram in Figure#2.19 shows how we might see social or collective creativity relative to the framework for individual creativity. Note that the artifacts they create help them to connect the ideas of individuals. The artifacts serve as 'boundary objects' that provide an interface between different communities of practice (Star and Griesemer, 1989).

Figure#2.19: The framework for individual creativity takes on a whole new life when considered from the perspective of social or collective creativity. The orange dots signify materials and artefacts made by the participants.

Psychologists started conducting research on creativity in the 1950's with a focus on the creative individual because at the time it was thought that the source of creativity and innovation was the individual, the solitary genius. It wasn't until the 1990's that this narrow focus was challenged and the role of collaboration in creativity and innovation began to be explored. Keith Sawyer (2006 and 2007) does an excellent job of describing this new perspective on creativity and innovation and the impact that it will have on schools, organizations and industries in the future. Sawyer claims that all true innovation originates in collaboration rather than through the efforts of the solitary genius, supporting this claim with numerous contemporary examples.

With the increase in collaborative ways of working and with the Internet's ability to connect people, it is clear that social creativity will become an even more important area of research in the future. As was discussed in the Introduction, the only way we will be able to address the challenges of wicked problems and fuzzy pathways are through collective forms of creativity and generative design thinking.

Creative teams are made up of a diversity of people. There is evidence that team creativity is founded on diversity and difference (Nijstad and DeDrue, 2002). In other words, the more diverse the members of the team, the more creative the team has the potential to become. Diversity is not always easy because different perspectives often lead to disagreements, but it is a powerful precondition for creativity. Different people bring different ways of thinking and doing to the table. The following sections describe some of the ways in which people differ in thinking, decision making and reasoning.

Balance left and right brain thinking. Brain research in the 70s and 80s pointed out two seemingly complementary sets of thinking skills, which have been associated with left and right brain hemispheres. One set (most often associated with the left brain hemisphere) contains skills in dealing with words, numbers, logic and sequences. These are the skills that have traditionally been pushed forward in academic education. The other set (most often associated with the right brain hemisphere) contains skills in dealing with rhythm, color, Gestalt, graphical composition, and visualization. These skills have received attention in arts curricula. Recent wisdom supports the fact that both sets of thinking skills are important, and that in facilitating people to use their minds, we should attend to the needs and powers of both 'channels' (e.g., Pink, 2005).

Utilize Henry Mintzberg's three strategies for decision making. Different types of problems call for different strategies. Mintzberg sketches three different strategies for decision-making that can be used in different situations: 'thinking first', 'seeing first' and 'doing first'.

	THINKING FIRST	SEEING FIRST	DOING FIRST
Features the qualities of..	science planning, programming the verbal facts	art visioning, imagining the visual ideas	craft making, trying it out the visceral experiences
Works best when..	The issue is clear The data are reliable The context is structured Thoughts can be pinned down Discipline can be applied	Many elements have to be combined into creative solutions Commitment to those solutions is key Communication across boundaries is essential	The situation is novel and confusing Complicated specifications would get in the way A few simple relationship rules can help people move forward
As in..	an established production process	new product development	companies that face a disruptive technology

Figure#2.20: A comparison of three strategies for decision making from Mintzberg and Westley (2001).

Thinking first works for situations where we understand the situation well, and have good models such as in a high school science assignment, where the teacher knows the right answer. But it doesn't work well in cases where there is lots of missing, uncertain or conflicting information.

In the latter case, seeing first (e.g., sketching a vision or using the approach typically trained in art) works better. Seeing first works well in creating future scenarios on the basis of incomplete data. Finally doing first (creating a prototype, and trying it out, and improving it iteratively) works best if we have very little experience with the situation at hand, i.e., we know very little. For example, if you want to learn about building sand castles that can withstand a wave, build one on the beach and notice how and where it goes wrong. Mintzberg explains that people tend to have a preferred strategy for decision making and that they may benefit from being exposed to and being able to practice the other strategies.

From the perspective of social or collective creativity, it is ideal to have a team made up of people who together have all three strategies for decision making as their preferred mode.

Understand Charles Peirce's three modes of reasoning. Charles Sanders Peirce, an American philosopher, logician, mathematician, and scientist, introduced three modes of reasoning that provide another window into the workings of the mind in action: deduction, induction, and abduction. The table below gives examples of each mode of reasoning.

	DEDUCTIVE REASONING	INDUCTIVE REASONING	ABDUCTIVE REASONING
Before	Shops sell goods only from 9 to 5 & This cake was bought in a shop	I looked at many ways of making cakes & Always the cake was made with flour	A birthday cake should be sweet & Honey can make things sweet
After	Certainly, the cake was bought between 9 and 5	Probably flour is a necessary ingredient for making a cake	Perhaps this birthday cake could be made with honey

Figure#2.21: A comparison of the three modes of reasoning

Deductive reasoning starts from a general rule such as 'people always do something in this way', combines it with a particular statement 'this person does this something' and ends up with a particular conclusion such as 'then this person must have done it this way'. Deductive reasoning is a purely logical thing. If you accept that the two statements are true, then the conclusion must necessarily be true. It requires no looking at the world. Of course, if the starting rule is wrong (e.g., there are shops whose opening hours exceed 9-5) the conclusion may not be correct (or it may still be correct, but not because of our reasoning).

Inductive reasoning happens when researchers try to establish general rules based on observation in the world. This is how the experimental sciences work. One typically cannot, e.g., see all the possible cakes that exist. So research methodologies have been developed over the past 200 years, often involving statistics, to guarantee that 'looking many times' can be sufficient to show that the conclusion can be trusted with a sufficient degree of confidence.

Finally, abductive reasoning is closely related to creativity and design. It is radically different from the other two, because it is about inventing a possible solution for a problem. If you want to explain how a birthday cake can be made to taste sweet, honey can be one explanation but other explanations (sugar, ginger syrup) are also possible. Abductive reasoning is finding an explanation, not proving it is the only one. Abductive reasoning is a form of inference or a leap to a conclusion. Abductive reasoning has recently gained a lot of attention as a core element in design thinking. Unlike deduction and induction, where the conclusion follows from the inputs, creativity is an abductive process of finding a new and possibly fitting solution from 'somewhere'.

In summary, the primary advantage of social or collective creativity is that people with many different ways of thinking, decision making and reasoning can be brought together, increasing the chances that connections and new insights will occur at many levels. But at the same time, with all these people having different ways of seeing, thinking and doing, it may be hard for them to come to agreement. The generative design tools and techniques can help here too. They can support people in developing a common language, a transdisciplinary design language that everyone can use to express their ideas.

MOVING ON

In this chapter we have presented ideas about thinking and creativity in order to provide a foundational layer for understanding how and why generative tools and techniques work. We reviewed key principles and theories about thinking creatively, first from the perspective of individual creativity and then introduced principles and findings that describe social or collective creativity. As a generative design researcher, you need to understand both perspectives because sometimes we ask people to work alone and at other times we ask them to work together.

We discussed that we cannot ask people to become instantly creative. They need time for immersion and for spreading activation to take place in order to build from the past and present and into the future. The path of expression is a means by which the journey to the creative expression of meaningful ideas can be scaffolded.

How can we invite ordinary people, whose creativity is probably latent, to join the design development process? First, we must learn to respect their creativity. Then, we need to provide them with experiences and tools so that they can exercise their creativity and participate directly in the design process. The next chapter gets very much more concrete about putting all this thinking about creativity into action.

THE CHANGING ROLE OF PROTOTYPES

There is little general agreement on what constitutes a 'prototype', and the word is often used interchangeably with the word 'model'. In general, anything that someone builds to represent a 'product' or experience before the actual artifact or event is completed can be considered a prototype. Prototypes can take many forms. They can be two or three-dimensional, at a smaller or larger scale, high or low fidelity, handmade or machine-made. A choreographed experience can also be considered to be a prototype.

Contributor

George Simons Jr.

George Simons Office for Design

Seattle, Washington USA

www.id-ahh.com

WHY PROTOTYPE?

Design Possibility	To inspire design thinking
	To experiment/explore ideas
	To learn by making
	To evaluate and enhance understanding
Technical Feasibility	To identify problems
	To decrease development costs
	To refine ideas/concepts
Business Viability	To establish functional criteria
To test ideas/concepts	To sell the idea to the client

A SHORT HISTORY OF PROTOTYPING

Yesterday - Prototypes to Communicate and Sell a Design

Phase One / Pre- to Mid-1980's

> a prototype is an artifact to represent a designed object's visual language.
> most prototypes are hand built of common materials such as wood, plastic and foam.
> there is a high level of integration between the designer, engineer and model builder.

Phase Two / Mid-1980's to Late-1990's

> prototyping starts to move beyond hand built 3D objects, to include computer modeling.
> CAD enables machining beyond hand controls to include CNC machine control.
> designers begin to move one step away from the modeling process.

A nice progression from really fast and rough, to fast foam (full scale), to a more refined mixed material model, to a 'looks-like' model with some foam core experimentation

1.

2.

> prototypes are mostly 'works-like' or 'looks-like' with little integration of the two.

Today - Prototypes to Learn and to Inform Design
Early 2000's to Today

> prototypes are not only artifacts, but a process to learn.
> prototyping begins to include social and cultural issues that surround a product.
> prototyping begins to be a collaborative design effort with other stakeholders.

Moving Forward - Prototypes to Invite Participation

The conventional notions of prototyping to communicate and prototyping to learn begin to blur. Three paths of prototyping emerge to integrate researchers and designers with all stakeholders in a fluid development process.

1. High fidelity 'Looks-like' and 'Works-like' Prototypes
   > highly accurate machined parts made from CAD data are more easily produced.
   > technology once available only to manufacturers is now affordable to even small consultant firms.

2. Rapid and Rough Prototypes
   > rough and un-precious prototypes are used to illustrate an idea.
   > rough prototypes are used to enable others to participate in the process.
   > ways to prototype experiences are explored by interaction, experience and service designers.

3. Paper-based Prototypes that Focus on Experiential Visions
   > prototyping to learn is seen as a means to integrate diverse perspectives, and to increase the value of a design by considering the interests of all stakeholders.
   > prototyping is as much a mindset towards how design gets done as a 'phase' or result in the process.

3.

4.

5.

6.

SUR-FACE	WHAT PEOPLE:	METHODS	KNOWLEDGE
	SAY THINK	INTER-VIEWS	EXPLIC-IT
	DO		

OVERVIEW OF CHAPTER THREE

OVERVIEW OF CHAPTER THREE

In the previous chapter we talked about how people think creatively. In this chapter we describe how to put the principles and theories of creative thinking into action. We introduce a wide range of tools and techniques that can be used in generative design research, organized according to a simple, people-centered framework: What people say, what people do and what people make. Tools and techniques for 'what people say' and 'what people do' have been practiced for many years, so we will not attempt to describe those in detail. To do so would take us beyond the scope of this book. Instead, we will focus on the category of tools and techniques that fall in the 'what people make' category which is unique to this book. We will also discuss the importance of the interplay of all three categories. This chapter serves as the springboard for Part Three where the details of planning, executing, documenting and analyzing generative design research are covered.

CHAPTER 3
HOW IT WORKS: GENERATIVE TOOLS AND TECHNIQUES

AN INFINITE SET OF TOOLS AND TECHNIQUES

Over the past decades a wide variety of techniques have been employed in learning about people, and in learning from people about their everyday experiences. These techniques have come from a variety of practices, both in industry (marketing) and in academia (psychology, anthropology and sociology). Some techniques and tools have crossed over between practices, and have been refined and enhanced in the process.

First, let's make clear the difference between the terms 'tool' and 'technique'. By *tool* we refer to a physical thing that is used as a means to an end. By *technique* we refer to the way in which this tool is employed. Pencils, pens, and markers are tools for the techniques of sketching, drawing, or annotating. With a description of a tool, we tend to focus on its form; with a technique, on the way it is used.

A workbook is a tool, typically in the form of a small book with exercises and assignments, containing text and images. The workbook can be used in different techniques, e.g., it can be sent to people who carry out the exercises and return the results by mail without the researcher having direct contact with them. In another technique, filling out the workbook is seen primarily as a way of preparing the participants for later activities. So even though the tools may have the same physical form, the manner in which they are used can differ. Such differences can have large consequences for the insights that are gained and for the way the design process gets informed or shaped.

SAY, DO, AND MAKE TOOLS AND TECHNIQUES

There are dozens of techniques and hundreds of tools to work with the techniques. Techniques can be classified by different criteria, e.g., the way they depend on a theory about the topic being investigated, the type of data that they deliver, or the level of academic rigor, training or financial investment they require. In our experience, the most helpful perspective from which to organize tools and techniques is people-centered, focusing on the activities of the participants rather than those of the researcher or the data. One can look at what people do, what they say, and what they make. Many studies (particularly in market research applications) include only Say techniques, but it is becoming increasingly common to find combinations of Say and Do techniques being used.

As you might expect from reading Chapter Two, it is the latter category, what people make, on which we lay the most emphasis in this book. That is in part because it's the newest in the context of research techniques, as it borrows from design. It's also because the Make category provides more opportunities for exploring experience at a deep level. But as we will explain later, Make tools and techniques should not be used in isolation. A generative study almost always has elements of all three: Say, Do, and Make.

For example, if you're conducting a generative study on future kitchen experiences of people, you can visit their homes and observe what they do: how do they use the kitchen? You can ask them questions and listen to what they say: interview them about what they do in the kitchen, with how many people, for how long, and when. You can get them to recall earlier kitchen experiences and reflect on those. And you can study what they make when given an 'ideal kitchen experience construction kit'; what ideas do they have, and what reasons do they give for these. The path of expression (page#57) guides the way in which you weave together these inputs from people to construct valuable concepts about possible futures.

All research techniques in use today for exploring people's experiences fall into one of three categories – what people Say, Do or Make – or they fall into the areas of overlap between the categories.

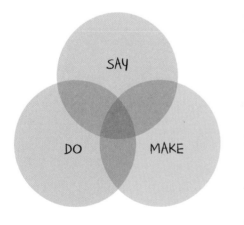

Figure#3.1 Say, Do, and Make tools and techniques complement and reinforce each other.

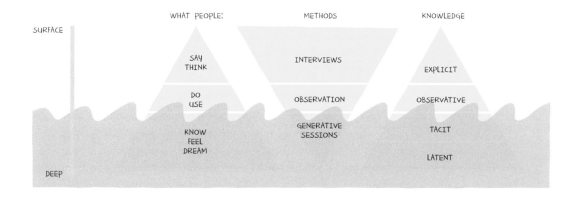

Figure#3.2 Methods that study what people Say, Do, and Make help access different levels of knowledge.

WHAT PEOPLE DO

With Do techniques, somebody observes people, their activities, the objects they use, and the places where they conduct these activities. This somebody doing the observing can be the researcher, or it can be the people themselves. Self-observation and self-report may, in fact, be the only option available for certain everyday activities such as those involving personal hygiene, since this is a domain that people prefer to keep private. Of all three categories, the Do category seem closest to scientific practice, because it can be conducted by an unobtrusive researcher 'objectively' observing and recording the behavior of people. In practice, though, there are limits to the level of unobtrusiveness that can be attained, e.g., for legal reasons of privacy, and for practical reasons. A great number of tools and devices can be used for making observations of people and recording traces of use. For example, photo- and video-cameras, note-taking paper for writing and sketching, tally sheets, voice recorders, etc. Viewing and documenting the place of the action itself, even without people in it, is also of great value. Gosling and colleagues (2002; cited in Gladwell, 2005) showed that looking around someone's living room for fifteen minutes can give you a more reliable impression of that person's character than spending a day with the person him- or herself.

There are a vast number of options available for studying what people do. Three salient dimensions to consider are the observer, the level of intrusion, and the recording media used in the study:

> **Who does the observation?** The answer can vary from researcher-as-observer to participant-as-observer with the points in between describing hybrid conditions along this scale.

> **How intrusive is the research?** On the one end, the observations are so low-key that the people being observed don't notice (e.g., with hidden cameras). On the other end, the observations may be very visible, e.g., when the researcher accompanies the participant as a photojournalist. The obtrusiveness of the observer may depend on where the research takes place (e.g., at people's homes vs. public spaces), and whether it is a planned activity or not. If you are documenting the observation of people, informed consent is a legal requirement (see contribution on page#176).

> **What media are used to document the phenomenon?** Again, there are many options and various media through which one can document behavior and traces of human activity: eyes, words on paper, diagrams on paper, photography, video, etc. The new communication technologies such as picture phones with video-recording and text messaging are opening up the possibilities along this dimension.

Two useful resource for learning more about the Do techniques include *Doing Anthropology in Consumer Research* (2007) by Patricia L. Sunderland and Rita M. Denny and *Ethnography: A Way of Seeing* (2008) by Harry F. Wolcott.

WHAT PEOPLE SAY

It's hard to imagine a reader of this book who has not been a respondent in a Say technique. Questionnaires, polls, and interviews are different ways of getting answers from people, usually by asking them questions. The form of Say technique that you've probably witnessed most often is the closed form of the questionnaire, in which all questions have been unambiguously formulated, and you are provided with constrained opportunities to answer. For example, 'do you own a bike? (yes/no)', 'what's your gender? (male/female)', 'your age?' (a number range between 20-80)'. The advantage of this form of questioning is that the data can be obtained without the researcher's being present and it can be processed very efficiently. The data can also be subjected to quantitative statistics (e.g., 43% of the respondents were male and owned a bicycle; on average the female bicycle owners were 3.4 years younger than the male ones; etc.).

Say techniques come in gradations of 'objectiveness'. Questions can also be framed more subjectively, e.g., 'how often do you travel by bike? (very often, frequently, rarely, almost never, absolutely never)'; 'indicate on a scale how comfortable your current bike is (1-7)'. Here also, descriptive statistics can be used to summarize the data. Another difference in the range of Say techniques is the amount of openness permitted in the answer. In the examples just described, the respondent could only fill in a limited set of answers to the questions. The researcher had prepared not only the questions, but also the answers he or she expected to get, with very little possibility for initiative on the part of the respondent. However, all of us have experienced questionnaires where none of the answers were appropriate and we've wanted to fill in something completely different but were not given the opportunity to do so. The closed-form questionnaire is one extreme within the Say spectrum.

Interviews are Say techniques that allow more freedom to learn from people, and for them to shape the direction that the questions and answers go. Interviews can also be closed in form, but are usually structured more loosely. For example, the interviewer can come prepared with a list of questions, or with a list of issues that serve as a starting point from which the conversation develops in a free form. The value of the loose structure is that the researcher can learn in unexpected directions. However, the price is that he or she has to cope with unexpected responses that cannot be classified and organized right away. And the researcher must be aware of what the boundaries of the question are in order to sufficiently steer the conversation in order to end up with usable insights.

The Say techniques go beyond the superficial layer of behavior; participants can express opinions, voice needs, indicate reasons, and report on events that occurred before the interaction with the researcher. Also, the Say techniques feature not only acts of behavior of a person on his own, but acts of communication of a person toward another. The receiver colors the message, e.g., by his or her own interpretation. And the sender colors the message, e.g., by answering what he/she thinks that the receiver wants to hear. This results in the say/do dilemma: what people say is different from what they do. In other words, people may not practice what they preach, and the views they express may be biased by a basic inclination to please the interviewer. Or they may express views to make themselves look better than they actually are. And worse yet, they might express views to deliberately sabotage the research findings.

There are several dimensions along which to take a position when considering Say techniques. Three prominent ones include the people who do the talking, the amount of pre-determined structure, and again the media/form that are used for the 'conversation'.

> **Who talks?** Interviews can be one-on-one, but there are many variations, both regarding the number of interviewers and the number of interviewees. A pair of interviewers can interview a single participant, a single interviewer can facilitate a group of participants, and sometimes participants are given tools with which to interview each other.

> Is there a **pre-determined structure?** Some interviews are no more than interactive questionnaires, with the interviewer guiding the interviewee through a fixed set of questions. A less fixed form can be an interview where the interviewer has a list of focus points ready, or even an open-ended interview with very little demarcations beforehand.

> The **media/form dimension** addresses the form that is used to carry on the conversation such as interviews, group sessions or surveys that can be conducted face-to-face, online, through the mail or on the telephone. The media dimension also describes how the Say techniques are documented including audio-recording, video-recording, or note-taking, etc.

A useful resource for learning more about the Say techniques (that also has a brief introduction to the Do techniques) is *Real World Research: A Resource for Social Scientists and Practitioner-Researchers* by Colin Robson (1993).

WHAT PEOPLE MAKE

Finally, you can have people make things to express their thoughts and feelings. The Make tools and techniques borrow from design and psychology, and involve participants by having them perform a creative act with respect to the subject under study.

An important part of generative techniques are toolkits for expression. These toolkits are carefully developed by the research team to support the participants in a pre-determined activity such as recalling memories, making interpretations and connections, seeing and explaining feelings, or imagining future experiences. Creating a toolkit that is fit for the study is a key skill and key factor to success. Equally important as the physical toolkit is the instruction that is given to the participants, and the way the participants are supported by the facilitator. In the remainder of this chapter we'll give some general principles and guidelines on how the toolkits are constructed. The external contributions throughout this book also show many different examples of toolkits used in practice. They also emphasize the fact that there is not 'a single toolkit' that can be used everywhere and that constructing the toolkit is part of the generative design research process. Chapter#6 describes how the toolkits are put to use.

The generative techniques discussed in this book rely on the creative process and usually result in the making of an artifact. In creating artifacts by engaging in an act of design, we are forced to take into account competing ideas and to resolve ambiguities to make a good enough single, embodied, solution. This is a powerful way of reasoning, which forces confronting all ingredients in a problem, choosing (even if only temporarily) an idea for a solution, and making explicit statements on all its ingredients. It prevents us from 'hiding in abstractions', and forces us to commit to an idea. In this making process, important insights arise, which can be made explicit in the presentations that generally follow the creative process.

As to the dimensions of Make tools and techniques, again there's plenty of choice. For instance, dimensionality, content, and time.

> **Dimensionality**: toolkits can help people to create artifacts with two-dimensional or three-dimensional materials. People can also create artifacts or scenarios that unfold over time.

> Topic **content** can be cognitive and functional on one end to emotional and expressive at the other end.

> **Time** can be an important choice to make: do you focus on mapping how events might unfold over time or do you focus on a single point in time?

INGREDIENTS OF MAKE TOOLKITS

There is an infinite set of toolkits, and a great variety of types of ingredients. Figure#3.3 shows a set of examples of trigger sets which have been used often in toolkits. Trigger sets are sets of elements designed to trigger associations and/or memories. Elements can be 2D or 3D, words, photos or a variety of other pictorial forms, they can be abstract geometrical forms or representational manikins; each of these types has its own advantages and limitations.

Trigger sets are not generic. They are created for a specific study. The form of triggers suggests certain ways of using them, but the openness leaves great freedom to the participant to use them in expressing his or her intended meanings. The participant can choose whether or not to use all elements of the trigger set in the Make exercise.

Photos tend to elicit emotions and memories, suggest complete situations and stories, and carry many different layers of meanings and associations.

 Systematic sets can be used to suggest and express values across an entire dimension, such as a systematic collection of emotional expressions, or a set of body postures.

 Words are powerful at expressing abstractions such as symbolic meaning or emotional content. Words are also good starting triggers for people who are more accustomed to using words vs. thinking with pictures.

 **Puppets** can be used to provoke storytelling and to set the stage for exercises in empathy.

 **Symbolic shapes** support making abstractions and formulating general relations, patterns, and rules.

 **Velcro-covered 3D shapes** can be quickly assembled into rough product 'prototypes' and smaller add-on functionality.

 Cartoonlike expressions often leave room for a variety of interpretations. They can also add an element of fun.

 **Raw collections of scrap materials** can be used for constructing objects or for embellishing rough prototypes.

 **Legos and other construction kits** are also useful for prototyping concepts.

Figure#3.3 Some ingredients that can be used in Make toolkits and where we have observed them to work well

The composition of the set is important. The trigger set should be sufficiently:

> **varied in content.** For instance, a photo collection can contain pictures of places, things and people in certain states, moods, activities, or roles.
> **varied in abstraction**, e.g., including both abstract phrases like 'staying in touch' and concrete things like a picture of a specific mobile phone.
> **varied in levels of ambiguity and openness**. A trigger is rarely characterized by a single meaning. It may suggest different meanings or ways of using it; the participant can decide which to use. For instance, a photograph of a running person can show gender (male), role (policeman), activity (running), mood (tense), feeling (stress), dress (uniform), function (authority), and can be picked for any of these reasons by the participant. Similarly, we've seen the blue rectangular frame in Figure#3.4 used to stand for 'a house', 'a painting', 'a frame', 'a jacuzzi', 'a black hole', 'a cubicle',...
> **varied in aesthetics**. Participants should feel free to express themselves in their own style. Having a trigger set with a variety of aesthetics encourages them to do so.
> **varied in form**. For instance, words in a word set can be presented in randomized order, colors, and fonts.

FRAME

Figure#3.4 An ambiguous figure such as these frames contains many meanings; a very specific picture will only support very few meanings.

BACKGROUNDS AND BACKDROPS FOR MAKE TOOLKITS
A backdrop or ground plane is usually provided for the making activity. The backdrop may be blank or it may carry a suggestive structure to guide or to focus the participant's efforts (See Figure#3.5). Whether the participant actually uses the structure provided (or prefers to work on the blank reverse side) can often be left to the participant's discretion.

BLANK   PRESTRUCTURED

Figure#3.5 Various backgrounds can be used to suggest or evoke structures to help people get started and to help focus the creative process.

TYPES OF MAKE TOOLKITS
Trigger sets, together with a background and supplies such as scissors, colored markers and glue (or tape) form a toolkit, which is administered according to specific instructions. As we said, the ingredients of the toolkit are important but the way you introduce it to people is equally important. Instructions for administering Make toolkits will be covered in Part Three of this book.

Toolkits themselves are varied in composition, and participants vary greatly in how they will (want to) use the toolkits. For example, an emotional collage toolkit consists of both photographs and words. Many people will use both, but an occasional person will only use words; yet others prefer to write words themselves, or make small sketches. Figure#3.6 shows some types of toolkits.
There are many factors to be considered in creating a toolkit, such as:

Emotional toolkit: Photos and words (or phrases) are used for eliciting memories from the past. The backdrop might be blank, allowing the participant to define its structure. Or the backdrop may be predefined to elicit specific content. For example, good memories inside the circle, and bad memories outside the circle.

Dolls' house toolkit: For focused applications, especially later in a session when attention is drawn to creating concrete solutions, toolkits can be more representational instead of abstract. They can also be scale models, or 1:1 models.

Storyline toolkit: This toolkit optimized for the expression of a story. A timeline running from left to right defines the flow of time. Visual and verbal elements might be included to facilitate thinking and expression.

Cognitive toolkit: A range of simple and symbolic shapes combined with words can be used to express relationships between ideas or components. For example, how does team-work work?

Group cognitive toolkit: When a toolkit is created for group use, its elements must be bigger, so that it can be handled by multiple people at the same time, and be read from a distance.

Figure#3.6 Some types of complete toolkits we have used many times

> **time and budget** available (both from the time needed by the participant in making the expression, and the time needed by the researchers in creating the toolkit)
> **location of use** (the lab, participants' homes, or public spaces lead to different opportunities, e.g., in available surface area, or freedom of movement)
> **topic of the study** (whether you are looking for concrete descriptions of work practice, or emotional recollections of past experiences)
> **comfort level** (some participants may be at ease in expressing something about the topic, others may be more restricted)
> **what you intend to do** with the findings (e.g., will this drive design of a product, service, organization or communication strategy?)

The size of the toolkit is also very important. It should not be overwhelming, burdening the participant with too many things to consider. For instance, a word-and-photo set which is meant to be used in 10 to 15 minutes collage-making, typically consists of about 100 words and 100 images.

APPLYING THE MAKE TOOLKITS

Make toolkits can be used in different settings: by people on their own in preparation for a meeting, in a group, or in a 1:1 interview setting. There are an infinite number of ways to use the toolkits and many different techniques to facilitate their use.

Figure#3.7 and Figure#3.8 illustrate some of these techniques that come from our most recent personal experiences. There are many other examples of Make techniques in use from other contributors throughout the book.

SAY, DO, MAKE AND THE PATH OF EXPRESSION

Depending on the topic of study, the time and the budget, all three types of research tools/techniques (Say, Do and Make) are likely to be used to different degrees. Combinations of the types can provide extra value because one finding may corroborate the other. For example, a Make activity is generally followed by a Say activity: people make a collage expressing their feelings about a topic, then describe in words the reasons behind the choices they made in creating the collage. And a session may begin with an emotion toolkit (to evoke memories), followed by a cognitive toolkit (to explore underlying motivations), and the doll's house kit (to create desired futures).

And often, techniques have ingredients of multiple types. For instance, the researcher can observe interactions between participants when a group of people makes a collage together (e.g., Postma & Stappers, 2006). Contextual inquiries contain interviews with people, conducted in their workplace environments. Such inquiries focus on activities in which the respondents perform actions and discuss these with the interviewer. Another example is in moblogging, for example, sending people a text on their mobile asking 'what are you doing now?' This technique contains both do and say, because people will tell you what they are doing.

In Chapter Two, the path of expression was explained as a strategy for taking the participant from observing the present, then back to their memories of earlier experiences, then forward to dreams for desired futures (and possibly to nightmares of feared futures). The three categories of techniques play different roles in the path of expression, as shown in Figure#3.9.

Do techniques are about observing the present. They can be very factual

Figure#3.7 Nurses co-creating a concept for ideal workflow on a patient floor. Note that the toolkit components are round, helping them to think in terms of zones and activities, not rooms. This session preceded the one shown below. (NBBJ/rev with Moffitt Cancer Center, 2006).

Figure#3.8 Nurses co-designing the ideal future patient room using a three-dimensional toolkit for generative prototyping. (NBBJ/rev with Moffitt Cancer Center, 2006)

WHAT PEOPLE...

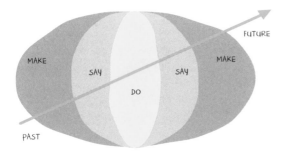

Figure#3.9 The three categories of research tools/ techniques address different portions of the timeline of experience. That is why it is important to use techniques from all three categories.

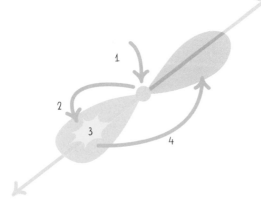

Figure#3.10 There are four steps in the path of expression across the timeline of experience

and precise. But they are also tied down to this present: they contain no 'what if's...'. Say techniques ask for expressed opinions and interpretations, and therefore allow a wider scope about experience that is beyond the present. But Say techniques are limited to that knowledge which participants can readily recall and which they can put into words.

The Make tools reveal deeper levels of understanding and can access both tacit and latent knowledge. The Make tools are essential for encouraging people to engage in associative, bisociative and creative thinking. For these reasons, the Make tools are better able to support the jump to imagining the future on the basis of deeper interpretations of the past.

In a generative session, the jump to the future may be facilitated by having the participants take part in the following series of activities, following the path of expression, as shown in Figure#3.10:

1. start with observing and documenting their *current* activities (what people do) around the topic of the study
2. then recall memories from *earlier* experiences using a Make exercise that includes photographs and other evocative triggers
3. reflect on those memories and possibilities for the *future* with a make exercise that allows for abstract and/or experiential expression
4. then express in a make exercise with a Make tool such as Velcro-modeling to create artifacts for future experiences.

In this chapter we described the tools and techniques of generative design research and their underlying principles. The external contributions throughout the book provide a view on the variety of shape, complexity, and aesthetics that these can take. In Part Three, especially in Chapter#6, we go into detail on how to use them in practice.

A SENSITIZING TOOLKIT

These sensitizing packages were sent out to participants. The client, Sara Lee, produces shoe care products (Kiwi) and wanted to get a deep understanding of their consumers. A contextmapping study was conducted to explore how people actually take care of their shoes today and how their feet feel over a day.

'Me, my feet and my shoes' was the topic of a contextmapping study conducted in collaboration with Kiwi Global Shoe Care. Kiwi wanted to get new inspiration for the development of innovative concepts for footwear products. For this study, 14 participants were selected. The rich material (such as photos, videos, workbooks and collages) that resulted brought this topic alive for the New Product Development (NPD) team.

The standard procedure of a contextmapping study was followed. The sensitizing packages consisted of a workbook, Polaroid camera, and material to express their experiences around footwear. Two members of the design team delivered the packages door-to-door. This was a time consuming act, but since participants are not always used to making expressive things about their own lives, some time for individual explanation is needed, for example, why the package is like this, to emphasize that it is about their personal experiences while it helps the research team empathize with their participants. Assignments in the workbook were divided over a week. Each day the participant was asked to reflect on something concerning footwear. This could be 'how many pairs of shoes do you actually have?' (The interesting thing was that they almost all realized that they had more shoes than what they thought before counting them), 'how do your feet feel over a day?' or 'where are your shoes, socks in your house?'

Contributor

Froukje Sleeswijk Visser

Assistant Professor

Faculty of Industrial Design Engineering

Delft University of Technology, The Netherlands

f.sleeswijkvisser@tudelft.nl

and

Director of ContextQueen

Rotterdam, The Netherlands

Reference

Sleeswijk Visser, F. and Stappers, P.J. (2007) Who includes user experiences in large companies? *Include Conference, London, RCA April, 2007*

Assignment in the workbook: where are my shoes in the house? This participant used her own digital camera and printed the photos.

By giving the participants these assignments they started to realize their own routines, habits and feelings around a topic, which seems not so rich in information initially. When these participants came to the group sessions, they were already sensitized with their own experiences around footwear, and were able to express their experiences to the group.

Two members of the team, one researcher and one designer, delivered the packages in person at the participants' homes.

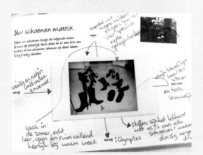

Assignment in the workbook: my shoe matrix. The participants were asked to place their shoes along two dimensions (daily- rare use, formal- informal) and then take a photo.

The toolkit consisting of a box with printed instructions, a workbook, a Polaroid camera, and stickers with images expressing emotions etc., colored pens, pencils, scissors and glue.

HELPING DESIGN STUDENTS UNDERSTAND GENERATIVE TOOLS

Weaving design understanding through the conversation about generative tools helps design students take ownership of the tools and use them skillfully.

With the sensitizing activity, I emphasize the design ideal of paring things down to the essential minimum. A good design has clarity of purpose - consider how the success of Apple comes from clarity of design. Adding too many steps or features to the sensitizing activity can interfere with the primary objective of helping a co-creator pay attention to something in their life.

Tobias Ottahal and Lydia Cambron designed a clear and minimal sensitizing activity when they worked with a co-creator who had advanced cerebral palsy. The sensitizer/primer used a post-it-note dispenser on each wrist. When the co-creator had a satisfying communication with someone he tore a note from his left wrist (the blue notes) and disposed of it. The red notes on the right wrist were for when he had a frustrating communication moment. Ottahal and Cambron could have tallied post-its left in each dispenser but that would be beside the point. The point was that when they met with their co-creator to do a (modified) collage activity, he had been paying attention to communication in his life and was ready to discuss it. This effective sensitizer is an example of good design.

The collage activity can be related to some of the 'aha' moments of learning to be a designer. Most design students can recall that first time they discovered an unexpected idea by simply producing a volume of sketches and sketch models. I remind them how the act of drawing and prototyping activates creative thought - it is generative. By making the link between their own experience and the collage activity, students understand collage as a short-cut visualization method for someone who has not acquired design skills. They can see how helping lay people access their own generative and creative potential allows them to partner in the design process.

Contributor

Louise St. Pierre

Assistant Dean in Product and Interaction Design

Professor of Industrial Design

Emily Carr University of Art and Design

Vancouver, BC, Canada

lsp@ecuad.ca

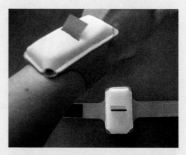

This sensitizing activity is designed to meet its purpose: helping a co-creator pay attention to something in their life. It avoids feature-creep by being minimal. By Tobias Ottahal and Lydia Cambron.

Design students work with various methods of rough collage and sketching. They often make unexpected discoveries through this process.

Contributor

Robert Strouse

Cognitive Scientist at Applied Research Associates

Fairborn, OH 45324

robert.strouse@ara.com

At the time of writing this contribution, Rob was a
Principal at REVES Studio in Columbus, Ohio USA.

Credit

This project was done in collaboration with New
Product Innovations (www.npi.com) and a client
organization that cannot be named due to the
confidentiality of the project.

TOOLKITS HELP PEOPLE ENVISION NEW TECHNOLOGY

New technology can change the way we live. Generative toolkits can help people envision how a new technology might fit into their lives before that technology
is fully realized - giving the design team invaluable
direction to focus their development resources. In this
case, the client wanted to investigate opportunities
for products that will support and facilitate the use of
portable electronic devices by people in the future.

The purpose of this toolkit was to give people the ability to build feasible and desirable options for extend-
ing the usefulness and desirability of their electronic
devices. People were asked to use the toolkits to create
something that would make their daily lives easier and
then share thoughts about how this technology would
fit into their lives in the future. The toolkit enabled the
participants to tell powerful stories about where their
concepts would live in their home, how they would
use them, and how much they would help them stay
organized.

The new technology toolkit included all
types of portable electronic devices (white
forms in the lower middle) together with a
wide range of additional components that
the participants could use to envision and
make their new technology ideas.

A TOOLKIT FOR BOARD GAME DESIGN

This toolkit was developed to inform the design and development of an educational board game promoting diabetes awareness. The project functioned as a graduate thesis case study, and was a collaboration with the Central Ohio Diabetes Association (CODA) of Columbus, Ohio USA.

CODA proposed to The Ohio State University's Department of Design a collaborative project developing a board game to educate and inform people about diabetes. The participatory approach was found to be a natural fit with game design, because games are participatory by nature. People think about and often change the rules of games when playing to alter their gameplay experience (Rollings & Adams, 2003). The goals of the toolkit were to combine designers' expertise with the expertise of people knowledgeable about diabetes (i.e., experts from CODA) to develop ideas for game play functionality. The toolkit also served to uncover systems-based functions and details in the diabetes management process. Participants collaborated in a Strategic Visioning Workshop, working together to create artifacts, which also allowed them to express their ideas and dreams (Sanders, 2000).

The toolkit was conceptualized by assessing existing information from previous discussion sessions. Participants who would participate in this workshop

Contributor

Erik A. Evensen

Owner+Principal

Evensen Creative

Bemidji, MN, USA

www.evensencreative.com

eaevensen@gmail.com

and

Adjunct Faculty at Bemidji State University

Bemidji, MN USA

Workshop participants began by selecting words to use as conceptual starting points. The words were related to aspects of games and diabetes.

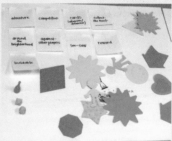

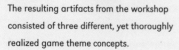

The resulting artifacts from the workshop consisted of three different, yet thoroughly realized game theme concepts.

Eric's contribution is based on his Master's Thesis in Design at The Ohio State University.

Evensen, E. (2009) *Making it Fun: Uncovering a Design Research Model for Educational Board Game Design* The Ohio State University, Department of Design. Committee members: Peter Kwok Chan, Elizabeth B.-N. Sanders and Paul J. Nini.

References

Adams, E, and Rollings, A. (2003) *Andrew Rollings and Ernest Adams on Game Design*. Berkeley: New Riders Games

Sanders, E. B.-N. (2000) *Generative Tools for CoDesigning* in Scrivener, Ball and Woodcock, Eds., Collaborative Design. London Limited: Springer- Verlag.

preferred a very verbal mode of expression, which served as the starting point for the toolkit. The toolkit also incorporated non-specific Velcro modeling shapes to be used once participants had specific ideas to express. Also included were several game-related components, to make things more familiar and comfortable for the participants as well as give substance to some of the more abstract parts of game systems. This included timekeeping devices, randomizers, dice of different sizes, and a wide variety of small plastic pieces. Some of these were defined in a specific way, such as inch-tall action figures, robot toys, and inexpensive playing pieces. The remaining components were generic items such as balls, Koosh-style balls, colored cotton balls, abstract game pieces, colored pipe cleaners, bottle caps, sticky notes, and colored paper of different shapes and sizes.

Splitting into three teams, participants began by using categories and key words from the toolkit to frame their initial exploration. They then selected components from the modeling part of the kit to assemble their game artifacts. At the end of the hour-long session, each team in the workshop had produced a different, yet thoroughly realized game theme.

The toolkit included Velcro modeling pieces for participants to express themselves.

Among the toolkit's many components were non-specific, colorful objects, and specific plastic pieces and game parts.

GENERATIVE TOOLKITS AND OCCUPATIONAL THERAPY

My training as an occupational therapist has provided me with an awareness of how activity and participation can facilitate healing, health and well-being. A person's engagement in activity provides a greater understanding of their context, thoughts and feelings. I have found that using toolkits with children and their parents allows for a wealth of information about their needs to be discovered through a motivating and engaging activity, in a shorter timeframe than a traditional interview might entail. The adaptability of the toolkit's contents and activities allows for the creation of an inclusive toolkit with the potential to be used by a greater number of people regardless of age, gender or ability, and enables their participation in the design process. Toolkits also have the potential to empower children's abilities to make decisions and avoid trivializing the importance of their unique ideas and opinions. Often, this can result in expressive and imaginative designs that best meet their needs and offer a sense of increased understanding, awareness and empathy.

Contributor

Jen Gellis, B.Sc.OT, MAA Design
Occupational Therapist
Sunny Hill Health Centre for Children
Vancouver, British Columbia, Canada

Jen's contribution is based on the work she did for her thesis at Emily Carr University of Art + Design. Gellis, J. (2009) Play Imagined: Enabling Children through Explorations into Creative Participatory Design Methods. Emily Carr University of Art + Design, Faculty of Graduate Studies. Committee members included Louise St. Pierre, Deborah Shackleton, Jim Budd and Ron Wakkary.

Images, colors and textures are placed on lightweight foam pieces to allow participants with decreased fine motor abilities to easily grasp and pick them up. Other paper images have perforations between them, so that they can be torn apart rather than using scissors. The pieces also have a magnetic backing to allow them to stick easily (without glue or tape) to the walls of the pretend play space, decreasing the physical demands of the activity.

Picture communication symbols showing emotions are used to enable the children to share their feelings. These symbols were chosen because the children who participated in the activity were already familiar with this form of low-tech augmentative communication.

The surfaces of the pretend play space can be used with both magnets and dry erase markers, allowing the toolkit to be re-usable.

Contributor

Pieter Jan Stappers

Professor

Faculty of Industrial Design Engineering

Delft University of Technology, The Netherlands

p.j.stappers@tudelft.nl

References

www.staples.com

www.officemax.com

www.hobbylobby.com

www.michaels.com

www.unitednow.com

A STOCK OF LIKELY-TO-USE PARTS CAN BE BOTH PRACTICAL AND INSPIRATIONAL

There are many different kinds of things that can be used in making workbooks and toolkits, quite a few of which will find a role in more than one project. Stationery shops and office supply stores sell various sheets of address stickers that you can print on, colored circle stickers, little envelopes, etc. Toy shops often have relatively inexpensive basic shapes and building materials. Art stores carry ranges of colored paper, clay, and small shapes of foam or wood for use in modeling exercises. Paper, pens, scissors, and post-its are general supplies needed for sessions and workshops. Good images, words, or partial exercises are also valuable assets for reuse.

When developing workbooks or sessions, your stocks can serve as inspiration as well as a physical supply of parts. But beware of duplicating your materials from one study to the next into a generic toolkit or set of exercises. These quickly lose freshness, invite mechanical and uninspired activity, and dull the associative sensitivity of the researcher. This same dullness can then become contagious for participants, as well.

Keeping up your own 'supplies store' saves time on shopping, but be sure to go shopping several times a year as inventories change. 'Back-to-school' time is a particularly good time to shop, as is the Christmas season.

Office supply stores are a good place to start when building your own 'support store'.

A METHOD TO REVEAL AIRPORT STORIES THAT INSPIRE NEW PRODUCTS

The primary focus of this research toolkit is to gain an in-depth understanding of travelers' experiences on their way through the terminals of North American airports. The findings are used to improve the accessibility of international airports.

The travelers' experience toolkit is the first of a sequence of seven consecutively developed generative tools. The findings of these tools are used to inspire and inform the development of new products or services to improve the accessibility of international airports in North America, while not modifying mandatory procedures or airport architecture. The goals are to identify traveler segments that would benefit from new products or services and to reveal design opportunities. The research is focused on the traveler's point of view throughout the airport experience and how to engage designers with peoples' individual airport stories. Originally, the tool was developed to capture predominately rich qualitative data such as travelers' aspirations, needs, desires, and anxieties, but the toolkit is sufficient to analyze quantitative data as well, such as the impact of time pressure on travelers' experience.

Several methods such as interviews, questionnaires, and flow-chart surveys were used to establish the terminology and concrete categories of events, activities, emotions and procedures used in the developed toolkit. A set of icons was developed for these main categories. These icons were presented as self adhesive symbol stickers together with guiding questions on an introduction page. The participants used the stickers to create story pages for their experiences at each airport. The participants started to tell their story by putting symbol stickers, starting on the left side of the page with entering the airport. The participants were encouraged to use pens to draw additional symbols and to add comments.

Contributor

Boris Bezirtzis

Senior Design Researcher

SAP

Walldorf, Germany

borisbez@gmail.com

Boris' contribution was written based on the work he did as a Masters (MFA) Student at The Ohio State University Columbus, Ohio USA.

Reference

Boris G. Bezirtzis (2006), *Generative Tools Used to Search the Design Solution Space: Lessons Learned from Exploring Travelers' Experience in Airports.* MFA Thesis, The Ohio State University.

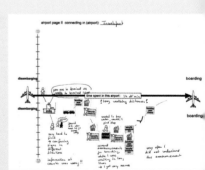

Stories progress from left to right on the story page. Stickers placed on the top side of the page indicate increasingly good experiences. Negative experiences are located on the lower half of the page.

departure	connections	arrival

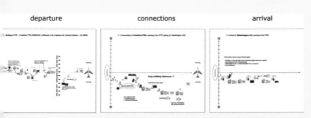

One story page is used for each airport on the way: Usually a departure, one or two connecting, and an arrival airport.

The participants enjoyed the storytelling sessions and the guiding structure of the toolkit made it easy and interesting to share their experiences. Additionally it is very easy for the researchers to prepare the material and to set up the sessions. The sticker and story pages are pre-labeled, easy to carry, collect, analyze and file. In comparison to the storytelling sessions of the pilot test, the time needed was reduced from about 1hour to 30min. The stories became richer in detail and depth and the participants and researchers had much more fun as well.

The story pages are developed to gather qualitative data, but they can be used easily to analyze and visualize quantitative data as well.

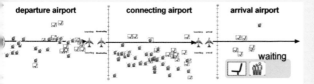

Patterns such as the impact of waiting on the traveler experience, can be discovered by isolating the relevant categories (icons) of the traveler stories.

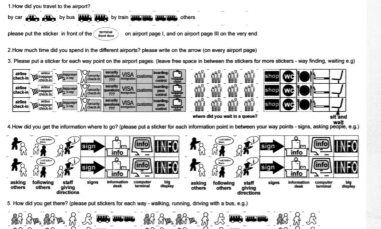

The sticker page provides guiding questions and reminders (the icons) to include specific areas of interest in the stories.

EXPLORING SMELL AS A GENERATIVE STIMULUS: THE IDEAL CAFÉ EXPERIENCE

Relying on visual and verbal stimuli in generative toolkits has proven to be effective in eliciting past and ideal future experiences. However, these have tended to produce more considered responses owing to the nature of the stimuli (symbols, words etc.). Odors circumvent the cognitive functions such as logic and judgment. Utilizing smells in a generative toolkit can help stimulate responses with a decidedly emotional aspect to them.

In a workshop, participants explored their ideal café experience. They prepared by filling out a workbook that got them thinking about smells. They were then provided with a set of 20 odors and 'odor-cards' and were asked to write associations they had for each odor. The cards were then used as generative stimuli in a collage describing the experience for the proposed café. It was observed that participants used emotion-rich phrases to describe their vision of the ideal café. The odor- inspired descriptions were different from the descriptions based on images and words.

Contributor

Amar Khanna

Senior User Experience Designer

Online Computer Library Center (OCLC)

Dublin, OH USA

khannamar@gmail.com

Amar's contribution is based on his MA thesis in the Department of Design at The Ohio State University in Columbus, Ohio USA.

Khanna, Amar (2006) *Exploring Human Response to Odors as a Design Research Tool: A Qualitative Investigation.* MA Thesis in the Department of Design, The Ohio State University. Committee members: Heike Goeller, Dr. Elizabeth B.-N. Sanders and Dr. Candace Stout.

The smell of ginger "Reminds me of a Chinese grocery store my mom used to take me to when I was a kid, I don't know why but I always felt a sense of novelty going in there."

Contributor

Mark Palmer

President and Founder

Geneva, LLC

Coral Springs, FL, USA

mark@geneva-sciences.com

At the time of writing this contribution, Mark was
the Director of Design Research / Human Factors at Motorola in Plantation, FL, USA .

SAY, DO, MAKE WITH PUBLIC SAFETY

Developing communication products for public safety users requires in-depth understanding of current experiences - through observation and structured interviews (say and do). However, defining new possibilities for communication can be effectively done through participation with users in imagining a new future (make). Storytelling within a group of fellow firefighters brings clarity and bonding, as well as primes them to open up to new possibilities. Projective techniques, such as collaging, allow firefighters to more clearly understand how they feel, and more importantly, how they want to feel. 3D modeling techniques allow users to explore new ways to communicate beyond what they have experienced in the past. It is the combination of these techniques that provides true insights for innovation.

Say

Do

Make

HOW CAN ELEMENTARY SCHOOL TEACHERS LEARN TO BE BETTER TEACHERS?

The National Staff Development Council (NSDC) and the Eisenhower National Clearinghouse (ENC) jointly published a CD-ROM designed to support teachers in creating individual professional learning plans. A generative session was conducted to explore:

> Where does professional development fall within a teacher's life?
> How and when do teachers use professional resources and information?
> When should the CD-ROM be delivered?

ENC is a national organization with a potential audience of approximately 2.4 million math and science educators, including all elementary teachers in the US. Four groups of math and science teachers from Ohio, Illinois and West Virginia participated in the generative sessions. They prepared for the sessions by filling out a workbook that made them aware of how and where they used professional resources and technology tools today. They were also asked to bring in valuable professional resources. The session began with a sharing of the resources and tools for teaching. We then invited the teachers to express their 'thoughts, feelings, and dreams' about professional development in the coming year using a generative toolkit. They were asked to create a map of future experience along a one-year timeline and to show where different activities would take place (i.e., home, school or other). The toolkit contained images, phrases, words and a large variety of simple and abstract shapes. The educators enjoyed expressing themselves with the toolkit materials and presented their future maps with enthusiasm.

We learned that teaching is not a day job. Most of the teachers indicated that they are always on the job (24 hours a day and 7 days a week), preparing lesson plans at home in the evening, thinking of ways to better reach their students while driving, or taking 'educational' vacations. The boundary between home and work is blurred for them, and most indicated

Contributor

Liz Sanders

Founder

MakeTools, LLC

Columbus, Ohio USA

Liz@MakeTools.com

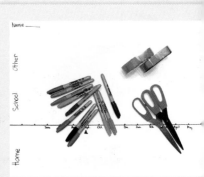

The posterboard background specified the timeline and scope for the experience maps. Scissors, glue sticks and colored markers encouraged creativity.

Jackie's future experience map reveals how she will balance home, work and other activities in the year to come.

Paula's future experience map shows a strong positive movement up toward her ultimate goal for the year.

that the time to explore, plan, and reflect comes only twice a year, during the summer and the winter break. This '24/7 blur' may be the most overlooked factor in teacher professional development.

And although the educators did not know one another before the workshop, by the end of the session they all had exchanged email addresses to continue the sharing of ideas, dreams and resources. We learned later that some of the teachers began to use mapping and collaging methods with colleagues and/or students after they had been to one generative workshop. One of the participants told us that "At the beginning of the year, my elementary special education students made a collage about themselves".

The ENC team members participated in all stages of the planning and conducting of the workshops. After the project was over, the maps and transcripts of the teachers' presentations were posted on the walls of ENC for everyone in the organization to see and to read. ENC continued to return to the maps and workbooks to inform their ongoing work.

The experience mapping toolkit had a wide variety of components including images, phrases, words, shapes, frames and arrows. The CD-ROM icon was a required component.

GENERATIVE DESIGN RESEARCH WITH CHILDREN IN CAMBODIA

Generative tools were used to understand the needs and preferences of children using prosthetic legs in Cambodia. This is a part of a research project conducted for the International Red Cross Committee. The results will helps designers develop prostheses that contribute to social integration and better quality of life for amputees.

It is a widespread belief in Cambodia that disabilities are a result of bad deeds in previous lives (karma). Having a disability is therefore associated with stigma and shame. This influences how people with disabilities are treated and how assistive devices are perceived. To understand the aesthetical and emotional needs of people with disabilities is, therefore, a key to developing functional solutions.

Three children using prosthetic legs in provinces on the outskirts of Phnom Penh took part in the study: a 10 year old girl, a 12 year old boy, and a 16 year old boy. An important part of the preparations was to visit the children several times to give them the opportunity to get to know the researcher and get used to taking part in research activities. All sessions took part in the users' homes. This is an expensive and a time-consuming experience for the researcher, but it made it easier for the children since they did not have to travel. Additionally, they were in a safe and familiar setting.

To get information about the children's daily lives and how using a prosthetic leg affects them, the children were asked to describe 'a normal day'. Using drawings and words from the toolkit provided to them and supplemented with their own drawings and words, children explained what they do from the time they wake up until they go to bed. They were also asked to distinguish between 'good things' and 'bad things' that happen.

Contributor

Sofia Hussain

PhD candidate

Department of Engineering Design and Materials

Norwegian University of Science and Technology (NTNU)

Trondheim, Norway

sofia@ntnu.no

Related publications

Hussain, S. (2010) Empowering marginalised children through participatory design processes. *CoDesign* 6(2), 99 –117.

Hussain, S. and Keitsch, M. (2010) Cultural semiotics, quality, and user perceptions in product development. In S. Vihma (Ed.), *Design Semiotics in Use*, 144-158. Helsinki: Aalto University, School of Art and Design.

Hussain, S., Keitsch, M. and Støren, S. (2007) The Know Your Product Method. Developing a Prosthetic Leg for People in India. In *Proceedings of the International Association of Societies of Design Research Conference*, Hong Kong 12-15 November, 2007, China.

The 16 year old boy's preferences for how to dress at home and at school.

The 10 year old girl's description of her day. She explained that she likes doing household chores, such as pumping water from the well, washing dishes and cooking, because she knows that these tasks are necessary to do. In Cambodia children have problems with understanding the unhappy smiley face because the concept of not liking something is in conflict with Buddhists' norms on accepting your fate and staying positive.

Paper dolls were used to help children express their aesthetic needs. They were given the option between three dolls with different drawing styles. They could select a name for the doll or let the doll represent themselves. Through dressing up the dolls with clothes and prostheses, the children explained how they would prefer to dress and how visible they want their prosthetic leg to be when they are outside playing with friends, at school, or at home.

These two simple generative tools were effective techniques for encouraging children to share their thoughts about sensitive issues in a playful way without being distressed. Both techniques initiated insightful conversations with the children.

Boys' and girls' paper dolls. The children could choose the styles of their clothes and their prosthetic leg.

A GENERATIVE TOOLKIT FOR CROSS-CULTURAL COMMUNICATION

A generative toolkit was used during a collaborative research trip to Chile to help children "Visualize a Future" for revitalizing the City of Lota. Student researchers engaged with a school class to explore the children's feelings about their city. The toolkit exercise led to a deeper engagement with the children.

The Institute Without Boundaries (IWB) at the School of Design at George Brown College, Toronto initiated a project with the Municipality of Lota, Chile to design a strategic plan for revitalization after recent disasters. IWB collaborators included design students from the School of Industrial Design at Carleton University, Ottawa, Canada and from DuocUC in Concepçion, Chile.

Initially, the two Canadian teams met at Carleton University and participated in a cognitive mapping activity. Using project-specific toolkits, they completed the sentence, "In Lota, Chile I see myself...". This acquainted the students with the use of toolkits for the mapping of experiences, their assumptions about the project, and each other.

Prior to traveling to Lota for a week-long charrette organized by IWB, the Carleton students explored ways to establish a meaningful dialogue with the people, given cultural and language differences. They designed a Lota-specific generative toolkit as a potential research instrument, not yet knowing who would participate. In Chile the student researchers from each institution split up into four teams to study the Economy, Place, Communication, and Community. The toolkit proved most valuable for team Community who visited a classroom of thirteen-year-old children in la Escuela Adventista.

The question "What do you like about Lota?" was introduced in Spanish to the children, as they paired up to make their mappings and discuss their ideas

Contributors

Lois Frankel

Associate Professor

School of Industrial Design

Carleton University

Ottawa, Ontario, Canada

Lois_frankel@carleton.ca

Alëna Iouguina

Industrial Design student

School of Industrial Design

Carleton University

Ottawa, Ontario, Canada

alyona.iouguina@gmail.com

Samantha Serrer

Industrial Design student

School of Industrial Design

Carleton University

Ottawa, Ontario, Canada

samantha.serrer@gmail.com

Related papers

Caruso, Christine & Frankel, L. (2010). Everyday People: Enabling User Expertise in Socially Responsible Design. Paper presented at the Design Research Society: Design and Complexity. Montreal, Quebec. 7-9 July.

Sanchez, Maria G. & Frankel, L. (2010). CoDesign in Public Spaces: An Interdisciplinary Approach to Street Furniture Development. Paper presented at the Design Research Society: Design and Complexity. Montreal, Quebec. 7-9 July.

Credits

Many thanks to team members Miki Seltzer and María José Casanueva; Isaías Irán Barra Barra, Camila Núñez Benítez, and the children of La Escuela Adventista; the City of Lota; Michelle Hotchin and Monica Contreras of the Institute Without Boundaries.

Each Canadian participant received a toolkit consisting of pictures, stickers, word-sets, and a sheet of Bristol board. As designers, they came prepared with their own markers, scissors, and glue.

The children used most of the images and words that were provided in their toolkits. Rich qualitative data emerged when they told their story with the help of translators.

together. Many of them highlighted the recent severe earthquake. The children also included many images and words about family, food, beaches and parks of Lota. In retrospect, a few carefully crafted questions could have been tested in advance to determine what sort of stories might evolve with a given image set. This activity warmed the children up to the researchers and led to deeper discussions, with the help of translators.

The class was then divided into two groups. Researchers in the first group conducted interviews with children briefly referring to the mapping exercise. Children in the second group discussed the maps in greater detail and shared thoughts on their ideal city prior to engaging in the interviews. The researchers commented on the importance of paying attention to body language, facial expressions, and vocal tone in understanding the children's messages.

This creative map made by one of the children also provides qualitative data about Lota. It focuses on and contrasts the effects of the earthquake with the abundance of fresh produce at the outdoor market.

The researchers made it obvious to the children that they were listening to them and that what they said was important to them. This opened the door for future communication.

QUICK AND PORTABLE TOOLS

Some research must be done quickly, or be done in contexts where there is little space to spread out a set of generative tools or engage participants in a drawing exercise. Image decks can work in both of these situations.

A stack of photos, carefully tailored to probe issues under investigation, can encourage otherwise taciturn participants to tell stories revealing essential knowledge. Images representing iconic, abstract, or metaphorical topics related to the research goal work best. Animals are often useful, as they carry symbolic or metaphoric meaning. We usually laminate the cards to make them sturdy and easier to handle. Art Center students Pengchong Wang, Katie Weiss, and Xun Ye used an animal deck to study what motivates buyers and sellers at swap meets. This T-shirt salesman describes himself as a puppy that needs to be friendly and open to engage his customers.

Contributor

Katherine Bennett, IDSA

Associate Professor

Art Center College of Design

Pasadena, California, USA

kbennett@artcenter.edu

Contributor

Michael Muller

Research Staff Member and IBM Master Inventor

IBM Research

Cambridge, MA, USA

michael_muller@us.ibm.com

References

Lafreniére, D. (1996). CUTA: A simple, practical, and low- cost approach to task analysis. *Interactions 3*(5), 35-39.

Muller, M.J. (2001). Layered participatory analysis: New development in the CARD technique. In *Proceedings of CHI 2001.* Seattle: ACM

Muller, M.J., Carr, R., Ashworth, C.A., Diekmann, B., Wharton, C., Eickstaedt, C., and Clonts, J. (1995a). Telephone operators as knowledge workers: Consultants who meet customer needs. In *Proceedings of CHI'95.* Denver CO USA: ACM.

Muller, M.J., Tudor, L.G., Wildman, D.M., White, E.A., Root, R.W., Dayton, T., Carr, R., Diekmann, B., and Dykstra-Erickson, E.A. (1995b). Bifocal tools for scenarios and representations in participatory activities with users. In J. Carroll (Ed.), *Scenario-based design for human-computer interaction.* New York: Wiley.

Tschudy, M.W., Dykstra-Erickson, E.A., and Holloway, M.S. (1996). PictureCARD: A storytelling tool for task analysis. In *PDC'96 Proceedings of the Participatory Design Conference.* Cambridge MA USA: CPSR.

Tudor, L. G., Muller, M. J., Dayton, T., and Root, R. W. (1993). A participatory design technique for high-level task analysis, critique, and redesign: The CARD method. *Proceedings of the HFES'93.* Seattle: Human Factors and Ergonomics Society.

CARD – COLLABORATIVE ANALYSIS OF REQUIREMENTS AND DESIGN

The CARD method (Tudor et al., 1993) is a participatory practice in which users and analysts together describe and critique existing work practices, or envision new ones, by playing a "card game." Each card in the game allows the description of an object, person, or action in a work environment – including the user's strategies, experiences, and interactions with other people. Each card is strategically incomplete, requiring the user(s) and the analysts(s) to collaboratively describe the work and work components.

CARD has been used to analyze, critique, and innovate work and technologies on four continents, primarily in domains of Human Computer Interaction and Computer Supported Collaborative Work. CARD provided crucial evidence of knowledge work among low-status workers (Muller et al., 1995a). The method was extended into a more formal framework (Muller et al., 1995b; Muller, 2001), and has led to critical adaptations in different language traditions (Lafrenière, 1996; Tschudy et al., 1996).

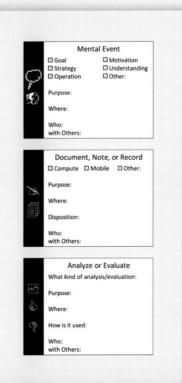

PART2 COMPLETE CASES FROM PRACTICE

INTRODUCTION TO PART TWO

The scale of generative studies can vary greatly, from a single immersion-meeting for familiarizing the designer with the user, up to a large research project taking place over several months with a complex setup, schedule and budget, and involving multiple stakeholders and researchers.

In this part we sketch this spectrum by presenting four cases. The aim of the cases is twofold: first, to give a sense of the possible scales of the studies, and of the different ingredients; second, to show the integration: all the ingredients, steps, roles, etc. are tightly and mutually dependent. Through the cases we try to give a taste for "the thing as it happens in the real world", to provide a backdrop and motivation for the more detailed 'how-to' focus of Part Three, and for the more theoretical focus of Part One.

The cases described in this part have happened to us, our direct colleagues, or students. The first two describe smaller scale student projects that are real. The other two cases describe larger- scale projects from industrial practice and are anonymized: we changed names, topics, and visuals for reasons of privacy and commercial confidentiality (which are important issues in the real world). We are also not able to show photographs of the research tools and materials in the second two cases and need to only refer to general results and outcomes. We also combined observations from different real projects in these cases, but we have seen all of these circumstances in practice.

The cases tend to focus on the positive parts of the stories in an effort to keep them short. You will, however, notice many tips and hints throughout the narratives. We should point out that many of the hints have come out of what *didn't* work, i.e., the lessons learned through experience.

The four cases can be read as stories from the field and as an introduction to how generative research can be done. If you already have experience in the field, you may want to go over the cases more briefly, or refer to Figure#4.1. Here you can compare the four cases side by side along all the primary characteristics. Going over the table should give you a sense for the variety in scale and content that each of the ingredients can take.

CHAPTER 4
FOUR CASES

	CASE 1 STUDENT EXERCISE	CASE 2 SENIOR PROJECT	CASE 3 INTEGRATION OF EXPERTISE	CASE 4 INTERNATIONAL PROJECT
Goals	Introduce design students to generative tools and techniques	Design something of real value for the lives of elderly people	Design for a human-centered healthcare experience	Explore unmet needs and dreams of family members around the world concerning leisure time activities
Objectives	› Hands-on learning for the students › Cross-team sharing and learning › Communication of project to larger audience	› Hands-on learning for the student › New product ideas for the sponsoring company › University/client relationship	› Integrate Lean Engineering and generative design thinking › Provide learning experiences for all the stakeholders	› Combine ethnographic and participatory design approaches › Idea generation and collaborative opportunity mapping for future products and services › Fast turn-around
Timeframe	4 days	Six months with two months for research	Six months with four people working part-time	Four months with 4 to 6 people working full-time
Budget	none	$200 for material	$180,000	$500,000 of which 40% is indirect costs including travel
Stakeholders	› Student team › Tutors › Eight travelers	› One student › University › Company › Elderly participants and their family members	› Generative Design firm › Lean Engineering firm › Physicians › Staff › Patients	› Design research firm › Client organization › International participants in China, India, UK and Germany: 28 families total

Figure#4.1 A comparison of the four cases that follow.

A STUDENT GROUP EXERCISE: THE EXPERIENCES OF TRAIN COMMUTERS

This case is a typical first encounter with generative tools and techniques. A group of five international students from different countries took part in a generative techniques workshop in a project week at the design academy in Germany where they were enrolled. They chose this workshop over the others because they were interested in what research methods could bring to widen their mostly arts-based education. A second reason was that they realized their future work would require more understanding of their clients and users. Finally, some of them had caught the 'co-creation' buzz in design blogs, and wanted to find out more about that.

The focus in this case was on learning and exploring the tools and techniques. Because no design would be made, the quality of the findings, and documenting these for future use were a secondary concern.

A WORKSHOP EXERCISE

As tutors we set up an open program for the week, beginning with two hours of introductory lecture on Monday morning. We introduced the mindset of generative design thinking, explained some of the principles, but spent most of this time showing and talking about lots of examples from practice. We divided the class into teams. Then, the teams were free to set up their own project, getting back to us for discussion about twice a day for feedback and advice. Two presentations were to be made at the end of the week. On Friday morning, the team presented to the other student teams in the generative techniques workshop. The exercise ended on Friday afternoon with a 3 minute presentation of the findings to the entire school.

First, the team decided on a topic and a participant group. The fact that none of them was a native speaker in that area of the country posed a hurdle in speaking to participants, so they chose 'the travel experience of train commuters' as they expected this to present opportunities for making contact with people who could speak English, and who would have time available. Learning how to make contact with participants became one of their biggest challenges.

CASE 1 STUDENT EXERCISE	
Goals	Introduce design students to generative tools and techniques
Objectives	> Hands-on learning for the students > Cross-team sharing and learning > Communication of project to larger audience
Timeframe	4 days
Budget	none
Stakeholders	> Student team > Tutors > Eight travelers

Figure#4.1.1 Overview of case 1

Figure#4.1.2 Word and Image Toolkit

Figure#4.1.3 Nine participants

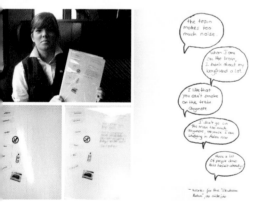

Figure#4.1.4 A participant with her present and future maps, and quotes of what she said

Hint#: Finding participants is often a challenging and time-consuming activity. In open-ended learning-based exercises choose your participant group first and then decide what topic to explore with them.

On Monday afternoon, the group made a collective mindmap of their preconceptions about the train commuting experience in an attempt to widen their view of how the participants might connect to the topic. They then brainstormed ideas for research activities. It turned out that many of their ideas might work well in larger sessions, or extended workbooks. But practical feasibility ruled out many ideas, as participants were expected to have 20 minutes at most to spare. Moreover, handing out 'homework' was beyond the scope of this project week, as a return post would easily take three days. A rough plan, preliminary roles and trigger materials were made in the evening, and discussed on Tuesday morning.

A REUSABLE INTERVIEW TOOLKIT AND A PLAN

One generative technique was chosen, which could be developed, deployed and analysed in the scope of one week. They developed a toolkit with pictures and words to support a 10-minute interview during a commuter's train journey. The participants received a one page A4 blank sheet of paper and two sheets of trigger stickers, both words and pictures associated closely or remotely with traveling.

They were asked to create a collage expressing what was good and bad about their current travel experience. After they had made the collage, they were asked to explain it, and then, on a transparency overlay, create a second collage to express their desired future travel experience, and again explain their collage. Students conducted the interview in pairs, one student asking the questions, the other one making notes. For speed, simplicity, and to avoid privacy issues, no audio recording was made, but participants were asked to pose for a photo with their collage.

Hint#: Work backwards from your goals for presentation to determine how best to document your fieldwork.

To cut costs and production time, the students created a reusable toolkit. By first wearing out the adhesive on the stickers, these would hold, but could also easily be replaced again on the trigger sheet (as one of the students proudly said "it quickly gets weaker if you stick-and-pull them on your jeans a few times"). Two copies of the interview kit were made. When a group of three students were doing the interviews, one could photograph the collages and restore the kit while the other two were interviewing a next participant. Because each student wanted to experience both the roles of interviewer and note- taker, they decided to make sure they had at least ten participants.

MEETING PEOPLE

Toolkit production took place on Tuesday afternoon. On Wednesday, they went into the field: to the railway station. They quickly found that it was difficult to approach people during the peak of the rush hour itself, because people were tired, space was cramped, and the large number of bystanders made both interviewer and participant uneasy. Therefore, the group decided to try commuters outside the peak hour itself. Their first participant, luckily, was curious and quite willing to try out something new. This broke the ice, and encouraged the group to approach others after that.

WORKING THE DATA

At the end of Wednesday, a total of eight participants had been interviewed, and the students returned to school with photos, notes, and impressions, both regarding the travel experience of commuters, and their own research experiences. Only one day was left to draw conclusions and prepare the results. Going through their notes, they identified some possible themes for conclusions. But they had the feeling that the overall themes lost something of the individual quality of their participants, and decided this was an essential part that should be saved and communicated. Therefore, they

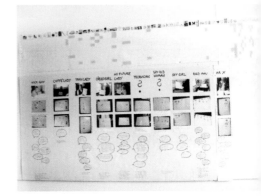

Figure#4.1.5 Counting how often each trigger word or image was used by each participant

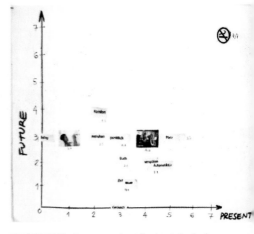

Figure#4.1.6 The frequency chart (horizontal axis shows frequency in present map, vertical axis shows frequency in future map) for words and images revealed that the 'no-smoking' sign (in the upper right-hand corner) was the only item used by almost everybody in both maps.

made a short summary for each participant, consisting of the photo of the participant posing with his or her collage, and larger photos of each collage (present and future), with about half a dozen salient quotes taken from the notes and added in the form of text balloons.

FURTHER ANALYSIS

In looking over the collages, it appeared that some triggers were used consistently more than others. To see more clearly what the patterns in the data were, sheets of paper were stuck on the wall to make an analysis area, and a big grid was drawn over over them. See Figure#4.1.5. Every participant was a row, each trigger word or picture was a column, and each cell in the grid received a mark if that participant had used that trigger. Separate grids were made for the 'present' and the 'future' collages

Hint#: Analysis on the wall lets the whole team participate in finding the patterns.

A summary chart was made to compare the current and future trigger choices. The result can be seen in Figure#4.1.6, and showed there was one clear winner: the no-smoking sign. Seven out of eight participants had used this image, both for the present and for the future collages. Clearly, smoking (or not) was a crucial ingredient of their commuting experience, and several notes and quotes addressed this issue. About half the participants had chosen the no-smoking trigger to indicate how happy they were with the recent ban on smoking on the train, the other half to indicate that they experienced the ban as a problem. Although their stories were different, clearly issues of smoking were prominent.

THE FINAL PRESENTATIONS

Students were required to make two presentations. On Friday morning, the team exchanged their findings with the two other student teams in the generative techniques workshop. Each group gave a presentation of 15 minutes followed by questions and discussion. Students and tutors together reflected on what was learnt and made within the limitations of a short workshop week. Most of the students felt they had made their first steps, and were encouraged that they would be able to make use of the techniques in their further work. They also indicated that it was very helpful to explore these challenges as a team. Then they quickly set to work on finishing a very high-level presentation (to be no more than 3 minutes) for the plenary presentation with all 200 students and tutors to celebrate the end of the workshop week.

A STUDENT PROJECT: COMMUNICATION NEEDS OF ELDERLY PEOPLE

INTRODUCTION

Design for Interaction Master students at TU Delft conduct a research-and-design project in their final, 4th, semester. This is a full-time project, in which the research phase can take two or three months. By then, the student will have learned the basic theory of generative techniques in a theory course, and had the opportunity to apply the techniques in a solo design project in the first semester, and in an interdisciplinary group project in the 3rd semester, but in each of these, the time span for the research was usually limited to a few weeks. For those who choose to dive deeply into generative tools and techniques, the graduation project offers an opportunity to do an intensive study into user needs, and design a product to fulfill those needs as well. The students' work is often sponsored by a client.

PROJECT ORIGINS

The company who was the student's client, Vodafone, had recently learned of generative techniques, and had invited students to apply for a graduation internship. Several students had applied, and Sanne had won the call, because her letter and interview were well-structured, and because she showed herself to be knowledgeable in and enthusiastic about exploring the new techniques, although her experience with applying them was limited.

Sanne was thrilled that she was accepted. The project brief was to 'design a communication support aimed at the elderly'. This appealed to her interests, both social and commercial: to design a product for a target group that had a need, and for a market that was large enough. Most products for elderly at the time seemed very limited in the attention for that user group, typically fixing some localized problem, e.g., phones with bigger buttons, than really taking their needs as starting point.

GATHERING DATA FROM LIFE

The market research department of Vodafone had already conducted background literature studies, including demographic studies and several studies regarding the life situation of elderly people. This information was valuable for choosing the target

Goals	Design something of real value for the lives of elderly people
Objectives	> Hands-on learning for the student > New product ideas for the sponsoring company > University/client relation-ship
Timeframe	Six months with two months for research
Budget	$200 for material
Stakeholders	> One student > University > Company > Elderly participants and their family members

Figure#4.2.1 Overview of case 2

Figure#4.2.2 Workbooks, camera and supplies

gure#4.2.3 Participant during her interview

gure#4.2.4 The social interactions map, with a
ansparent overlay used in the second interview.

group and helping to set the overall goal, but it remained at
the level of abstract statistics. The generative study's primary
goal would be to bring to life this target group. A main starting
point from the literature, supported by her own talks with elderly
people she knew, was that the family plays a large role in the
life of the elderly. Sanne had a good relationship with her own
elderly family members, but she was aware that choosing people
too close to you brings risks to the objectivity of the results.
Therefore, she decided to find three families to participate in the
study, and to involve primarily the grandmothers, but also some
of their children and grandchildren.

Recruiting participants was done through informal contacts,
and was not difficult. Participants liked to get the attention, were
happy to participate and talk about history and their pride: their
family. They enjoyed the interviews as a pleasant social activity
in itself. To keep the emphasis on the grandmother, the data
gathering part consisted of an interview followed by a generative
session, conducted at the grandmothers' homes. For each visit,
a familiar relative was also present, to join in the discussion, and
to make the occasion less formal.

Hint#: *Participants who feel comfortable are better participants.*
Travel to meet with them in the places they are familiar with.

In the first session, the grandmothers made a collage using
pictures and words to trigger associations, concerns, and
memories. The topic of the exercise in the first session was 'communicating with people in general', and in the second session
it was focused on 'communicating with family'. The resulting
discussion confirmed the importance of family relations, which
was corroborated by observations, e.g., the presence of photos of
the grandchildren in the house. Also, insights surfaced regarding
the speed of life, the importance of conversations, the role of
technology in their lives, and the amount of free time.

Sanne was surprised about how quickly the time would pass, and
that the whole time could easily get filled if a favorite topic was
addressed. Clearly, learning to facilitate sessions and interviews
requires its own skills, and Sanne had to learn quickly.

Hint#: Elderly participants have a lot to share and have the time for sharing. Plan on sessions with the elderly to take up to twice as long as sessions with younger people. It takes some practice to decide when to steer the conversation, and when to let it go its own pace and direction.

The second round was a session with three families, held at the university, and based on the learnings from the first set of sessions. These sessions were preceded by a small workbook of exercises and photo assignments. In the second session, members of three generations took part. The grandmother, grown-up child, and grandchild together created a family tree, and indicated the exchanges, interactions, and joint activities that they undertook. The family members also presented what they had made to each other, which constituted another chance for her to observe their dynamics. Sanne was surprised about how honest and open the participants were about emotional bonds between them, even though they were talking in each other's presence. Sanne noted that observing how the participants interacted when making the family tree was as informative as the content of what they said, but was more difficult to capture in findings.

ANALYSIS

Soon after the session was conducted, Sanne transcribed the audio from the interviews and the session, selected passages, categorized these, and scanned them for themes and patterns. Although she was the single researcher (and designer) on the project, she regularly shared her findings with both families of participants, the company and university tutors. She distinguished insights along several themes. For example, the grandmothers wanted to have initiative in communication, but didn't want to use computer media such as internet chat channels, both because they lacked contemporary computer skills that their children had, but also because they wanted to communicate at a slower pace.

Figure#4.2.5 Final prototype in use

Figure#4.2.6 The final prototype consisting of the family book, and an extended TV remote control.

VISION, PROTOTYPE, AND EVALUATION

Based upon her findings, Sanne created a vision for a future communication service, a family weblog with a special interface for the grandmother. This concept made use of asynchronous communication styles, because of the different speed preferences of the family members. A special interface device would allow the grandmother to view the website on her regular TV, to contribute content by writing letters on paper and posting these letters and pictures in a book which would automatically scan and place the content on the website. The younger online generation could contribute via Internet.

The concept was communicated through a storyboard and discussed for feedback with all stakeholders (elderly, families, and university and company tutors). The participating elderly and grandchildren were so enthusiastic about the concept that support was given by Vodafone to implement the family weblog and input devices in a working prototype. The prototype was subsequently evaluated with three families (two new families who had not taken part in the generative sessions were recruited as independent evaluators). Each family used the prototype at first for one week. As she continued to develop the design and prototype, Sanne regularly involved the participating families (each time both a grandmother and a grandchild) to collaborate in further solution development and evaluation. When the lessons from the first week trials were incorporated, the prototype was used by the three families over a period of several weeks, and Sanne began writing her final report.

She was eager to learn if the families could and would use it, and how much they still remembered about the generative sessions that had taken place about three months before. The test was a success. The families were enthusiastic, and their use of the prototype showed hoped-for effects. For example, a web-posting led to not just reactions on the website, but also phone calls and discussions during visits. Moreover, the remarks made by the participants about the product showed that they were still very aware of the considerations that had been raised in the earlier generative studies.

PRESENTATIONS AND DELIVERABLES

At the graduation session, Sanne presented her project to Vodafone and the university. In the 20 minute PowerPoint, the data from the study served to illustrate the project's relevance to motivate the design direction and to frame the presentation of the concept prototype. Afterwards, she received several reactions from earlier participants and other potential future users, including a letter from one grandmother who wanted access to such a product to communicate with her grandchildren in Canada. Many people recognized the value of both the need and the solution. The project received a Dutch Design Award 'Design for All' in 2007.

INTERMEDIATE CONSULTANCY PRACTICE: NEW HEALTHCARE SERVICES

Hint#: The application of human-centered approaches for affecting future healthcare experiences is a very rapidly growing domain. The interest is likely to increase as the Baby Boomer generation ages.

This case describes a hypothetical project that might be handled by small to medium-sized design research consultancies. It represents a situation likely to become increasingly evident in the future as clients demand the best of all worlds by integrating diverse approaches to research and design. This case shows the integration of Lean Engineering (an approach for systematically removing all activities which do not result in end-user value from the production process) and generative design thinking. This integration has the potential to improve both the efficiency and the experiential qualities of a progressive and collective healthcare practice

Group/MD is a group of eleven specialist healthcare practitioners who share an office building in a city in the Midwest United States. In view of the overall discontent with US healthcare practices, they saw an opportunity to challenge the status quo. They could not and did not want to compete on price. What could they do to differentiate themselves? They dreamt of being able to pursue a truly human-centered healthcare practice, one that simultaneously meets the needs and aspirations of patients, family members, physicians, nurses and other staff. The two most business-minded of the physicians investigated current and emerging approaches to service design and manufacturing process innovation and saw the relevance of two very different approaches. One was the Lean Engineering approach. The other was the experiential/contextual approach as described in generative design thinking. Wanting the best of both worlds, they decided to put out an RFP (Request for Proposal) that described a collaborative effort

CASE 3
INTEGRATION OF EXPERTISE

Goals	Design for a human-centered healthcare experience
Objectives	> Integrate Lean Engineering and generative design thinking > Provide learning experiences for all the stakeholders
Timeframe	Six months with four people working part-time
Budget	$180,000
Stakeholders	> Generative Design firm > Lean Engineering firm > Physicians > Staff > Patients

Figure#4.3.1 Overview of case 3

Figure#4.3.2 Each participant shared his or her imagined ideal experience

Figure#4.3.3 Each team created a visual strategic plan for moving forward

Figure#4.3.4 Impressions from the immersion day

between two companies, each having expertise in one of the approaches. Twenty firms applied to the RFP. After a long and in-depth interviewing process, Group/MD selected BlueBoat, a small design research firm from Denmark, for their strong experiential perspective and a US-based consortium called Lean Team, Inc. for the Lean perspective. Both companies expressed a strong interest and willingness to join their separate areas of expertise to offer an integrative approach that would best meet the needs of the client to make a truly human-centered healthcare practice.

The founders of BlueBoat, Eva and Marco, practiced primarily from a design-led and participatory perspective, and had deliberately brought people trained both in design and in design research into the company. Most of Eva and Marco's client work to date had been in healthcare, starting with the industry-sponsored initiatives they were involved in during their graduate school experiences. BlueBoat had worked primarily in Europe, although they did have plans to expand to the US since there was so much interest there in the design-led, participatory approach and not enough consultancies with experience in delivering on it. The project with Group/MD formed the perfect opportunity to start to build their practice in the US and to bring in two students from US universities as interns to work on the project to provide the American perspective while keeping travel costs to a minimum.

The Lean Team, Inc. is made up of seven Lead Engineering consultants who each had from three to fifteen year of experience implementing Lean thinking, tools and methods inside various manufacturing organizations. They were excited by the opportunity to apply their expertise in the growing area of healthcare. They were well aware that Lean practices were being applied inside hospitals and with mixed success. They were familiar with the case studies of failed attempts that were discussed openly by the 'victims' of the approach on the Internet. So they were excited by the prospect of collaborating with a group of researchers from a human-centered perspective because they believed that this perspective would alleviate the risk of designing an efficient but heartless system.

Group/MD wanted the consultant teams to explore the introduction of EMR (Electronic Medical Records) and the use of other new technologies for tracking supplies, information and people. BlueBoat realized that it would be important to talk with Group/MD about the possibility that the research would provide insight into not only how technology might best be applied but also where technology should not be applied.

Hint#: Don't assume that the introduction of new technology is always a good move.

EXPECTATIONS AND GOALS

Three of the Group/MD physicians were particularly interested in learning about the design research process by being involved in it at every step of the way. BlueBoat encouraged them to participate as actively as their time would allow. BlueBoat also made the request that the other eight physicians be involved in the process whenever requested, estimating that this would be about one day a month over the next six months. All the physicians agreed.

The budget was quite limited, so agreements were made in the proposal stage to distribute the workload and expenses between the three organizations in the most time- and cost-effective manner possible. Since BlueBoat was stationed in Copenhagen, it was decided that Group/MD would handle the recruiting of people for the participatory sessions. This would include nurses, medical assistants, administrative staff, patients and family members of patients. The Lean Team would procure all the technology for documenting the research and would pilot test it in the field.

The project relied on a collaborative effort between three groups of people who had never worked together before. BlueBoat suggested that a full week be set aside for a kick-off meeting at Group/MD to ensure that the team members get to know each other and have the opportunity to work face-to-face to map out the detailed schedule and deliverables. Then they planned to make extensive use of Skyping via their laptops throughout the project to a minimum in order to keep the costs down.

Hint: Consider using the new communication technologies to increase the amount of "face-time" between the collaborating partners

THE KICK-OFF MEETING

The three groups met together for the first time at Group/MD. The activities that took place each day that week are described below. Evenings were also put to good use. The people from out of town (i.e., BlueBoat and Lean) broke into smaller groupings to relax, eat dinner and get to know one another. The relationships they established in the first week set the stage for successful long-distance collaboration later.

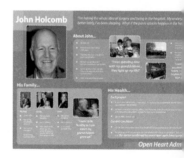

Figure#4.3.5 All participants collaborated on the collective workplan

Figure#4.3.6 One of the personas that was made to represent future patients

Figure#4.3.7 Puppets were used to help the participants explore future scenarios

Hint#: Always take the opportunity to collaborate face-to-face before attempting to collaborate via on-line tools.

Day 1: Visioning

BlueBoat prepared the plan and the materials for the Visioning Workshop in which participants developed an imagined ideal experience of the future situation. It was a story of how it would feel to be a patient in the new facility.

In the Workshop each participant had the opportunity to share his or her imagined future experience as a patient or family member in Group/MD's new facility. After each person had presented his/her future experience, a discussion took place. Then the participants broke into three teams (with representatives from each organization together on a team) to work collaboratively in creating three potential strategic plans for moving forward.

Each team received a strategic planning toolkit to inspire ideas and to visually document their thinking. BlueBoat had also created these materials using the generative design thinking process. After each team presented their strategy, everyone discussed the advantages and disadvantages of each strategic plan but they did not attempt to reach consensus on an approach on Day One. BlueBoat recorded the Visioning Workshop in both audio and video formats, so they could refer back to the session later.

Day 2: Immersion

This was the day for BlueBoat and Lean to begin to immerse themselves in observing how work gets done currently in Group/MD's offices. The physicians went back to work in order to keep up with their patient workload. Before beginning the immersion, BlueBoat and Lean shared observational tools and methods with each other. They conducted the observations with their peers, but met as a whole group several times during the day to share thoughts and observations on preliminary patterns of behavior.

Day 3: Introduction to Lean and Generative Design Thinking

The Lean group provided an overview of Lean Manufacturing, in which the focus is upon improving the 'flow' or smoothness of work. They then presented case studies of former projects that showcase the various techniques to improve flow such as production leveling, 'pull' production and the 'Heijunka box'. BlueBoat also provided an overview of generative tools and techniques in the context of some of their previous work.

Day 4: Development of the workplan

Day four began with a sharing of ideas and insights from the first three days of working. All team members participated in the creation of a collective project workplan. They then created a dynamic calendar to keep the plan flexible during its creation. The entire six month process was documented on the dynamic calendar, in order to keep the project alive with the client and to motivate their participation in it.

Day 5: Reflect and refine

The final day was set aside for filling in the details of the workplan and for reflecting on the process to date. The three groups reviewed the workplan in the context of the visions and the strategic plans that were expressed on the first day and they reflected on the activities of the week. For example, they discussed the observation that Lean was best for coming up with ways of improving the current situation, whereas BlueBoat's approach was best for exploration of future possibilities.

Hint#: Build on your strengths.

They worked out the final details of the workplan including the structure of two shared databases that they would use to document all the data that was planned to be collected in the fieldwork phase.

FIELDWORK

BlueBoat and Lean then executed their fieldwork activities according to the plan. Lean focused on the research needed to construct 'value stream maps' that show current material, people and information flow. BlueBoat focused on the research needed to create experiential maps that show scenarios of people using information, supplies and materials.

They posted observations, photos, videos and field notes to the databases on the shared server. They also met weekly, via the internet, to discuss preliminary findings and emerging opportunities.

INTERIM WORKSHOP

The BlueBoat and Lean Team members met again three months after the kickoff meeting for a two-day workshop to construct a common mapping of fieldwork experiences. Lean presented a detailed value stream mapping of the current system as well as some preliminary suggestions for workplace improvements. BlueBoat presented a visual comparison of current and hypothetical future flows of people, supplies and information. After a discussion of similarities and differences, they constructed a collective representation, one that reflected all the insights and opportunities found in the two approaches. The representation covered both the current and the future states. They used this representation as a framework on which to generate opportunities for change. Each opportunity was identified as short-, medium- or long-term. The final step was to prioritize all the opportunities using a 'dot-voting' exercise.

Hint#: Collective creativity is best in a face-to-face format. This may change in the future as online tools and social networks proliferate and advance.

On the second day of the workshop, BlueBoat led the team in an exercise utilizing personas and scenarios. They introduced personas of future patients, family members, nurses, physicians and staff. They then created scenarios (involving these personas) that might occur in the future given the planned application of EMR and other new technologies. The persona/future scenario approach is very useful for keeping the human center in focus. BlueBoat introduced the use of hand puppets to facilitate the storytelling. Everyone had fun. They explored both 'light' (optimistic) and 'dark' (pessimistic) scenarios. The combination of light and dark scenarios helped to expose unforeseen and/or unanticipated consequences of change.

Figure#4.3.8 The final workshop was attended by all

Hint#: Be sure to consider both light and dark sce-narios when exploring the implications of introducing new technology into the workplace.

CONCEPTUAL DESIGN

They decided to split the conceptual design phase responsibilities according to their respective strengths. Lean's primary responsibilities included recommendations for application/deployment of new technology, and managing people-flow, material-flow, and information flow. BlueBoat's primary responsibilities included both the products and service of workplace design as it was informed by the patient and family member experiences, and the physician, nurse and staff experiences. With the collaboratively developed scenarios as inspiration and direction, BlueBoat and Lean returned to work on their respective parts of the design. They stayed in touch frequently using various forms of internet-based communications.

FINAL WORKSHOP

All the physicians attended the final one-day workshop. BlueBoat offered an immersion session on the preceding day for the eight physicians who had chosen not to be fully involved in the ongoing project. This way they were brought up to speed with the rest of the team and were prepared for the final workshop. The presentation of findings and recommendations on the final workshop day was short and high-level since the physicians had been involved, one way or the other, in the process. As promised in the plan, the presentation included short term and long-term considerations for:

> 'Product' implications (e.g., space and physical layout)
> Service implications (e.g., staff roles and responsibilities, etc.)
> System implications (e.g., flow of people, information and materials)
> Recommendations for application/deployment of new technology.

Most of the time in the final workshop was spent discussing the next steps of concept refinement and system implementation. They decided collectively that the Lean group should remain involved in the implementation phase to provide additional feedback and to conduct usability testing as the design and service development progressed.

EPILOGUE

All three organizations benefited from their collaboration. Group/MD continued to practice Lean-human-centered thinking as they moved into their new spaces and the plans were put into practice. Patients and family members started to notice the positive difference in the healthcare experience there.

BlueBoat and Lean Team continued to correspond and bring each other in on projects in the healthcare domain. They also made plans to share and cross-train student interns. BlueBoat and Lean talked about publishing their work as a case study for others to learn from but no one had the time to commit to this goal. So, instead they put together a 10 minute video which they posted to www.youtube.com in hopes that it would be noticed by design and engineering students and faculty as well as by healthcare professionals. Fortunately it got blogged and the word spread rapidly. Together they won work in bringing this approach to dentists' offices as well. BlueBoat and Lean continued to practice in both doctors' and dentists' offices, working together as well as with other partners.

Lean Team had gained dramatically in their ability to understand and address experiential and future concerns. BlueBoat had increased their ability to see things from a system's perspective and to quickly identify and address concrete, near-term opportunities.

Hint#: Sharing cases with other practitioners is a way of helping to grow generative design research for everyone.

A LARGE INTERNATIONAL PROJECT: FAMILY LEISURE TIME

Hint#: You will need to have several years of experience in generative design research before attempting a project like this one.

The final case, a hypothetical one about a study on Family Leisure Time, is situated on the 'large' end of the generative design research scale. It was the sixth project in an ongoing relationship between GDT, a generative design research consultancy in Boston Massachusetts, and VERGE, an international supplier of communication products and services. The Family Leisure Time Project was large in scope and aggressive in its timeframe: it needed to be completed within a four month period. It was also a global project, with fieldwork occurring in four countries. GDT's past relationships had been with several of the product development teams in VERGE's US headquarters and the first five projects had been targeted toward people in the US only. GDT had successfully delivered insightful and useful design opportunity frameworks to VERGE on all the previous projects, so there was a strong level of trust and mutual respect between the companies. VERGE's product managers who had collaborated with GDT to date had been quick to embrace generative design thinking, but had had difficulty in finding the time to actively engage in the process. GDT had compensated for VERGE's lack of full participation by staging elaborate participatory events at the end of the research projects to ensure that the bridge between research and design was crossed.

Hint#: Ensure the client is able to use the research findings in their work. Simply producing a report will probably not be enough. It may go unread, its findings unused, and your research might be regarded as unusable.

INTRODUCTION

THE FAMILY LEISURE TIME PROJECT
Family Leisure Time was a global strategic initiative headed by Julie, Project Manager for the Family Future Experience Group at VERGE. Julie had been challenged to go beyond VERGE's current focus on family communication experiences and to explore the unmet needs and dreams of family members during leisure time

CASE 4 INTERNATIONAL PROJECT	
Goals	Explore unmet needs and dreams of family members around the world concerning leisure time activities
Objectives	> Combine ethnographic and participatory design approaches
	> Idea generation and collaborative opportunity mapping for future products and services
	> Fast turn-around
Timeframe	Four months with 4 to 6 people working full-time
Budget	$500,000 of which 40% is indirect costs including travel
Stakeholders	> Design research firm
	> Client organization
	> International participants in China, India, UK and Germany: 28 families total

Figure#4.4.1 Overview of case 4

activities. Julie felt immediately that GDT would be the ideal consultant group to bring into the up front exploration phase, but she was required to write a Request for Proposals (RFP) and get at least six competitive bids. Julie wrote the RFP but she did not outline exactly how the project was to be conducted. Instead, the RFP focused on how the research results would be used and who would be using them. Julie was interested in seeing how each of the six firms would address the RFP and approach her challenge. The RFP went out to GDT, two large market research firms, and three consultancies specializing in applied ethnography. All of the firms besides GDT had had extensive experience in conducting global fieldwork, whereas GDT had only limited experience in doing so, with no previous global research projects for VERGE.

SIX PROPOSALS

Three weeks later, Julie had six proposals to consider. She would select two or three of the firms to interview in a face-to-face meeting since this was such a large and important step for her career and for VERGE. She eliminated one of the market research companies for their over-reliance on traditional focus group methodology. She also eliminated two of the ethnographic firms; one for a poorly written proposal and the other for a perceived lack of understanding of how the outcome would be used, thinking "Way too academic!" The face-to-face meetings would take place with three parties: GDT, one of the market research firms and one of the companies specializing in applied ethnography.

Hint#: Never deliver poorly written or edited documents to clients.

Hint#: Understand your clients, their expectations, and make sure you connect to those.

INTERNATIONAL FIELDWORK CONSIDERATIONS

Julie was reassured to see that GDT's estimate of outside costs for recruiting, screening, translation,

session moderation, travel, etc. were right in line with the other two firms still in the running. She was aware that outside costs on this type of work can run up to 40 % of the total, sometimes even more. What Julie learned was that GDT was able to quickly generate an accurate assessment of the expenses for global fieldwork by relying on their international network of friends, colleagues and former co-workers to get very practical advice and hints. GDT was able to compensate for their limited experience in international fieldwork by tapping into the collective online intelligence. All of the international research partners that GDT had arranged to collaborate with came very highly recommended from others who had recently utilized their services.

Hint#: There are a number of active and resourceful on-line communities of designer researchers. Refer to them when you need help but be sure to return the favor.

WINNING THE WORK

The three remaining firms were all invited to come to VERGE to present their workplan and research approach on the same day at two hour intervals. Julie invited all the people in the Family Future Experience Group to attend the meetings or participate via web cameras on their laptops. She prepared an evaluation form so that everyone attending (or viewing) would have a voice in the final decision.

GDT was the last firm to present. They brought three team members along for the presentation: Phil, who would be the project manager, Sophie, who was trained as a designer and Bob who was trained in research. GDT presented their plan clearly and graphically, leaving plenty of time for the many questions from Julie's team members.

Two days later, GDT received the good news: they had been selected for the Future Leisure Time project. Phil asked for feedback about this decision and learned that they were selected over the others because of: their ongoing client relationships with VERGE, their sound, yet eclectic, approach to research, their ability to address the questions asked, and their respectful attitude towards the people around the world who they would bring into the generative design home workshops. GDT's approach, however, was their key differentiator. Their plan included both contextual interviews (in this way similar to the market research firm) as well as ethnographic observations (similar to the applied ethnography firm). But GDT offered another perspective that the other firms did not. Their approach relied on the results of the initial research methodologies to inform generative, hands-on workshops with families in their homes. Many of the VERGE team members already had first-hand experience seeing the power of the generative tools to allow family members to express their dreams for the future. They were eager to see how this approach would work in other cultures.

STARTING UP

STAFFING UP
GDT's proposal was quite detailed in terms of the specifics of activities, time and locations. They were able to use the proposal to structure their workplan for the next four months. Because a number of other smaller projects were already underway, Phil decided to bring in three freelance practitioners for the four months in order to ensure that they could meet the schedule. GDT's network of colleagues and former employees was large and diverse so it was quite easy to find the right people for the job. They were able to hire international graduate students from the local university who had grown up in three of the countries they would be visiting in the fieldwork phases. The students had recently graduated and were looking for field research experience.

THE KICKOFF MEETING
The first meeting with VERGE took place at VERGE's US headquarters (a two hour flight away) so not all of the members of GDT's team were able to attend. Phil, Sophie and Bob attended. This session, as well as all of the other VERGE/GDT meetings, was video-taped so that those not attending could watch it later. Before the meeting, GDT prepared first draft guides of all the research materials for the entire project. They also came prepared with mockups of some generative design tools. By proto-typing all the research tools and materials ahead of time, they could use the meeting not only to talk about schedule, but also to talk very specifi-cally about research methodology and content. The GDT team members

Figure#4.4.2 The kickoff meeting took place at VERGE headquarters

Figure#4.4.3 The entire four months schedule could be seen at a glance

asked the attending team members from VERGE to try the toolkits out as though they were participants in the generative sessions. In this way the VERGE team members were informed about the research and were also able to give useful and constructive feedback about the toolkits. The research materials and generative toolkits would be pilot-tested again later by the international team members to ensure that they were not culturally biased in any way.

Hint#: *Asking the client team members to respond to a rough draft of the research materials is a good way to get useful input. It is also a good way to ensure that they feel ownership of the plan and the materials.*

ONGOING COLLABORATION
After a full day of meeting, discussing and decision making, GDT had all of the feedback they needed to proceed with further detailing the research plan. Decisions had been made about:
> anticipated deliverables (content and format)
> schedule for the fieldwork
> meeting schedule
> roles and responsibilities for the people in all stages/phases in the research plan

The combined teams also decided to establish a blog for tracking and posting project-related information and any interesting ideas that popped up. GDT volunteered to create the blog and to begin by posting the revised and detailed workplan on it. GDT team members knew that it was ideal for the VERGE team members to take an active role in the research but realized that it would be difficult due to everyone's busy schedules. The blog would allow people to review progress and to contribute at any time and from any location.

Hint#: *Try publishing the research progress on a (secure) blog to keep the client informed throughout the process.*

INTERNAL PLANNING WITH A LARGE MATRIX OF POST-IT NOTES
Once back at the office, GDT mapped out the four month schedule against internal staff and resources. They needed to do this in order to ensure that they had the right people scheduled at the right time. Working backwards from the final deliverables, they described all the activities and necessary time requirements. They mapped the entire project out on large wall-sized matrix with the weeks across and people/roles down the side. They used color-coded post-it notes to differentiate and to indicate:
> activities (Who was doing what? Who is going where?)
> materials/tools (What needs to be produced? When to make it? When to ship it? etc.)
> meetings (Internal or external? Where?)

With post-its, the team could update the plan very quickly. They displayed the matrix on the main wall of the project team space in order to keep the project top of mind. They also put notes on the matrix to remind themselves to photograph it every week and post it to the blog for the VERGE team members to see.

PROJECT OVERVIEW
The project was to take place in six phases:
1. Literature search
2. Preliminary fieldwork in four countries with a focus on contextual interviews and quick ethnographies to understand the current situations and contexts
3. Analysis of preliminary fieldwork data and preliminary opportunity mapping
4. Generative design workshops with family members in the four countries to explore future experience domains
5. Full analysis of all the data
6. A participatory event with VERGE to identify additional opportunities and challenges as well as to decide upon action steps

Hint#: *Planning for two phases of research lets you address both the 'big picture' and areas of focus in one project.*

Delivery of the final documentation was planned to follow the participatory event by about one week in order to be able to capture the event's activities in the final document.

DUMPING PRECONCEPTIONS

The very first step in every research project at GDT is the 'mind dump'. The mind dump is a team meeting in which each person on the team makes a mindmap of what they know about the domain that they are about to explore. It includes hunches about what kinds of opportunities they expect to find. Each team member presents his or her mindmap and the presentations are audio-recorded. The team discusses how their preconceptions might bias or direct the research. These are things they would watch out for as they proceeded. Then the maps would be put away, so that they do not stand in the way of new insights emerging from the analysis work. They are not referred to until a week before the final meeting, to check if anything was forgotten, and to see where the greatest surprises had come up.

Hint#: *Always dump project preconceptions in a mindmap; it will show you afterwards that what you found was maybe obvious in hindsight, but not apparent up front.*

LITERATURE SEARCH

All the GDT team members took part in the initial research phase, led by Anthony who was considered the best researcher of secondary literature sources in the firm. They mined both historical and current information sources on a cross- section of relevant topics including leisure-time activities, entertainment, family life, television, gaming, vacations, shopping, hobbies, etc. They posted a selection of the materials to the blog for VERGE team members to see.

Hint: *Be sure not to overload your client with too much information unless they ask for it and return the favor.*

Ideas and opportunities for family leisure time products and services started emerging instantly. Anthony took responsibility for catching, categorizing and storing the ideas for later use.

(Idea catching was not something that GDT had done before, but by the end of the project, it became apparent that idea catching would become a part of every GDT process in the future).

Hint#: *Don't lose track of any ideas that pop up during the research process.*

The literature review was documented in the form of a small booklet communicating the main themes to date. It was organized in this type of structure:

VIEWS ON FAMILY LEISURE TIME

	Historical	Current	Trends
US			
China			
India			
Germany			
UK			

Figure#4.4.4 Main findings from the literature were summarized in a table

Team members were asked to keep the small booklet with them and use it for reminding, reflecting, and note-taking. The secondary research activities continued throughout the length of the project, but shifted more to Anthony's hands. He continued to ensure that ideas were caught and stored and that new themes or issues were disseminated via the blog.

INTO THE FIELD

FIRST ROUND OF FIELDWORK

The preliminary fieldwork took place over a three-week period with two field research teams working in parallel. One team went to China and then India. The other team went to Germany and the UK. Each team had four people: two senior researchers with years of experience in observational fieldwork and participatory design workshops, and two junior researchers. The recent graduates from China, India, and Germany were assigned to the teams visiting their native countries. Each team was gender-balanced, making it easier to make observations in different types of contexts.

The plan for the preliminary fieldwork was relatively unstructured (i.e., the agenda was outlined day by day, in contrast to the later fieldwork that would be outlined minute to minute). Goals were set for each day, but the plan for the day emerged somewhat opportunistically.

Hint#: *Start with an open and flexible observation plan so that you don't miss any unanticipated opportunities.*

Team members paired off and used different strategies for immersion into the local culture including: observing, attending, participating, chatting with locals, photographing, and visiting. The pairs met daily to share notes, tips and observations. They updated the blog daily with photos, thoughts, and feelings from the observations and informal conversations. The blog worked well for keeping those at home in the loop. It also proved to be a good way for the Asian and European teams to share with each other. Although the agenda was somewhat loose, the documentation of field findings was rigorous. Data (e.g., photographs, video files, and fieldwork notes) were downloaded every evening to the GDT server in such a way that team members back home could begin to document and categorize the data before the field researchers returned. This was necessary because of the tight schedule.

While overseas, the GDT team members met with the market research companies that they would partner with for the generative in- home workshops in order to finalize plans for recruiting, moderating and translation services.

Hint#: *Take advantage of 'face time' whenever possible.*

ANALYSIS OF THE FIELDWORK DATA AND PRELIMINARY OPPORTUNITY MAPPING

Analysis ramped up as soon as the team members returned to the US. The plan was for analysis to take place simultaneously on the walls and on the computer. This would go on for the next four weeks as work began on preparing for the next round of fielding. Analysis on the walls followed an inspirational approach and let others in GDT get involved in the project. Analysis on the computer was data-driven, systematic and highly structured. The team members divided up the responsibilities according to their strengths in various types of analysis.

For example, Bob and one of the interns focused on analysing the photographs from all the countries. Phil, Sophie and the other interns focused on the written field notes and the blogging trail. They all met daily to compare notes and to talk about patterns emerging in the data. The purpose of analysis at this stage was twofold:
> to identify themes and ideas and to map potential product or service ideas
> to revise and refine the next stage in the design research process

The analysis on the wall followed these steps:
> First, all the photos taken in the field were printed, labeled with identifying information and posted on the walls.

> Fieldworkers then annotated the photos with background information and observations.

> Others reviewed and commented by posting notes of a different color. Ideas were noted on post-its of a special shape and Anthony added them to the ideas database as they appeared.

> Key themes from the secondary research were added to the wall and the photos and notes were clustered around them. New themes emerged in this process of clustering and re-clustering and they were added to the wall as well. The process continued to grow and to change.

Hint#: *Start the analysis 'on the wall' so everyone can participate. Move to analysis on the computer when you run out of wall space or you need help to see the patterns.*

The analysis in the computer followed these steps:
> The photo jpg files were renamed according to a consistent scheme to enable sorting by category. They were placed into a database that is specialized for sorting and organizing visual information.
> The audio-recorded conversations were transcribed and translated.
> The transcribed conversations and field notes were entered into linked spreadsheets that are designed for exploratory sorting along dimensions including:
  > country
  > region
  > city
  > family lifestage
  > family member type
  > family type (e.g., couple no kids, couple with 2+ kids, etc.)
  > gender
  > age of participant
  > time of day
  > day of week

Once all the data had been entered into the computer, Phil and Sophie were able to use the database functionality to look for patterns among the dimensions. Other dimensions emerged during analysis and were added to the spreadsheets. The new dimensions included values, motivations and routines.

Figure#4.4.5 Analysis on the wall started with the collected pictures

Figure#4.4.6 Continued analysis on the wall

As always, the ideas that emerged in the analysis process were collected, organized and stored. The team put together an interim insights and findings report and posted it to the blog to keep Julie and her team at VERGE up to date on what they found. Anthony had been tracking activity on the blog (with VERGE's permission) to see if and how it was being used. He could see that three people from VERGE checked it daily and posted occasionally. Others from VERGE checked it occasionally and never posted. The GDT team decided to try to step up VERGE's participation on the blog, so they came up with a faster and easier way for VERGE team members to post comments and questions in context. They also emailed each of the VERGE team members to notify them about the interim report and the new, easier way to make comments.

SECOND ROUND OF FIELDWORK:
GENERATIVE WORKSHOPS WITH FAMILIES
Preparing for the workshops
To prepare for the in-home sessions with family members, the first step was the recruiting of participants. The recruiting process would take several weeks since the requests being made of the families were ambitious:

> each family member (who is able to read and write) would be asked to complete a workbook before the home session.
> the home visits, to take 2 to 3 hours, would need to be done with all family members present and participating.
> the home visits would be audio- and video-recorded and photos taken.
> an interpreter would come with the team to facilitate conversation.

The plan was to visit with five families per country for each of the four countries. In order to ensure that five visits be completed, the recruiting companies would recruit seven families per country, with two serving as back-ups in case of cancellations. If there were no cancellations, GDT would do extra home visits. The recruiting process differed slightly across the countries, so Phil needed to track the recruiting progress on a daily basis to be sure that all questions were answered and the appropriate types of families were recruited.

Hint#: When working with outside recruiting organizations either ask them to provide a daily update or check in with them to discuss their progress on a daily basis. Don't assume that "no news is good news".

Hint#: Recruiters make first contact. Make sure that they understand the research approach, so they don't raise wrong expectations in participants. For example, the recruiters need to understand that a generative design session is not the same as a traditional focus group. Participants must come to the session having completed their homework, for example, or they will be turned away.

Hint: You will need to communicate carefully with the recruiters so that they do not provide more information about the goals of the project than you intend to share.

PLANNING THE RESEARCH ACTIVITIES

Once recruiting was underway, the GDT team revisited the research plan, materials and generative tools that they had discussed with VERGE at the kickoff meeting. They reviewed everything, from the workbook activities to the in-home generative exercises to be sure that the flow of events would facilitate ideation and expression of new ideas on the part of the family members. The overall plan held up to scrutiny and the GDT team members were able to make many good refinements based on their findings from the earlier ethnographic research. For example, they had a clearer understanding about day- to-day family activities and were able to probe more into the reasons and the emotions behind such activities. They were able to bring more focus to the planning of the generative

toolkit exercises as well. The moderator's guide was also further developed and refined. Every minute to be spent in the home visit was accounted for. It was very important that the moderator's guide be descriptive and detailed so that the interpreter could use it to guide the conversation.

Hint#: Use of a common moderator's guide and toolkit materials for distributed teams will ensure that all teams come back with comparable data.

Refining, producing and distributing the workbooks. The next step was the finalization and production of the workbooks to be sent to the family members. Workbooks were designed to serve several purposes:

> to sensitize the family members in thinking about and reflecting upon the experience being researched, in this case, family leisure time activities.

> to provide an effective and efficient way for the research team to collect some basic background information about the participants without taking valuable time away from the home visit.

Hint#: When planning for workbook production, plan time to carry out changes that emerge from the piloting, and count on time for the printer to break.

The GDT team decided to make two types of workbooks: one for the adults and one for the children in the household. The kid version was much shorter and visually informal than the adult version. The workbooks were translated and then pilot-tested by international students from the university community to make sure that they were culturally relevant and sensitive.

The workbooks underwent one final revision before they were produced in the quantities needed for distribution. Once the families were recruited, the workbooks were sent out. The schedule allowed for a one week time period for the recruited participants to fill out the workbooks.

REFINING AND PRODUCING THE TOOLKITS

Once the workbooks had been sent out, the GDT research team pilot-tested, refined and then translated the generative toolkits. Because it was going to be important to be able to compare the results of the generative exercises across countries, it was important for the toolkits be culturally sensitive to all the cultures. Verbal toolkit components were translated and adjusted, but the visual components were selected to have one, universally acceptable, set for all the countries.

Hint#: Creating toolkits that work across cultures is not a trivial assignment. Be sure to provide for this in your plan with appropriate time and cost estimates. We have found that international students from nearby universities can be very helpful in pilot testing for cultural acceptability.

Pilot testing of the toolkits proved to be very helpful in the final selection of a set of photos with the cultural diversity to work across all the countries to be visited. Thought was given to the organization and packing of the toolkits, because a lot of local travel was involved. The toolkits needed to fit into carry-on luggage for traveling and they needed to be organized so that the research team members could simply pull out toolkits as needed with everything ready to go.

CONDUCTING THE GENERATIVE DESIGN WORKSHOPS

With the in-home visits scheduled, the research plan finalized and the toolkits ready to go, the research teams went back to the field. Again, two research teams worked in parallel with one team going to China and India and the other team going to Germany and the UK. The research teams were smaller in this round with only two people per team plus the interpreter in the non-English speaking countries. When going into people's homes, it was important that the research team not outnumber the family members because this might cause an uncomfortable social situation. This is particularly important when the family's home is small.

Each team conducted one, two, or sometimes three in-home visits per day. The in-home sessions went well with just a few last minute cancellations. One of the teams had prob-lems with their video camera, but was able to purchase a new one between sessions. And because they were recording audio and video separately, they were still able to record the whole session.

Hint#: Carry back-up technology for documentation and be prepared to replace equipment on the go.

The families enjoyed the sessions and it was often difficult to end the session on time because they wanted to keep talking. A number of the participants commented on how fun it was to make things together, using the generative toolkits and how much they learned about themselves and the others in their family.

Hint#: Schedule in-home sessions with at least one hour of extra time between them to allow for unplanned events. This means one hour in addition to the travel time needed.

The digital audio files were uploaded to a secure server between sessions or in the evenings so that the transcription companies could begin as the sessions were completed. The final transcriptions needed to be translated to English so that the GDT team could analyze them. Photos were taken of the artifacts made during the generative toolkit exercises. The photos were also uploaded to the server during the trip. In that way, the data would still be available in the event that the artifacts were lost in transit.

FULL ANALYSIS

The full analysis started as soon as the team members returned to the US. Analysis of the in-home sessions was primarily computer-based. As in the earlier phase, the data were entered into linked spreadsheets designed for exploratory sorting. Additional dimensions emerged during analysis and were added to the spreadsheets. The team members divided up the responsibilities according to their strengths in various types of analysis. In this stage of full analysis, the responsibilities split into qualitative or quantitative expertise. Even though the sample size was not large, quantitative methods of analysis were useful for pattern identification. For example, multidimensional scaling programs are effective for identifying and showing relationships between items used in generative toolkits such as collages.

The GDT team members met daily to compare notes and to talk about emerging patterns in the data. As always, all ideas that emerged in the analysis process were collected, organized and stored.

Figure#4.4.7 Participants enjoyed the in-home sessions

PARTICIPATORY COMMUNICATION EVENT

Phil, as program manager, had reserved a portion of budget for the activities he felt would be needed to make the bridge from research to design with the VERGE team members being an integral part of that process. He was also aware that although there was a fair amount of blog activity on their part (especially after they made the changes to make commenting easier), only a few people were responsible for most of the activity.

Hint#: Don't count on your blog as an immersion tool for all the client team members. Some people will be too busy to contribute.

The GDT team planned a two-day participatory event to immerse the VERGE team members in the findings and expose them to the insights obtained through analysis. Even though they identified many new product/service ideas and new business opportunities based on the research, Phil felt that it was important for the members of the VERGE team to take part in the bridging process. So the GDT team decided that they would conduct a generative session to facilitate the transition from insight to idea and opportunity identification, with GDT and VERGE working collaboratively and collectively.

Hint#: Client team members need to be immersed in the rich sources of data in order to internalize the research findings.

FINAL DOCUMENTATION AND DELIVERABLES

The final documentation was delivered a week after the final workshop so that the results of the workshop could be incorporated. The documentation consisted of five paper copies of the final presentation and a hard drive that contained 'everything'.

The 'Everything' hard drive contained:

'LEAD' MATERIALS

> the final presentation
> synopsis of the final workshop with video highlights
> field notes and summaries of the field notes
> secondary research overview

BACKGROUND' MATERIALS

> annotated and well-labeled photos from the early fieldwork
> audio files of all recorded sessions and visits
> transcripts made from the audio files
> video files of all recorded sessions and visits
> the databases used for pattern identification
> photos from the in-home sessions
> photos of all the artifacts generated
> guides used in the field
> toolkit materials

Hint#: *Determine from the start whether or not the client is interested in keeping the raw data.*

The final presentation was a high-level Powerpoint of 50 slides with an audio track as well as footnotes to facilitate the presentation to other audiences within VERGE. It outlined short-term, mid-term and long-term opportunities for both products and services. Five paper copies (with CD enclosed) of the main presentation were given to Julie to share with her core team. In addition, the core team received informal curiosity triggers, such as mugs with participants' faces on them, and some mini-posters of key findings to hang in the elevators. It was hoped that these would incite others at VERGE to ask about the project, and remind the project team about their understanding of the family leisure activities around the world.

Figure#4.4.8 A reminder mug, featuring one of the personas from the findings.

THE ONGOING RELATIONSHIP

Julie and her team at VERGE were quick to continue with the results of the Family Leisure Time Project. Immediately after the final workshop they were able to apply insights and ideas to some of the near-term projects underway. They also initiated three new longer-term research efforts. Julie decided to keep the GDT team members involved in the planning meetings for all three of these efforts. The GDT/VERGE relationship continues today.

Hint#: Underpromise and overdeliver to maintain positive client relationships.

ROUNDING OFF THIS CHAPTER

The four cases narrated in this chapter illustrate the range of using generative tools and techniques in practice. There is not a single, fixed recipe. A great deal is determined by the attitude of the people involved, their skills and availability, and the particular constraints and opportunities of the situation. In the first two cases, the main goal was to learn how to conduct a generative design research study and, in case 2, to carry the findings through into design in a client relationship. In the last two cases, the emphasis was on producing insights and, in case 3 facilitating a change in the delivery of healthcare services.

As the first case shows, you don't need a huge project to work with the techniques, but can start with a situation that is familiar. The same mindset, together with the associated tools and techniques, can be applied not only on a small, personal scale, but also a large and still personal scale. The stories in this chapter provided a feel for the 'whole' of a generative study. In Part Three we will take generative studies apart in order to describe how to plan for, execute and analyze them.

PART3
HOW
TO

INTRODUCTION TO PART THREE

In the third part of this book we discuss how to put everything we have discussed so far into action. We describe what you need to know and what you need to consider for projects as small as the one week exercise for the students in the design school in Germany (case#4.1) to projects as large as the international exploration of leisure time activities (case#4.4). So there is a lot to cover.

We break down the steps for conducting generative design research and present them in a linear order: planning for the fieldwork, gathering data in the field, analyzing the data, communicating the findings, conceptualizing based on the findings, and bridging the gap between research and design. In reality, there would be significant overlap between the steps. And there would be iterative loops back again to previous steps. The four cases in Part#2 helped to communicate some of the various ways the steps can take place over time.

The first two chapters in Part Three describe how to plan for fieldwork and how to gather data in the field. The first chapter describes the big picture of planning and covers the entire project including the roles, events, timeline and anticipated end results (which we will call 'deliverables'). Of course, you could just go into the field and collect data opportunistically. However, we advocate the creation and use of a plan. Generative design research uses many different tools and techniques and a plan will help you have what you need when you need it. Generative design research is most useful very early in the design development process and so part of the plan is to be prepared for the unexpected. Think of it as anticipatory planning.

The second chapter describes the steps in the execution of the plan. Step by step. We'll cover steps relevant to both small and large projects. Refer back to the four cases for real-life examples of how the plans might actually unfold. The final chapters cover analyzing the data, and then communicating the research results. The final two chapters provide a brief description of conceptualization and the bridging of the gap between research and design.

CHAPTER 5
MAKING THE PLAN

INTRODUCTION

The success of a research project, especially complex studies involving multiple stakeholders or outside companies, depends on the quality of the plan. The plan is a concise and clear description of what the goals of the project are, what the different parties involved are expected to do, what resources are needed, what results are expected and how and when they are to be delivered. The plan is usually part of the contract in industrial research, and often comes with very detailed time and cost estimates. This chapter discusses the making of the overall plan, leading up to the winning of the contract. But each of the activities within the plan, covered by the next chapters, will involve its own activity planning. Figure#5.1 shows the relationships between components of the plan. We'll first discuss the columns, then the rows.

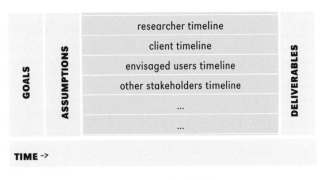

Table#5.1 The components involved in making the plan

We will use the word '**goal**' to refer to the expected result(s) of the research effort. We will use the word '**subgoals**' to refer to the mini-goals that must be addressed along the way to meeting the end goal. For example, the primary goal of conducting a generative research study may be to: (i) provide an understanding of the experiences (past, present and future) of the people whose needs and dreams are of interest, and to (ii) understand the context within which their experiences take place in order to (iii) identify opportunities that can be acted upon to improve their future experiences. This primary goal depends on the domain in which the research is taking place, and the uses to which the client wants to put the results. The goal is reflected in the deliverables that are produced at the end, e.g., a report with insights or a transfer workshop or product ideas, etc. Since the working relationship between the researcher and the 'client' (for students, this would be the supervisor) needs to be close and the responsibilities for activities shared, it is advisable to document in writing all assumptions about who will be doing which activities and by what date.

ASSUMPTIONS ABOUT CONTENT: FOCUS AND SCOPE

The first part of making the plan is deciding on the content of the plan and its application. For what purposes is the research done? To formulate a general strategy? To apply existing technology toward a target group? To fill a knowledge gap?

The fundamental problem of exploratory research is always the chicken-and-egg problem: before you set out to explore, you must know something about what you will find in order to make a plan that your client or supervisor can approve. So it is best to state your assumptions in the beginning of the plan. That way you can revisit them if needed.

In practice, it makes sense to define two areas of content: focus and scope. The focus is that area of experience which you want to 'fully' understand. Scope refers to larger fields of experience around the focus that provide important links and perspectives. For instance, if the focus is 'men's shaving experience', the scope might be: home activities, body care, social behaviour, etc. In a holistic worldview, everything can be relevant, but when you're on a budget, you need to set the limits somewhere.

Figure#5.2 illustrates the focus and scope. The large oval denotes the chosen scope, the smaller circle the focus. Often, generative research involves giving people assignments and toolkits that help them explore the surroundings of different starting points in the scope (e.g., day in the life, hygiene, bathroom activities...). These are shown as arrows radiating outward to indicate the directions of exploration. Because the assignments are open-ended, participants can take them into a direction of their choosing. As part of this, they may choose to 'wander into' the focus area out of their own choosing.

In conducting generative research in the fuzzy front end, it is advisable to keep the focus in the center of consideration, but broaden the investigation out to the scope. It is only by going 'out of bounds' that you can see where the boundaries lie.

TIME AND TIMELINES

Generative tools in the fuzzy front end can be used in a variety of ways, but the outline in Table#5.3 shows a basic plan that is widely applicable and has been used many times before. The table also lists workable and comfortable time estimates for each step. These estimates cover the time needed to prepare for and to conduct the research. They are based on a small to mid-sized research project having data collection taking place with about 20 participants all living in the same region. The estimates assume that the research team has 3 or 4 people who are spending

Figure#5.2 Participants are given assignments in a wider scope around the central focus of the research.

50% to 100% of their time on this project. The four cases in chapter#4 described both shorter/smaller and longer/larger plans.

When you are starting to learn the techniques, or are entering a new domain of experience, you should realize that 'comfortable' planning is what you need. Once you are more experienced, the workable estimates should be considered guidelines to follow when making the research plan. On the other hand, experienced teams working with client teams that want to be very involved will also need to use the more comfortable timelines.

Hint#: *Data documentation and analysis are a part of the plan too. By thinking about documentation and analysis at the start of the project you can often prevent hours of tedious work from having to be done or redone.*

PEOPLE AND TEAMS

For each of the parties involved, you will need to map out a timeline to ensure that the goal and various subgoals can be met: the client timeline, the participant(s) timeline and your timeline as researcher or research team. By mapping them out simultaneously you can see that the relationships between them are working.

In general, the less experience you have in conducting research, the more detailed your map should be. But even if you have many years of experience in conducting this type of research, a good map is important in order that all the parties – the other team members, the client, etc. – know what is expected of them, when it is happening and where they are expected to be.

ACTIVITY	WORKABLE	COMFORTABLE
Kick-off meeting	1 day	3 days
Secondary research focus	2 days	2 weeks
Making observations in the current context(s) of use	2 days	2 weeks
Planning and strategy	1 day	1 week
Making sensitizing packages	3 days	2 weeks
Letting participants work with packages	1 week	10 days
Conducting the workshops	4 workshops all in 1 day	6 workshops over 3 days
Analysis, reflection and interpretation	1 day to 3 weeks	2 to 5 weeks
Communicating the results	1 day	3 days
Various preparation activities in between	2 days	6 days
TOTAL TIME	**ABOUT 6 WEEKS**	**ABOUT 16 WEEKS**

Table#5.3 A typical plan that has been used many times with time estimate ranges by activity

THE 'CLIENT' TIMELINE

Let's consider the 'client' to be the recipient of the research. So the client might be someone paying for your research work or someone who is supervising you in an academic setting. There are many different characteristics of clients that will have a direct impact on how you plan to involve them in your process. Are the results to be used toward a product or a service? Did they commission the research for the insights only or do they want to learn about the research process? Have they been through this kind of process before? What kind of attitude do they hold about this way of doing research? How open/ comfortable are they to new tools and methods? Each and any of these considerations can occur and will change the basic plan and the timelines.

It is very important that the communication with the client is based on an open and trusting relationship. If the client team is not familiar with the use of generative tools in the design development process, it is best to prepare them by asking them to participate in a small generative session at the start of the project.

Hint#: Use the generative tools to facilitate creative collaboration in your meetings with the client, too.

For example, you might arrange for the client team members to go through a similar workbook/ workshop process that the participants will go through, and use the results as part of the **preconception dump** (see page# 116). Another very revealing exercise is to ask the members of the client team to make a collage that predicts the type of collage that people in their target audience might make. Later, you can compare the client team's predictive collages to the actual collages. When we have used this exercise in practice, we have never seen a person on the client's team come even close to predicting what their target audience creates. Asking the client team members to take part in the process in this way will help them better understand the process, be more understanding of what the participants will be going through, and be convinced of the value of the findings. The process is also quite likely to give you some important insights into your client's needs and aspirations. Valuable results often seem trivial or obvious if the client's team hasn't made their expectations explicit beforehand!

You will also need a plan for communicating with your client about the results of the project as it moves forward. This is easier when the client works nearby and is involved directly in the process. But it is more often the case that your client's involvement is limited because of time constraints on their end or because they live and work in another city or perhaps even in another part of the world. It is best to make explicit in the proposal the amount and frequency of communication that is expected on the project. Creative use of websites, blogs or Twitter for ongoing communication with the client can also help keep the costs down. Case#4.3 and Case#4.4 describe how online tools can be used to support communication between the research team and the client.

Regardless of whether the budget is large or small, it is generally best that the client be involved in the data collection phases of the research (i.e., making observations and applying the generative process through workbooks and workshops). In particular, being there to take part in the workshops is always a very good use of their time. A very involved client will be immersed in the process which leads to their owning and using the results of the research. But clients will not always take the time to be involved. The chapter on communication offers some other ways to get the client involved.

THE PARTICIPANT TIMELINE

The participant timeline describes the involvement of the participants in the research and includes:
> screening in order to obtain the right cross- section of the target group
> being recruited, and signed up (which includes signing consent forms)
> receiving workbooks and/or other sensitizing materials
> filling out workbooks and/or other sensitizing assignments
> getting feedback e.g., by mail or website
> attending the workshop and receiving incentives (if applicable)

The activities along the participant timeline will be described in more detail in chapter#6.

Hint#: To help keep your participants motivated during the sensitization period, you should consider providing them with multiple feedback moments.

THE RESEARCHER TIMELINE

The research team's timeline carries their activities, as well as the many connections to the client and to the participants over the time period of the project. Gantt charts can be used to organize and communicate this type of information. Computer versions can be easily modified, sent by email to all members of the team, or managed on a project website. Shared calendars and filesharing services such as Dropbox (http://www.dropbox.com) are also good tools for sharing data.

Architectural firms who work on very large, complex and long-term projects sometimes use a Post-it note version of the Gantt chart to help keep all the team members aligned to each other and to the schedule, as shown in Figure#4.4.3 on page# 114. The latter has the advantages of being easy to modify as a joint action by people who are present, and being large enough that all the members of the team can see it from a distance. It can be photographed with a digital camera to be sent to others.

Establishing the field research portion of the timeline requires skill and expertise in scheduling and organization. This is particularly true when the fieldwork takes place out of town. A checklist that describes the following in detail is an essential part of a good research plan.

> who needs to be where and when
> what they need to bring
> what they need to do there
> when they must be done
> where they go from there (including driving instructions)
> contact information for everyone on the fieldwork team

Hint#: Learning how to estimate the timeline and the cost of projects gets easier with experience.

DELIVERABLES

It is important that the deliverables (i.e., the end products) of the generative design research project be described as clearly as possible in the plan. But that does not mean that they should be described in too much detail because there is no way of knowing exactly what you will deliver before the research has started. For example, you may want to offer as one of the deliverables *"insight into the current and past experiences of people who choose to spend their leisure time gardening."* But you would not want to offer *"10 to 12 major insights into the current and past experiences of people whose choose to spend their leisure time gardening.."*

The deliverables should deliver on the objectives of the research. So a good way to begin to outline the deliverables is to revisit the objectives and go from there. But don't forget that with generative design research it is likely that deliverables will also come from the co-designing process, especially if the client's team has been integrally involved in the process. Such process-oriented deliverables might include a learning experience in co-designing for the client team, empathy with the end-users, as well as ownership of the results.

Hint#: Be sure to estimate the time it will take to involve your client in the research process and include that time in the overall cost estimate.

FINANCES

The cost of the project can be estimated by multiplying the time it takes to accomplish the planned activities by the billing rates of the team members involved. The cost estimate will vary based on the manner in which potential outside services (i.e., the recruiting of participants, the incentives given to those who participate, travel costs, cost of transcription services, etc.) are handled.

When the budget is low, it is advisable to request that the client take on some of the activities that might be outsourced such as recruiting and scheduling the participants, producing and distributing the workbooks, providing the room in which the workshops are held, etc. Getting the client involved in the project even in these small ways has benefits beyond cost-savings. Involved clients tend to have much greater ownership of the results than do uninvolved clients. There is also an unconscious flow of information through contact for all of the people actually interacting in the study. Involvement of the client's team throughout the process takes additional time and effort that is generally well worth the effort.

Hint#: Take a hard look at time costs and constraints. Build in emergency funds for time + cost just in case unforeseen incidents deter the plan.

VARIETIES IN PROJECTS AND PLANS

Projects vary greatly and their plans reflect this. They depend on a multitude of factors such as: Who is doing the research? What is their level of experience? Are different parties involved? Who are the stakeholders in the generative process? What role will they play? Client? Observer? Opponent? Supporter? Participant? End-user? Are competing interests involved? Why is the client commissioning the research? What are the budgets for costs, involvement, and time? By whom will the results be used? What are their expectations for use of the results of the research?

The research planning diagram introduced earlier in this chapter can take on many different shapes and sizes. The smallest planning diagram might be used for a student project taking place in one semester that involves a small number of end-users as participants.

The largest planning diagram might be used to plan a very large and complex project that involves the collaboration of multiple companies involved over a year. The four cases in Part#2 illustrate the some of the variety of project plans that can be seen in the generative design research domain.

INDUSTRY

In industry, the objective of research that is conducted in the early front end of the design development process is usually to understand future experience and context in order to innovate and to thrive in the market-place. For example, what new product, space or service opportunities should the company pursue in the future? The research domain is usually not completely open when working in industry. There are at least three targets for which your client might scope the challenge:

1. from the perspective of the **marketplace** (e.g., "what is the next new thing in mobile communications?")
2. from the perspective of new **technology** (e.g., "what will people want to use this cool new technology for?")
3. from the perspective of the **envisaged users** (e.g., "how will today's Baby Boomers want to live when they retire? What will retirement mean to them?")

The first two perspectives are generally called 'market pull' ("the competition is doing it") and 'technology push' ("we can make it, who will want to use it?") (see, e.g., Scherer, 1982). The third is a relatively new addition, which puts understanding people's needs first, and has been called 'contextual push', or 'people push' (Stappers et al., 2009). The perspectives are not mutually exclusive. They can very well be applied together.

The marketplace and technology perspectives are most common in industry today. Their scope is limited, and emphasizes short-term application. The narrow scope limits the yield, but at the same time, it also serves to ensure that actionable results are determined within an affordable timeframe. In industry, time and cost are always of concern. And results of the research must be actionable, in the sense that it can be acted upon in a business context.

Only the third perspective, 'people first', describes a genuinely human-centered point of view. This perspective has the widest scope and is the perspective from which one can see and learn the most for the longer term. The 'people first' perspective can reveal opportunities that will become relevant in the longer-term future. This perspective might also reveal opportunities across many industries and/or marketplaces. And it may point to the need for new technology exploration. More companies and organizations are becoming interested in these issues lately.

ACADEMIA

In an academic context, generative design research can be used for different purposes:

> as an instrument to explore a new context (e.g., a research project exploring a new product category such as 'medical instrument design')
> as a means to inform a product design problem (e.g., for designing a vacuum cleaner which is particularly suited for the new elderly)
> as the object of methodological study in design research (e.g., "how can we encourage role play with shy Asian respondents?")
> as the focus of inquiry for a research program in psychology on theories of creativity (e.g., "how does visual/verbal thinking promote creativity in everyday people?")

We have encountered each of these examples and combinations of them in our experience. Compared to industrial contexts, where usually a more or less explicit company strategy is involved, academic contexts can be at the same time more open-ended ("it's only for training a student in the techniques") and more long-term ("it's for developing and validating more effective techniques").

STUDENT PROJECTS THAT ARE SPONSORED BY INDUSTRY

In the past few years we are seeing more and more companies sponsoring student projects at universities and/or art schools. This is particularly true for fuzzy front end research and product/service innovation processes. This is often the case because industries want students to bring them new, risky ideas and techniques, while not running the real risks of incorporating them on tactically important development plans, devoting costly staff resources, or releasing too much confidential company information to competitors.

The subgoals with regard to the use of generative tools and methods in this context include:

> making a contribution to knowledge in a specific domain,
> contributing to the education of students (some of whom may be considered as future employees),
> having a lot of innovative work done for a small investment of time or money, and
> learning about the research method.

These diverse perspectives have the potential to set up a conflict between the interests of the student (learning) and the client (insights). The more time and/or money the client invests in the student project, the more likely these issues are to arise. It is very important that all parties involved (i.e., student, supervisor, company) agree upon the primary subgoals and clarify roles and responsibilities before the work begins. Case#4.2 describes the successful results of company-sponsored student work.

CLARIFYING THE SUBGOALS UP FRONT

Clarifying the subgoals up front takes on different forms in the three contexts.

With work in industry, one or more meetings (face-to-face or via conference call or Skype) usually take place between the industrial partner (the client) and the research team to discuss the subgoals, timing and expected deliverables. Then documentation in the form of a proposal with very specific action steps, time and cost parameters and deliverables is written. We need to be able to predict the project timing in advance so that the client team will be able to mark their calendars as to when meetings will occur and when the results will be delivered. We need to be able to predict what costs will be incurred throughout the entire project. And we need to describe the deliverables in advance so the client knows what they are paying for. This can be quite a challenge in the case of generative research whose aim is to uncover insights and/or generate ideas for new products/services/experiences. How can you cost what you don't know?

In addition, the client generally invites proposals from several different research team/ firms. When the stakes are particularly high, a face-to-face interview is also held. For example, the interview is common in architectural practice where the project is defined over many years and will result in a 'product' that will serve generations of people. In architecture, the working relationship will go on for many years so it is more important that the chemistry between people involved is positive, as well. Case#4.4 touches on the process of winning a large international research project where face-to-face interviews played a role in the client's selection of the consultant firm.

In academic research settings, there will usually be a proposal or workplan as well. The time constraints are likely to be more generous and the budget possibly less generous than in the business world. In the teaching setting, the goals and subgoals differ depending on whether one is:
> understanding how the tools and methods work (as in Case#4.1),
> learning how to apply the tools and methods and their results within a design project,
> experimenting with new tools and methods,
> investigating domains that have not yet been explored.

In client-sponsored student work, the expectations with regard to learning and actionable results need to be discussed and agreed upon in advance. As is true with projects in industry, a proposal or workplan

should be generated at the beginning of the process. The deliverables need to be agreed upon in advance. Issues of ownership of the ideas generated will need to be settled up front, as well. For example, if a student project leads to a new patent, who owns the patent? When may the student or university show materials from the study in their portfolio or publications? A common arrangement is that the student learns skills, and can be the inventor of a patent, the company is owner of the patent on product ideas, and academics publish methodological insights (with limited reference to product ideas). It can be a win-win-win situation. But the anticipated balance between learning/growing and the harvesting of ideas must be addressed up front to avoid a mismatch of expectations.

LEARNING ABOUT MAKING THE PLAN

The best way to improve your skills in making good generative design research plans is to practice. Make the plan, execute the plan and then (most importantly) evaluate the effectiveness of the plan after the project is over. You should meet as a team after the project is over to review and discuss:
> were the objectives met? Why or why not?
> were the deliverables completed and delivered? Why or why not?
> was the schedule met? Why or why not?
> was the work done within the estimated budget? Why or why not?

It is also advisable to ask the client team for their feedback about the experience and the deliverables of the project.

The only way to get better at making plans is to get feedback on the execution of work that was previously planned or to work with others who have had many such experiences.

Contributor

Katherine Bennett, IDSA

Associate Professor

Art Center College of Design

Pasadena, California, USA

kbennett@artcenter.edu

DESIGNING DESIGN RESEARCH

Design research is sometimes seen as a constant set of tools and, as a result, some designers conclude that one process can work for all situations. The field has evolved into a complex landscape of approaches, however, and good design practice stays abreast of these developments.

To help our students break out of a narrow approach yet negotiate the complex landscape of methods in practice today, we acquaint them with a comprehensive yet manageable set, giving them an understanding of why, and in which situations, a particular approach would be effective.

We have developed a decision aid that asks the students what kind of knowledge they are seeking, and points them toward research tools that would be effective for that purpose. Once they've used the aid for a few projects, they begin to gain knowledge of the variety of approaches and see how different methods work in different cases.

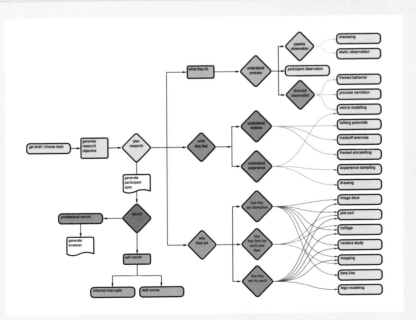

WORKING WITH SME'S VERSUS LARGE COMPANIES

Until Wakeford (2004), Small and Medium Enterprises (SME's) have been the forgotten child within academic research regarding participatory design. In comparison to the large international companies, SME's have specific characteristics and needs that distance them from large international companies. SME's often work with regular clients, know them well and invest greatly in the relations with their clients. Because of their close relation with their clients, SME's have a good picture of the users they are designing for; they feel involved. But that is also their pitfall, they think they know everything while in many cases, they need a fresh look at their current practice. This fresh look is also needed for the SME's dedication to the initial innovation that was the basis for the company's origin. Generative techniques can help in this aspect. They can provide strategic market opportunities, new product lines, a closer and better relation with their clients and new ways to get to know their clients.

Contributor
Christine de Lille
Utrecht University of Applied Sciences,
the Netherlands

References:
Wakeford, N., (2004), Innovation through people-centred design-lessons from the USA. DTI global watch mission report.

De Lille, C.S.H. Van der Lugt R., Bakkeren, M. (2010) Co-design in a Pressure Cooker. Tips and tricks for SMEs ISBN 978-94-90560-03-4

Table: overview comparing SME's and large companies

	LARGE INTERNATIONAL COMPANIES	SMALL AND MEDIUM ENTERPRISES	SMALL DESIGN AGENCIES
Budget	Large budget	Small budget	Small budget
Staff	Team or team members, or outside consultancies dedicated to design research	No dedicated staff	No dedicated staff
Involvement with user	Large distance to user	Close contact with user	Contact with user through client
Communication challenges	Communication between researcher and designer; communication between departments	No communication problems	Communication problems with clients
Knowledge on user research methods	In specialized departments	Often not aware of need	Aware of need, but often lacking in skills

Contributor

Pieter Jan Stappers

Professor

Faculty of Industrial Design

Delft University of Technology

The Netherlands

p.j.stappers@tudelft.nl

Reference

Buzan, T, & Buzan, B. (2000) *The Mindmap Book,*
Millennium Edition. London: BBC

MINDMAP YOUR PRECONCEPTIONS

At the start of a project, it is important to try to map an overview of what (you think that) you know beforehand. This serves two purposes: at the start, it helps you set the initial directions you wish to explore in the study, guiding areas that should be covered, and issues that should not be forgotten. At the end, it helps you recollect what you thought about the issues before the study, as the 'shaving' mindmap of Sleeswijk Visser shows. Very often, your insight grows dramatically during the study, and your findings will seem 'totally obvious' in hindsight: but these 'obvious' things are the value, the things that would have been overlooked.

Mindmaps, as developed by Buzan, are an efficient and inspiring way to collect and organize your thoughts, using visual and verbal skills. Starting from a central concept, you keep adding branches connecting associations and specifications, using words and pictures. Although they are personal expressions, mindmaps can very effectively support communication, too.

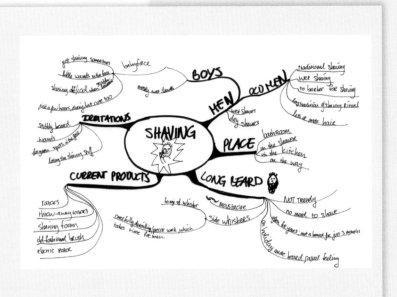

THE PATH TOWARDS A SIGNAGE SOLUTION FOR MIAMI VALLEY HOSPITAL

When Miami Valley Hospital (MVH) decided to develop a new 12-story patient tower on an existing urban campus located in Dayton, Ohio, they knew immediately that the new campus would be composed of complex navigational paths. Over the course of many decades, the campus had grown up and grown out; adding one more building would most certainly contribute to the wayfinding complexity. MVH concluded that a comprehensive signage solution would be required to enable people to find their way.

The signage design team hired by MVH recommended that the best path for determining the solution required an in-depth understanding of the campus, the organization and the various stakeholders involved. Two primary stakeholder groups were indentified: a cross-functional team from MVH (including executives, managers and front line staff) as well as MVH's 'expert users', including patients (both frequent and infrequent), family members and visitors (both frequent and infrequent).

The signage design team included researchers and designers working closely together. They took a participatory approach to the challenge in order to draw upon the vast knowledge possessed by the MVH team and the expert users with regard to wayfinding on the MVH campus. They began with an open-ended discovery process including: visioning, observing, interviewing, surveying, and a series of participatory workshops.

The same research plan was used for both the cross-functional MVH team and the expert user team. In this way it was easy to see where the perspectives overlapped or contradicted one another. The MVH team understood that the needs of their customers came first with regard to wayfinding and signage. The key components of the research plan included:

Contributor

Trudy A. Cherok

Consultant

Design I Research I Writing

Columbus, Ohio USA

trudy.cherok@earthlink.net

Trudy's position at the time she wrote this contribution was an Associate at NBBJ Architects in Columbus, Ohio USA.

Credits

Thanks to Nikki Burns, Miami Valley Hospital Southeast Addition Project Director, for her continued support and facilitation of this nontraditional approach to signage system solutions!
The design/research team was working with NBBJ Design when this project took place.

The Primer Workbook was used for collecting data and demographics from the two participatory groups. It also helped to prime them for participation in the cognitive mapping workshops.

An expert user presents his cognitive map; the map captures his mental image of the existing Miami Valley Hospital campus and is based upon on his personal experiences.

Members of the MVH executive team build a cognitive map based upon on their collective personal experiences.

In an unanticipated outcome, members of the executive team embrace and deliver the final outcomes to the full executive team in a resulting succession plan.

Priming Workbooks to prepare participants for the workshops
> Cognitive Map Making: *Getting There, Current Maps and Future Maps*
> Change Willingness Diagram
> Wayfinding Prowess Diagram
> Wayfinding Personas
> Linear and Circular Wayfinding Journeys
> 'What if' Cards
> Surveys and Interviews.

The level of in-depth understanding generated by the research effort resulted in many reliable outcomes: principles for strategy and design, discernable wayfinding types, quantifiable data for spatial use and navigation, experiential hierarchies, information hierarchies, language splits, transition plans, a new wayfinding/wayfollowing theory, chains for optimized wayfinding performance and high level strategy and design for wayfinding/wayfollowing solutions.

An unanticipated outcome was that the process produced an owner-embraced succession plan. With the participatory approach, MVH and the design team learned together throughout the process and therefore gained the same depth of understanding - moving toward solutions at the same rate. The signage design strategy is now being implemented by MVH.

DESIGNING AND DEVELOPING ERGONOMIC INTERVENTIONS FOR IMAGING TECHNOLOGISTS

Several studies have shown that imaging technologists, including sonographers, x-ray technicians, and mammographers, are experiencing occupationally related musculoskeletal injuries. By using a participatory design process that engaged practicing technologists, we identified opportunities to develop tools, equipment, and procedures that could reduce the physical burden associated with imaging work.

The long term objective of this project was to reduce the high incidence of work-related musculoskeletal disorders (MSDs) and physical discomfort experienced by imaging technologists (I-techs). Prior research has shown MSDs to be a significant problem for this occupational group, due to patient interaction and other risk factors encountered on the job. Due to the shortage of imaging technologists and increasing demand for scans, the health status of imaging technologists is a critical factor in the availability of health care services.

Recognizing these issues, we implemented a four-phase design process with the goal of developing, through a participatory design process, usable and acceptable interventions that reduce the physical challenges associated with provision of imaging services in hospital and out-patient settings. The initial design concept phase engaged targeted groups of I-techs, including vascular, cardiac, diagnostic sonographers, diagnostic radiologists, and mammographers, in active ideation workshops. In preparation for the sessions, participating I-techs were asked to complete a sensitization workbook which had them reflect upon the more physically demanding tasks that they perform.

Contributors

Carolyn Sommerich
Associate Professor
Integrated Systems Engineering
The Ohio State University
Columbus, Ohio 43210 USA
sommerich.1@osu.edu

Steve Lavender
Associate Professor
Integrated Systems Engineering & Orthopaedics
The Ohio State University
Columbus Ohio 43210 USA
lavender.1@osu.edu

Reference

[1] Sanders, E.B.-N. (2002), From user-centered to participatory design approach. In Frascara, J. (ed.), *Design and the Social Sciences*. (London: Taylor & Francis Books Limited).

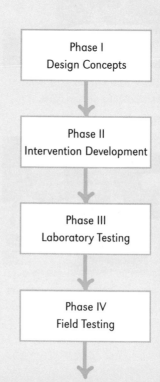

Phase I
Design Concepts

Phase II
Intervention Development

Phase III
Laboratory Testing

Phase IV
Field Testing

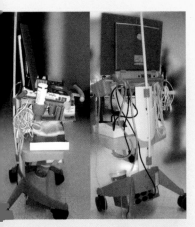

These pictures show the expressed needs of the I-techs for a portable equipment set-up that provides them with height adjustability for a larger display screen, on-board storage (for in-patient records, equipment cleaning supplies, and electrodes), and the capacity to burn CDs of sonographic exams on the spot.

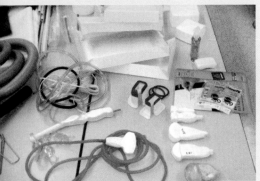

Some of the materials used by the i-techs in developing their interventions

Workbooks were reviewed with participants at the beginning of the ideation group sessions. Participants discussed and prioritized equipment, environmental, and situational issues that make specific tasks physically demanding. Participants were then asked to address the issues they identified in an active design process using the MakeTools approach. Participants expressed their ideas by assembling an assortment of common materials to form full size 3D representations of their concepts.

All workshop artifacts and the presentations that the I-techs made about them were reviewed by the research team to understand the needs and desires being communicated by the participants. Our challenge was to develop these needs into design concepts and then into interventions. In some cases the concepts represented products that were already available. In other cases, new solution concepts were developed. All potential intervention concepts were then brought back to the appropriate groups of I-techs to obtain feedback, including foreseeable usability issues that might present barriers to adoption. At the conclusion of these sessions, I-tech participants were asked to help us prioritize which interventions should move forward in the near term, through subsequent laboratory and field evaluation phases.

The laboratory phase validates, through controlled experimentation, that the intervention concepts reduce the physical demands placed on the I-tech. Subsequently, where possible, successfully validated interventions are being introduced into clinical settings to obtain usability and acceptability feedback from I-techs performing normal job duties.

CUSTOMER JOURNEY MAPPING: THE CLIENT'S LOOKING GLASS

A Customer Journey Map shows how the user goes through several stages when experiencing a product or service. It helps you design the several stages that make up the setting for a total experience. But it's also a great assessment tool. In our consultancy practice we hold Customer Journey Mapping sessions with our clients to help them assess:

> How do their different customers experience their services/products in each stage?
> What do they know about their different customers in that stage?
> And what don't they know?
> What prior research is available for each stage that might fill knowledge gaps?
> Where is there room for improvement and where are they facing challenges?
> Where lie opportunities for design or innovation?

Going through these questions and visualizing the answers builds the relationship with our client and gives a solid foundation for design research projects. It often is the basis for finding key areas the client thinks is important, but then realizes he knows little about, or doesn't know how dependable they are.

Contributor

Erik Roscam Abbing

Founder/Owner of Zilver Innovation

Rotterdam, The Netherlands

Erik@zilverinnovation.com

A customer journey mapping session with the team from Zilver Innovation and the developers, designers, purchasers, marketers and managers from the Dutch kitchen appliance manufacturer ETNA.

This consumer journey map describes the stages of the journey for users of ETNA kitchen equipment. For each stage of the journey the insights that followed from the contextmapping research were summarized. Next, the project team looked at why that stage is important to the user, how it contributes to the entire experience, what happens in the stage and when it takes place. Next, the team has looked at how the brand's innovation values can be made concrete in each stage. There is room to map ideas that the brand's designers and product managers may in have the coming years, stimulating them to come up with ideas for each stage of the journey.

Contributor

Preetham Kolari

Director of Research

Motorola Mobility

809 Eleventh Ave

Sunnyvale, California USA

pree@motorola.com

This contribution was based on work done when
Preetham was a Vice President at SonicRim,
Columbus, Ohio USA.

AN INTERNATIONAL RESEARCH PROJECT AT MICROSOFT

Microsoft Corporation wanted to improve its market size in the emerging markets, mainly the BRIC countries (i.e., Brazil, Russia, India and China). We went to nine different emerging market countries in three phases. The first phase was extremely generative and was intended to understand the value that a PC provided for the end user and the motivations involved. We started with participatory exercises that defined people's future computing experiences. The next phase was to prototype the user interface with the user. The last phase was to usability test a working prototype and benchmark it against previous versions.

Microsoft hired an external consultancy to help with the research. Very high participation early on during the generative phases of the project was key to a successful transition of knowledge from the consultancy to an internal Microsoft team. It also helped the team build empathy for people's aspirations. Immersion workshops helped the Microsoft team members who did not travel get a holistic view of the different cultural nuances and needs. Overall, the research helped Microsoft make the right decisions for the emerging markets and to conceptualize and ship the Windows Starter Edition.

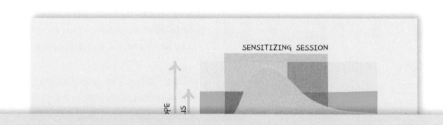

SENSITIZING SESSION

CHAPTER 6
GATHERING DATA IN THE FIELD

INTRODUCTION

Gathering field data is the most visible of the activities in the generative design research process. It is probably the activity that people would picture when imagining what doing generative design research will be like. But it is only one step out of the many steps that it takes to get ready for fielding and later to get the data documented in preparation for analysis.

Readers who are not already familiar with gathering field data may want to read one or more of the cases of Part 2 before reading this chapter. The cases contain realistic detail and can help you imagine what conducting the fieldwork will be like. This chapter is more instructive and was written under the assumption that the reader is not already skilled in planning and executing field research.

STARTING UP

GOING FROM THE PROJECT PLAN TO THE WORKPLAN

The project plan in the previous chapter was constructed for the purpose of describing the research in order to get approval to move ahead with the project. It is, in essence, a prediction about what the research will entail and what it will deliver. Prediction of the outcome may be necessary to catch the interest of the client and to get a sign-off on the work. Prediction is also needed in order to estimate the time and cost of the project. This can be tricky when the scope is relatively open and timeline is aggressive. As we mentioned previously, this is not an easy task. Estimation of the time and cost of generative design research projects is something best learned through experience. It is not something that we will be able to address in this book.

The project plan is not the same thing as the workplan. The workplan is usually far more detailed, with dates, names, places and deliverables indicated day by day. Table 6.1 shows the workplan outline that we will use to structure this chapter. This outline may be helpful to use as the starting point of the workplan for your next generative design research project.

PROJECT PLAN

Find and review what is already known

Initiate the team(s)

Understand the current context of use/experience

Screen and recruit the participants

Plan what the participants will go through

Create the materials
(e.g., sensitizing materials, session script, toolkits and checklist)

Pilot test the plan and the materials

Revise and produce the research materials

Sensitize the participants

Conduct the interviews or workshops

Document the data

Table#6.1 An outline for the workplan

WORK PLAN

The project documentation becomes increasingly detailed as the project progresses as is shown in Figure#6.2 The project plan needs to be as accurate as possible since it helps you get the job and it defines the overall budget and timing. The workplan maps out all actions of team members and their interactions over the course of the project. The session script details all the actions and the timing for a single session. The screener details who the participants will be and when they will take part in the action.

SESSION SCRIPT

FIND AND REVIEW WHAT IS ALREADY KNOWN
The first place to begin for any new project is to find out what has previously been learned about the scope and focus of the research topic. The focus is the core area of the topic that you are exploring, the scope is defined by the outside boundaries of where you want to go. The *focus* of a study should not be confused with its *goal*. The focus indicates a part of the topic, whereas the goal points beyond the study to useful insights.

SCREENING RULES & SCREENER

Figure#6.2
Documents of increasing detail.

Learning via previously published sources is called "secondary research". Traditionally, secondary sources have been books, papers and peer-reviewed articles but today there are many other sources (e.g., YouTube, documentaries, Wikipedia) available on the Internet. It is particularly important to track and credit all such sources since the credibility of the content varies quite a lot and websites come and go. Be sure to include the date on which you accessed Internet information.

Often the client will have relevant background research that should also be reviewed before the workplan is established. Some or most of this information may be proprietary so it is important to ask for it. It is often the case that the client does not want to give the research team the results of previous research for fear that it will point the research team in only one or the wrong direction. Try to persuade them otherwise. Reviewing information and research results provided by the client is useful not only for project-relevant content, but also as a means of better understanding the perspective of the client's team as well as the communication channels they are familiar and comfortable with. Secondary research also can provide some background quantitative information which some clients appreciate.

The review of secondary resources can and should continue throughout the project. Continual review of secondary resources is especially important for projects that focus on the use of new and fast moving technologies.

INITIATE THE TEAM(S)
First you need to select the team members. It is important that the team members be as diverse as possible as this will lead to better results. Some characteristics to look for diversity on include:
> research experience vs. design experience
> detail-oriented vs. big picture thinker
> creative vs. analytical mindset
> gender
> age and familiarity with the topic
> cultural differences

Even if the team has worked together before (and especially when they have not worked together before) it is important to begin the project with some activities that help build the team at the same time as they further the project content.

For example, making a mindmap (at the start of the project) of preconceptions about how the project will turn out is one such activity. The preconception mindmap can be done individually or collectively. Each person reveals, by mindmapping, what they think will be learned on the project, what challenges will be faced, etc. These predictions should be documented, shared and discussed. Preconception mindmaps expose the mindsets, expectations and biases of team members which can then be used to help the team stay objective in executing the research. The mindmaps often help to further define and clarify the focus and the scope of the project. And mindmaps may sometimes reveal additional issues to address in the workplan.

Hint#: Be sure to document, date and save the mindmaps. They are useful later in the process to see how "seemingly obvious" findings were not at all obvious at the start.

It is important also to prepare for the kickoff meeting with the members of the client team. They need to be immersed in the content for the project, especially if they are to play a big role in the execution of the research workplan. You may want to conduct the preconception mindmapping exercise with the client team members, for example.

Hint#: Early interactions with clients can teach you their language, jargon, and background, which comes in useful later in communicating the results.

Another idea is to use the kickoff as an opportunity to engage the client in the creation of the research plan and/or the generative toolkit materials. This type of collaboration with the client's team can be quite time consuming, so you may want to come to the kickoff with the plan and all the materials in draft form. In this case it is important to consider that the plan and toolkit materials must be complete enough to be presented clearly yet open enough so that all people

in the kickoff meeting feel free to comment on and to modify the plan and materials.

Hint#: Coming with a plan and materials for review at the kickoff meeting makes sense if you have done previous research in similar content areas but it may be risky if you are exploring a content domain for the first time. If you are unsure, have a conversation about it with your client.

If you are exploring a content domain for the first time you might consider bringing a research plan and materials from a previous project for discussion at the kickoff meeting. Be sure to maintain client confidentiality as needed. Another idea is to ask the members of the client team to fill out a workbook and/or engage in a toolkit-based activity as a way of familiarizing them with the process. This will give them a much clearer idea about the research process and will help them to gain empathy with the potential participants.

Figure#6.3 shows a typical agenda for a kickoff meeting that you may want to use as the starting point for your next generative design research project. The agenda should include time estimates for each activity to ensure that all items get covered.

Hint#: It is important to send a draft of the agenda to the client ahead of time in order to get feedback about content and timing.

It is very helpful in the kickoff meeting to map the research process visually in a flexible format and in a format large enough for the entire team to see. The use of generative tools applies to all forms of collective creativity, even transactional planning events.

UNDERSTAND THE CURRENT CONTEXT OF USE/ EXPERIENCE
It is important to take the opportunity to explore the experience domain at the start of the project. You

AGENDA	
9:00 am	introductions
9:15	objectives and scope
9:30	background
10:30	review research plan
11:30	discuss participants
12:00	lunch
1:00	review materials
3:00	discuss deliverables
3:30	establish roles
4:00	set key dates
4:30	end

location: Jonas' office

participants: Jane, Philip, John, Mary and Jonas

Figure#6.3 Kickoff agenda

need to get a sense of the lay of the land before you can finalize your workplan. This exploration can be done either formally (e.g., an ethnographic research phase at the start of the project) or informally (e.g., by making preliminary observations in the field).

Conducting informal interviews with key stakeholders related to the experience domain is another way to explore it. Keystakeholders may have the bigger picture of the scope or at least a part of it. They may even help you figure out what kind of participants to recruit or how best to recruit them.

PARTICIPANTS

SCREEN AND RECRUIT THE PARTICIPANTS

Screening refers to the activity of identifying and locating people who fit the profile you are looking to include in your research. Recruiting refers to the activity of establishing an agreement with people who fit this profile about their participation in the research. Sampling refers to how you will go about selecting the people who will serve as representatives of the population of interest.

Hint#: *Don't underestimate the time it takes to recruit participants.*

There are a range of options for gaining access and agreement to participate from potential participants, ranging from low outside costs (i.e., doing it yourself) which can be quite time intensive, to high outside costs (i.e., paying another party to do the work for you). With any of these options, however, you will need to have an agreed upon screener or, at the very least, a set of agreed upon screening criteria from which to work. A screener is a script that someone with no knowledge of the research plan can use to successfully identify people who match the profile you have established. It is usually designed to be conducted over the phone. A screener is made up of a series of questions along with directions that state what to do for each possible answer. Figure#6.4 is an example of one screener question. The series of questions in a screener form a flowchart of decision points and can quickly become quite complex.

'Terminate' means that the screening stops at this point since the respondent does not match the agreed-upon criterion of doing two or more of the bold-faced activities. It is important that the screener not give away the goal of the research project since some people will attempt to second-guess what the research is about. For example, the focus of the research for the screener item above was about smart phones. Some of the activities on the list are there to hide this fact, because you don't want to focus the participants' attention on the focus area until later in the generative session.

Working with professional recruiters or recruiting companies requires that you have funds to do so. This option is not usually available on very small projects or for student work. When working with a recruiting company you will most likely need to develop a full screener that includes all the questions to be asked and all the intructions for how to proceed based on responses to the questions.

Hint#: Writing an effective screener is harder than it looks. Seek the advice of a screener expert to review your screener before you put it in action.

Recruiting on your own relies on the use of personal networks (including those of the client) to identify possible participants. With the advent of social networking tools on the internet, the feasibility of recruiting in this manner has increased dramatically. There is always the possibility that people will misrepresent themselves, but that holds for any method of finding and securing participants. This type of recruiting may, however, turn out to cost quite a lot if the recruitment criteria are difficult and/or your social networks are not able to reach the people you are looking for.

If you are working with a set of agreed upon screening criteria instead of a full screener, the person doing the recruiting must have an intimate knowledge of the profile and be able to make informed decisions on the fly. This method of recruiting may be the best way to recruit professionals since the screening interaction can become more of a conversation than a survey.

5. Q: Do you personally own, use, and charge a HANDHELD device for the following activities? Please indicate yes or no to each activity.

> **Talking on the phone**
> Listening to music
> **Checking email**
> **Surfing the internet**
> Playing video games
> Watching movies

If yes to 2 or more of the bold-faced activities, continue. Otherwise terminate.

Figure#6.4 One question from a screener

It is important that you screen out 'professional respondents' or 'focus group groupies' i.e., people who misrepresent themselves in order to qualify for research groups. They will not be able to adequately represent the people whose experience you are seeking to understand. Screening them out is generally done by asking them how often they have served as respondents in the recent past and terminating those who have participated within the past 6 months to one year. They can, of course, lie about this as well. Requesting that participants do homework and bring their completed homework to the session with them is another way to weed out people who should not be in the interview or group session. Reviewing the homework (i.e., sensitizing materials) before the session can often tell you whether the participant is appropriate for the session.

Hint#: Keep in mind that when you hire an outside research service to do the recruiting, you will be responsible for the screener. If the questions are not right, you will not get the people you seek.

Sometimes clients prefer to work through an established pool of participants or a recruiter with whom they have a long-standing work relation. This has the risk that participants may expect your session to be more like a traditional focus group or interview, and the workbook to be more like a quantitative questionnaire with fixed answers and checkboxes. Make sure that the recruiter understands what kind of study you are conducting to avoid such mismatched assumptions.

Hint#: Most outside research firms are not yet familiar with generative design thinking and the use of toolkits in participatory sessions. They may offer services in the form of skilled moderators. These moderators are usually skilled at conducting traditional focus groups but these skills do not usually prepare them for the open-ended quality and the application of generative tools. It is best to do your own facilitating of the sessions.

INCENTIVES
People recruited by research firms who agree to participate in a research sessions are usually given an incentive for doing so. Most often the incentive is an agreed upon amount of money. Sometimes a small but useful gift may be given instead. In other situations, people will volunteer their time and energy, particularly when the topic is of interest to them. They may be willing to take part in the research session because they understand that they have been given the opportunity to influence something that will affect them in the future.

Hint#: For students and beginners, it is best to not be overly ambitious when estimating how much time people will donate toward your research. We have found that a small sensitizing packet (that takes no more than 20 minutes) and a one hour session is a good place to start.

SAMPLING
Sampling refers to the selection of people who will serve as representatives of the population of interest. The sample size is usually small in generative design research, so careful consideration of the selection of respondents is very important. The focus of this type of research is on the generation of relevant ideas so it is important that a diverse group of people be selected.

There are a number of different approaches to sampling (see also Figure#6.5):

OPPORTUNISTIC SAMPLING:
Here you would take as your sample the people you can get most easily (e.g., students asking friends and family, using the network of your client). Opportunistic sampling is not recommended when you are involved in professional work, but for students who are

just learning how to do design research, it is a reasonable approach. It is best if your participants are not well known to you since they may try to give you the answers they think you want (or possibly the opposite). One very useful approach is for students to recruit their friends and family for another student or team, who then do the same for this student. Another technique for efficient recruiting is 'snowball sampling': ask a participant to bring somebody else along (of course, this way you will lose control over who participates, and if people bring their friends, their relationship may be of influence on your session).

REPRESENTATIVE SAMPLING:

Here you would make sure that your sample accurately reflects the composition of the population that they are representing, e.g., you would recruit more participants for larger subgroups. Representative sampling is important for many types of research, especially quantitative studies for statistics-based decisions (such as having people evaluate prototypes for market success), but it is not a requirement for generative design research. The goal of generative design research is to explore and for that, diversity ('finding your blind spots') is more useful than representativeness (matching the people in the sample in order to make generalizations about the people).

PURPOSIVE SAMPLING:

Here you would try to cover most of the dimensions of variation in the group and maybe even take a few samples outside the target population to get a better understanding of the boundaries of the target. It is most often the case that purposive sampling is

used in generative design research since it is usually conducted at the beginning of the design process when a diversity of opinions is needed. For example, when conducting generative design research to explore the unmet need and dreams of everyday living in family situations, it would be best to recruit many types of families: single people, roommates, couples without children, couples with children of various ages, multiple generations within one household, single parents, empty nesters, etc.

Hint#: The cost of utilizing outside research firms can be very expensive, especially when considered on top of the cost of traveling to other parts of the world. Be sure to get several bids from outside research services (recommended by other field researchers if possible) before submitting a proposal to your client.

Recruiting can be quite time consuming. A general rule of thumb is that a professional recruiting agency will need two to three weeks to recruit twenty people for three workshops. Populations which are more difficult to find (e.g., people who admit to not washing their hands regularly) will take longer and be much more time-consuming (and therefore expensive) to recruit than others (e.g., people who say they wash their hands regularly). There are regional differences in the screening and recruiting process, but you will find companies all over the world who specialize in this activity. They often offer translation services and native speaking moderators as well.

Hint#: You will want to over-recruit, i.e., recruit more people than you need, to account for unexpected cancellations and other unforeseen events. A rule of thumb is to recruit 8 for 6 people to show. Of course you will need to be prepared (i.e., with chairs, research materials, etc.) for the event that all 8 actually do show up.

Hint#: If you are inexperienced in conducting generative design research sessions, aim for 6 people at most in a session.

OPPORTUNISTIC SAMPLING   REPRESENTATIVE SAMPLING   PURPOSIVE SAMPLING

Figure#6.5 Different approaches to sampling

ETHICAL CONSIDERATIONS:

The rules by which research is conducted vary between industry and academia. The rules also vary in different parts of the world. In the US, for example, human subjects research that is conducted by people who work for a university must adhere to the requirements of the Institutional Review Board. The Institutional Review Board (IRB) is a committee that has been formally designated to approve, monitor, and review biomedical and behavioral research involving humans with the aim to protect the rights and welfare of the research subjects. Also in the US, the Health Insurance Portability and Accountability Act (HIPAA) helps people to keep their health-related information private. Conducting field research in the healthcare areas in the US can be very time consuming as several levels of permission need to be addressed before even talking to patients in healthcare environments.

Design researchers in practice do not always have such 'rules' to adhere to and may not even be aware that these requirements exist if they have not been trained at the university as researchers. This is not an excuse for unethical research practices. Whatever the official rules for your country might be, you must be a good researcher.

> Treat your participants with respect and understanding.
> Do not deceive them.
> Do not surprise them suddenly with a consent form. Do it at the beginning, and explain why it is there.
> Tell them what you are doing and what their involvement will be.

> Be sure to get each participant's consent in writing for their participation and for your use of the audio recording, video-recording and photography of the interview or session. Do this before you start recording. A sample consent form is shown on page#176.
> If they agree to being photographed, video- recorded or audio recorded, tell them what the documentation will be used for and who will be reviewing it.

PLAN WHAT THE PARTICIPANTS WILL GO THROUGH

Now that recruiting is underway, it is time to plan the fieldwork activities and research materials in more detail. You probably have a good idea as to the overall agenda for the fieldwork, having written a project plan or proposal in order to get the funding and/or the approval to do the work. However, it is very important at this point to switch your perspective in order to see from the participants' points of view as you develop the project plan into a more detailed workplan. In creating the plan from the participants' points of view, you need to see it as a whole experience and not just a series of tasks that you ask them to perform.

In generative design research, we are interested in finding out what people's values and needs are in the future, and how these values and needs can be served by design through the development of new concepts for experiences, products or services. But it is difficult for most people to talk about their imagined futures. The best way to help them do so is to provide for them a path of expression. More information about the path of expression can be found in Chapter#2 starting on page#55.

Using the path of expression approach, the participants are led on a journey that takes them from the present situation into their past via their memories to the underlying levels of needs and values. The journey then takes them to situations in possible futures, and then back to the situations that can get them there.

The steps along the path of expression include:
1. immersion into current experiences
2. activating feelings and memories from the past
3. dreaming about the possible futures
4. generating and expressing new ideas relating to the future experiences

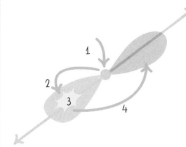

Figure#6.6 The path of expression (see also Figure#2.17 on page#55)

At the start of the journey, you will want to immerse the participants in the larger scope of experience. The scope is the context that surrounds the focal area that you want to fully understand.

To fully understand the focus of the experience, it is necessary to see it from the outside in and from the inside out. And for your participants to make the leap from their current situations into their dreams for the future, they will also need to have multiple contextual domains in play. Each activity you ask them to engage in will prime the next activity. You will want to plan their journey so that they reach the focus only at the end of the journey. In fact, they should not even be aware of the focus until closer to the end of the journey (see Figure#6.8).

In the period preceding the group session or interview, sensitizing takes place: the participant gets a feeling for the goals and topic of

the study, collects personal experiences and increases his or her understanding. So that when the session begins, he or she comes well-prepared but with an open mind. Figure#6.8 illustrates this build-up of awareness.

Hint#: *In sensitizing, be sure to invite people to explore both the scope and the focus of the topic, but do not let them fixate on a final opinion about the focus.*

In summary, each step in the journey should prepare the participant for the next one. The journey starts by expanding into the larger scope and later moves progressively toward the focus. As the participants move from the scope toward the focus, they are first immersed in the present situation, and then in the past. The context then narrows as they move toward future experience of the focus.

The homework activities (i.e., sensitizing materials) are very useful for covering the larger scope and for addressing people's thoughts and feelings about the current situation. Skilled design researchers can also create homework activities that elicit feelings about the past.

Figure#6.7 The central area represents the focus of the topic which is to be explored, the wider one represents the scope. The arrows show how different perspectives and exercises explore different parts of the focus and scope.

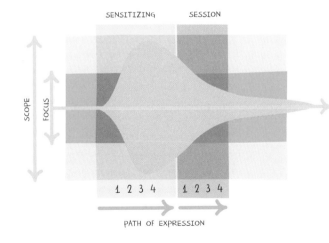

Figure#6.8 In the early steps of the process, participants are triggered to explore the wider scope of the topic from diverse starting points and perspectives; in later steps, we narrow down to the focus.

The exploration of future experience is best when done in face-to-face situations that take place in the sessions.

The ordering of the activities is a critical part of the planning process. The timing is also very important. People need time for immersion and for ideation and reflection. That is one of the reasons why pilot testing is such an important step in the generative design research process. You will quickly learn whether your time estimates are on track.

Hint#: Pilot testing will provide valuable feedback for your plan, your materials and for the timing of each activity.

WORKING WITH SPECIAL GROUPS

The format of your session should be tuned to the attention span and communication styles of the participants. Typical group sessions have 5-6 participants and this works well if your participants are adults talking about a topic familiar to them. For elderly people, or if the topic is emotionally more sensitive, smaller groups, or one-on-one interviews, may give the participants a situation in which they can express themselves better. Similarly, teenagers behave differently in smaller or larger groups as well as in mixed gender or same-gender groups. And people from different professions (e.g., builders or office workers) may thrive in different atmospheres. Consider carefully the group composition and potential group dynamics for your generative sessions. It is important that people put together in a group have something in common with each other (e.g. either experience, interests, occupation, age, etc).

Hint#: Elderly participants in generative sessions will need extra time (count on nearly doubling your usual estimate) since they will have so many experiences to share and often plenty of time for sharing.

CHILDREN AS PARTICIPANTS

Conducting research with children is a special situation and it may not be comfortable for everyone. You have to truly enjoy being with children to be an effective researcher in this situation. Here are some special things to consider when conducting research with children (anyone under the age of 18):

> You must have the written permission from their parent or guardian before they can participate. This is true even if you are doing the research at their school and you already have permission from their teacher or other caregiver.

> It is advisable to go with very small groups when conducting group sessions with children. The size of the group will vary with the age of the children. For example, you will want to work with only 1 or 2 preschoolers at a time, 2 to 4 school-agers and 4 to 6 teens at a time.

> The sessions need to be shorter and have varied activities. Again the length of time will vary by age.

> The activities need to be fun and engaging for the children. You will explain to them that they are free to leave if they do not want to finish the session.

> In doing generative design research with families, it is best to include children of ages 6 and above. They can usually participate in the activities, sometimes on their own and sometimes with a parent's or an older sibling's help. They usually enjoy the session quite a lot, especially the making activities with the toolkit materials. Be sure to bring extra toolkit materials for them.

Hint#: When working with families who have small children, be flexible and open to situations that may come up. Sometimes researchers need to be babysitters as well.

WORKING TOWARD THE SESSIONS

CREATE THE MATERIALS (SESSION SCRIPT, SENSITIZING MATERIALS, TOOLKITS AND CHECKLIST)

Think of the interview or group session as a journey, one that starts with the initial contact, then goes into the sensitizing phase, followed by the session and then on to closure. It is important when creating the research tools and materials to keep the journey in mind. To the extent that you are able to set the stage for the participants to have a positive and integrated experience, you will successfully engage them and learn the most from them.

The toolkits and materials need to be professionally executed in the sense that they are inviting and free from errors. But that does not mean that they should be expensive or overly designed. The more 'finished' the materials are, the less likely people are to engage with, play with and change them. The ideal design of materials for generative design research is simple and with a lot of white space. They should look 'easy' and possibly even playful or 'fun' if that is appropriate for your participants.

Focus on the participants' needs when you are creating the research materials. It's all about them, after all. Personalization is a good idea. You may want to include their name already printed on the materials. A good rule of thumb about the aesthetics of toolkits is that they should express the individuality of the respondent when they are filled out. If you lay the filled-in workbooks in a row, and they all look the same it's your aesthetic, if they are different it is more 'theirs'.

Hint#: Find the balance between 'sketchy' and 'designed' toolkits and materials to motivate and empower the participants.

Consider the usability of the materials. If you are asking people to make notes about their day throughout the day, the workbook should be small enough for them to carry easily. If some of the activities are open- ended, offer sample answers so they can have confidence in knowing how to respond.

WHY AND HOW TO WRITE A SESSION SCRIPT
The session script describes how the session should go. Use of a session script will help to ensure that each interview or session is done in a consistent manner. Having a script also gives the client and/or other team members an opportunity to add their input to the session plan in an organized way.

Hint#: The session script is very useful as an outline for whoever will be transcribing the audio files after the interviews and sessions are completed.

Both skilled and novice facilitators should be conducting the session or interview with a session script for all the reasons stated above.

A session script states:
> Introductory 'ground rules' including disclosure of audio and video recording
> The objective(s) of each part of the session
> The language you will use to give instructions or ask questions
> The timing for each part of the session
> Additional probes to cover as time permits

Figure#6.9 shows an example session script for a very experienced facilitator. In planning the session, you create a sequence of activities that follow the principles of sensitizing and the path of expression. A sequence that is used often is (i) start off with a collage toolkit to explore memories, (ii) follow that with a cognitive toolkit to discuss underlying structure, and (iii) round off with a Velcro-modeling or tinkering toolkit to express participants' dreams for the future and to let them emphasize their most important insights. Toolkits can also be combined or modified.

HOW TO MAKE SENSITIZING MATERIALS
The main purpose of using sensitizing materials is to immerse the participants in making observations and reflecting upon the experience domains that will be further addressed later in the journey. The sensitizing materials are the first stop along their journey (i.e., the path of expression). So the scope of content in the sensitizing materials should be broad. It should also be focused on their current and past experience. For example, if the focus of the experience is the use of computers in the home, the sensitizing materials should focus on what goes on at home. How does the family live? How do they spend their free time? What is important to them as a family? Has that changed since the children were born? How? Perhaps the computer is at the center of family life. Or the computer may be just a tool that is useful for work and

TIME	ACTION	CHECKLIST
5 min	Introductions	Goal: insight into experience, "You are the expert", basic rules
5 min	Warm-up	Images of animals; each participant selects a picture of an animal with which he can identify most and presents the animal and himself to the group
5 min	Instructions for collage making	Use the images and words to make associations and to bring back memories about shaving this morning or whenever
20 min	Collaging "the shaving environment"	Environment of shaving: where, what, who, when, situation, seeing, feeling, heading, scenting, tasting, mood? Thinks about the last time you shaved.
25 min	Present collages	Explain your collage to the group. You can react to each other's stories.
10 min	Group discussion	Reacting on each other's stories.
15 min	Collaging "feeling before, during and after shaving"	Why do you shave, how do you feel, how do you feel about shaving, what happens, are there changes: your feelings and state of being, what is the effect?
25 min	Present collages	Explain your collage to the group. You can react to each other's stories.
15 min	Group discussion: 'Ideal shaving' exercise with attributes for aliens	What would be the ideal situation? What should shaving be like in the future?
5 min	Closing comments Walk out	

Figure#6.9 An informal session script such as this (from Sleeswijk Visser et al., 2005) will work for experienced facilitators; for beginners, it should be more elaborate, e.g., include details as "write the assignment on the flipover".

homework. This is what you need to learn about. But if you begin by asking only questions about computer use at home, you may never learn how people live and how they wish to live in the future. You will never learn whether computers are a part of that future or not. The objective of the sensitizing materials is to stimulate participants' memories, and to provoke their observation and reflection of the current situation before asking them to take a leap into the future. Be careful not to ask too much of people in the sensitizing materials. You do not want to scare them away from participating in the session or workshop.

The sensitizing materials also provide an opportunity for the research team to gather some background information about the participants. It may be more efficient to gather this kind of information in written form than to take time out of the interview or session to obtain it.

The sensitizing materials will usually approach the broader content area from a number of different angles simultaneously. Some examples include:
> asking people to take pictures of where they spend time and where they wish they could spend more time,
> asking them to fill in open-ended questions about their everyday lives, and/or
> requesting that they fill out a diary of one day in their life, including how they feel throughout the day.

Sensitizing materials can come in a variety of forms. The possibilities are unlimited. Some that we have used on projects include:

> Workbooks with between 6 to 12 pages
> Small booklets
> A single sheet of paper
> A deck of cards with instructions for use
> Boxes with components and instructions for use
> Mobile phone with occasional sms-text messages as triggers for observation
> A sequence of emails with small assignments
> Cameras with instructions for use.

In fact, you can use toolkits as sensitizing materials also. This is not recommended for beginners, however, since it is difficult to write the instructions unless you have seen toolkits in use in a number of previous situations.

Hint#: *There are more examples of sensitizing materials shown in the sample projects throughout this book. These may help you better understand how you might go about sensitizing your participants.*

HOW TO MAKE A TOOLKIT

There is an art to making a good toolkit. The more toolkits you make and see the results of (in the form of what people make with them), the better you will become at making them. The feedback about the use of the toolkits is absolutely crucial for this expertise to grow. The toolkits exemplify a new form of visual literacy that is legible by all. Toolkit creation is one instance where having training in design might hinder the process. Toolkits need to make sense and appeal to non- designers so overdesigning the toolkit is something to be avioided.

Hint#: *There are a number of toolkit page spreads at the end of this chapter. You may want to take a look at those now.*

The steps below will get you started on the learning process. First you will need to consider why you will be using the toolkit:

> Is it for stimulating the expression of memories and feelings?
> Is it a means for the participants to share their understanding of an experi-ence, a product or an environment that they are familiar with?
> Is it for facilitating the expression of dreams and aspirations for experience?
> Is it primarily for the research team to gain empathy with the participants?

And where on the journey will the toolkit be used? Toolkits used early in the session are more likely to explore the scope that lies beyond the focus. Toolkits used later in the session are more likely to deeply explore the focus. For example, the contribution on page#91 shows a very focused toolkit. And the contribution of page#89 shows a toolkit for exploring scope.

Think about the path of expression that you have decided upon for the participants.
> What activities need to come before this toolkit to get them ready to use it effectively?
> And how will the use of this toolkit help to prepare them for later activities within the session?

Let's assume that the toolkit will be used for stimulating the expression of memories and feelings about past experience and that it will be used early in the session. The participants have already spent time being sensitized to their current feelings about the experience and we want them now to remember and think about their past experiences. We'll use an image/word collage toolkit as an example because they are quite effective for the elicitation of memories and feelings.

Step 1. Write the instructions. The first step is for the team to discuss, agree upon and then write the instructions for administering the toolkit. This is best done with the participation of the whole research team. Doing this collaboratively will help you see whether or not you agree on what the purpose of using the toolkit will be.

Step 2. Brainstorm a list of words. Then, based up on the agreed upon instructions, conduct a brainstorming session to generate a long list of words that relate to the topic (i.e., purpose of the toolkit). This step can also be shared with team members in other locations via email. It is a good idea to invite your client to take part in the brainstorming step as it can increase their interest in and ownership of the project. Make a copy of the resulting word list for each team member who will be searching for images.

Step 3. Look for visual material. Team members will then select photos and other visual materials for the toolkit using the brainstormed list of words as inspiration. The list is best seen as a pool of ideas that will stimulate image search, i.e., the goal is not to select an image for each word on the list. In fact, it is best to put the word list away (after reading it over several times) when looking for visual material so the hunt for images is not taken too literally.

Try to collect 4 to 5 times as many trigger items (words and images) as you will need. For example, if you are aiming for the toolkit to hold about 150 items, you will want to have at least 500 items (both pictures and words) to review. Where can you find the images? You can use or take your own photos. And there are many on-line options for finding images (e.g., www.flickr.com, www.google.com with Image Search, etc.) It is best to use images that are copyright free. Take care that the image quality is adequate. Images for collage toolkits do not need to be high resolution but you do need to be able to see what is going on in them. Often images for the web are very small and will not work well when printed.

Hint#: *When using Google Image Search, be sure to set image size to Medium in the Advanced Search mode.*

Step 4. Review the trigger items altogether.

Pin or tape up all the words and the images onto a large wall so you can see everything at once and it is easy to move the items around. A large table, as shown in Figure#6.10, also works well. Meet with a team of people to review, reorganize and narrow down the toolkit images and words. Be sure to review the instructions first. Revise them as needed and then continue with the organization and selection process:
> Eliminate duplications.
> Be wary of images that point to only one interpretation.
> Cluster similar items and choose the best from each cluster.
> Add notes about any content that you are missing.

Here are a few rules of thumb for deciding what to include and not to include in the toolkit trigger set:
> Have a balance of positive, neutral and negative stimuli.
> Include both ambiguous and concrete stimuli. The ambiguous items often provoke the most useful responses, but the concrete items are most helpful for giving people a familiar place to start.
> Include a variety of different visual styles, e.g., photos, line drawings, cartoons, artwork, etc.
> Be sure to include different ages, races and gender of people.
> Review the visual and verbal trigger items at the same time so that you can decide whether a given idea is best expressed visually or verbally.

Cultural relevance is very important. If you are making toolkits that are intended to be used by people from a culture (or subculture) other than your own, you need to do more thorough pilot testing and may even need to do preliminary research before you make the toolkits. An alternative approach is to invite people from that culture/subculture to join your team.

Hint#: Develop the look and feel of your toolkit and instructions to fit the language (jargon, aesthetics, expectations) of the participants.

Once you have organized all the items, removed redundancies, and selected the set that you will use, it is likely that you will discover holes in the set of images and words.

Step 5. Fill in the holes in the trigger set. Your trigger set should be broad and open- ended enough so that people can express a very wide range of memories, feelings, understandings or ideas. One way to discover the holes in the trigger set is for the team members to use the trigger set to express the widest range of experiences (related to the topic) that they can jointly imagine. Once the holes are revealed, one person can fill them in, providing they were a part of the team who reviewed all the materials.

Step 6. Review the final set. Take another look at the toolkit trigger set once the holes have been filled. Work as a team to negotiate the final selection of trigger materials. You will want to keep the total number of items between 150 and 200 words and pictures. The larger the toolkit, the longer it will take people to make use of it. A good toolkit will give them the open-endedness they need to express whatever they have in mind at a specific point on the journey.

Hint#: Here is a lesson learned after many years of experience in making toolkits. Intuition wins. If there is a trigger item in the set that one member of the team will not agree to eliminate, despite arguments from all the other members on the team, it is best to leave it in the final trigger set. More often than not, that is the trigger item that provokes or evokes the most useful and insightful ideas.

Hint#: You can "load" the toolkit with triggers that you have assumptions about. For example, you may have a preconceived idea about an idea for a new product or service. You can make it into a trigger and see if any of the participants expresses interest in it.

Step 7. Design the toolkit. Create the physical form of the toolkit. Consider the size, ordering, and layout of the trigger items. For example: You will want to make all the items of approximately the same size so that no single item draws the eye because it is larger than the others. You can print the words and pictures on sheets of paper, or on pre-cut sticker sheets.

Or you can pre-cut all the items. Pre-cutting the items will facilitate the serendipitous connections to be made between unrelated items. But it will take people much longer to view all the items.

Hint#: *Printing the trigger items on pre-cut sticker sheets will help make the making activity faster. But it will also add cost to the toolkits.*

Pay attention to how you arrange the items when printing on the sheets. Again, randomization will provoke connections, but require longer viewing time. Clustering words apart from images is a good strategy to promote quick viewing. Be sure to either randomize or alphabetize the word lists. You may want to vary the font and color of word stimuli to help spark connections.

Pay attention to image quality and paper quality. If your prints are too high in quality, people may hesitate in cutting out parts. If they are too low in quality, people may not use them either.

Step 8. Pilot test the toolkit. Give the toolkit a sample run. (See section 'Pilot test'). Ideally the toolkit will be tested in the context of all the other activities that have been planned for the interview or session.

Step 9. Revise and produce. Review the results of the pilot test. Were the instructions clear? Were there images that no one used? Consider eliminating them. Did the pilot testers ask for images or words that were not included in the toolkit? You will want to consider adding them.

PILOT TEST
A pilot test is a practice run of the planned session and a test of all the associated materials. Doing one or two pilot tests is essential for beginners in the generative design research process. It is also advisable for skilled practitioners especially when working in a new domain or with a target population that you have never worked with before. The results of the pilot test will give you valuable feedback about:
> the timing of the session,
> the order of activities within the session,
> the wording of the instructions in the homework/sensitizing materials and in the session activities and
> the composition of the toolkits.

The pilot test will give you practice in conducting the session, familiarize your with the tools in action, and will increase your confidence in having the real sessions go well. It will also provide practice in the use of technology for documenting the session. You will need to assess the results of the pilot test documentation and make changes as needed:

> How well did the video-tape capture the session?
> Can you use the segments of the video later for presentation purposes?
> Is the audio recording intelligible?
> Can you use the photos to tell the story of the session?
> Can you analyze this data?

The closer the pilot test is to the actual plan, the more useful your results will be. For example, the participants in your pilot test should match the population you are seeking to understand, if at all possible. But doing a pilot test with friends or family is better than not doing a pilot test at all! It is best to conduct the pilot test at least a few days before the actual fielding is to begin since it is very likely that changes will need to be made. You will need some time to make the changes before going into production mode to make the toolkits and gather the materials needed for the scheduled sessions.

Figure#6.11 A sample toolkit

PRODUCE THE RESEARCH MATERIALS

When considering how long it will take to produce enough sets of the materials for all the interviews or sessions, plan for twice as much time as it really should take. Disasters are likely to occur. For example, printers tend to break when you are in a hurry.

1. Revise. Before you can begin the production process, you will need to revise all the materials based on the pilot test results.

2. Consider cost and time tradeoffs. You will want to consider both the cost and the time implications of your choice in materials. For example, will you use paper or stickers for the toolkit trigger items? Stickers are more expensive but they will make it much faster for the participants to make their collage. If you use paper, will you have the items pre-cut or will you supply scissors?

Figure#6.10 Toolkit creation requires a large, flat surface or a wall.

Hint#: Look into outside services to save time and money (e.g., printing, copying, cutting, etc.). If you are making a large number of toolkits this may be the best way to produce them.

3. Produce. Batch mode is usually the best (i.e., most efficient) as long as you are well organized. In batch mode you will make all the materials for a given activity in a batch. Once all the material sets have been made, you will collate the sets for each partici- pant and then collate the participant sets by group. It is advisable to make a few extra sets in case you have more people attend the workshop than you had planned. Also, extra toolkits can be a useful planning device for the next project.

Hint#: You will want to put very small numbers on each of the images. This will greatly speed up data entry later on.

4. Organize and pack. When packing completed materials to take into the field, it is important to consider how, where and how often you will be unpacking them. For example, you will want to have sets ready for each session pre-packaged in the order that you will need to access them during the interview or session. Hopefully there is someone on your team that enjoys this kind of challenge!

SENSITIZE THE PARTICIPANTS
You will need to get the sensitizing materials in the hands of your participants about a week before the interview is conducted or the session begins. If that is not possible, they will need at least a weekend in order to have some free time to complete it. How is it best to get the materials to the participants? Should you send the sensitizing materials by mail or by email or hand-deliver them? If you use mail, will you use the Post Service or an express delivery service at an extra charge?

Hand delivery is ideal since it will give you an opportunity to meet the participant face-to-face and go over the materials with them, addressing any questions they might have. We have found that personal delivery also helps to ensure that the participants show up for the session, and to establish a relationship which helps in conducting the session. But it is often not possible or feasible to do a personal delivery of these materials.

It is useful to request that the completed sensitizing materials be returned to the research team before the session begins. If you do that, you will be able to review this material and can then revise the session script according to what you have learned. But if you get the sensitizing materials too far ahead of the session, their role in immersing the participants in the topic may be lost. It is best if you get the materials back a few days before the session and have an efficient plan for review of the materials.

CONDUCT THE INTERVIEWS OR GROUP SESSIONS
It is finally time to collect the data! We start with some general considerations, followed by more specific considerations for different contexts of use.

In preparing for the sessions, it is recommended that you make a checklist of all the things you need to bring. Here is one we have used before.

THE CHECKLIST
> The schedule for the day
> The session script or interviewer notes
> Note-taking paper
> 2 audio recorders and extra batteries
> Audio/video release forms
> Video recorder and charger (or extra batteries)
> Digital camera and charger (or extra batteries)
> Maps or directions (verified beforehand) to each destination for public transport, or GPS coordi- nates for the car
> Cell phone

> List of cell phone numbers for each team member
> Phone number(s) of the participants
> Toolkits for each respondent with 3 extras (just in case)
> Extra blank sensitizing materials (in case the participants lost theirs)
> Scissors, tape and markers
> Incentive and sign-off forms
> Umbrella
> Money and/or credit cards (just in case)
> Snacks and drinks
> Etc.

It is important to be on time. Start by introducing everyone on the research team and their role in the session. State your intent clearly and up front.

Hint#: *If someone offers you a breath mint, take it.*

This does not mean that you have to provide a lot of detail about what your intent is with the research. Describe your intent with enough clarity to satisfy the curiosity of your participants but also with enough generality so as not to reveal the focus or give confidential information away. Never lie.

You will need to get permission to record the session before you begin. You should have enough Audio/Video Release forms with you for each participant to sign (including a copy for them if they want to keep one).

Before beginning the session, be sure to thank the participants for doing the 'homework' (i.e., sensitizing materials) and show interest in what they have done. For example, it is often a good idea to begin the session by letting them tell about their experience with the sensitizing homework. This is a good time to let them voice concerns that the sensitizing materials may have triggered (otherwise, they may return to this throughout the session).

You will need to work with a research partner since facilitating the session and observing/ documenting both require full attention. During the session, both the facilitator and the documenter should try to pay attention to what the participants are doing as well as to what they are saying. The documenter will be responsible for recording each interview or session (video and audio). Both facilitator and documenter may also take some photographs as long as this activity does not interrupt the session.

At the end of the session, give the participants a chance to ask some questions. Then provide incentives (as relevant) and ask them to sign any forms required for receiving payment for their time. You might want to leave the audio recorder running until you need to pack up. Often people make very useful comments once they have had some time to reflect, and some afterthoughts pop up after the official session has ended.

WHERE TO CONDUCT THE SESSIONS
Fieldwork can take place in many types of settings. Here are some considerations to keep in mind when conducting fieldwork in three of the most common types of settings.

IN THE CONTEXT OF USE (E.G., HOME OR OFFICE):
Being in your participants' home or place of work can be an extremely valuable source of information. When doing the fieldwork in the natural context of use or experience, it is important not to disrupt the daily flow of activities, if at all possible. If you are conducting research in the home, you may want to ask people NOT to clean up before you come so that you can see how they really live. In our experience, this request is not always followed but it is worth a try.

Even though it is advisable to have the research team members not outnumber the participants, when going into people's homes you should always work with a research partner. A mixed gender team is the best situation, both for the research team as well as for the participants.

Hint#: Carry your cell phones and have an emergency plan worked out ahead of time if the fieldwork is in an area that you are not familiar with or have reasons to be concerned about.

ON NEUTRAL GROUND:

Conducting the field research on neutral ground, such as in a research facility, is the best option when the research is confidential and the participants must not be made aware of the sponsoring party. Research facilities are designed for the efficient handling of interviews and group sessions. They offer the opportunity for many people to observe the sessions because there is usually a one-way mirror with soundproofing between the room where the session is held and the 'back room'. Research facilities can take care of audio and video recording as well.

Hint#: Even if the facility is audio recording the session, you should also record audio yourself. Mistakes do happen.

They usually offer other amenities such as food delivery and errand running, at a price.

ON YOUR CLIENT'S GROUND:

Conducting the research on the client's ground is also a consideration. It can help to save money (i.e., no fees for facility rental) and it can help to get more people from the client's team to observe and/or attend the session. If the client's ground is a well-known local organization or facility, however, the anonymity of the research sponsor will be lost. Most clients prefer to remain anonymous when exploring future experience.

Sometimes conducting the research on the client's ground is the only option. For example, in doing generative design research with people who work in hospitals to inform/inspire the design of the new hospital, money is tight. Recruiting tends to be done by administrative people in the hospital and the participants come to the session over their break time or their lunch hour. They do not receive an incentive for their time but most are glad to be able to have a voice in the future of their workplace. One challenge that we have seen in conducting research with healthcare people in their workplace is that they may have to leave the session in order to deal with emergency situations.

Table#6.12 compares the three workshop locations across a number of dimensions.

	IN THE CONTEXT OF USE	ON NEUTRAL GROUND	ON YOUR CLIENT'S GROUND
Time	Time-consuming	Efficient	Efficient
Cost	Medium cost	High cost	Lowest cost
Maintains objectivity	Yes	Yes	No
Minimal distractions	No	Yes	No
Additional information available	Best	No	No

Table#6.12 Considerations for choosing the location for workshops

FACILITATING THE SESSION

Facilitating your first session can be a daunting task, especially if you're not used to speaking in public or leading groups. You have to be the host receiving the participants, then explain to them what they should do, keep track of time and process, and guide the group toward the topic of the study. One trap to avoid is becoming the 'teacher' who judges the quality of the answers of the class. It is important to keep in mind that the participants are the experts of the topic, and you, the facilitator, are there to help them express themselves.

In the beginning of the session you should clarify these roles i.e., that they are the experts and your role is to listen. Remind the participants that there are no right or wrong answers, and that you are very interested in their answers. It can help to give the impression that you don't know much about the topic itself. If you present yourself as an outsider, the participants will be more likely to explain seemingly obvious things, and bring out details usually left tacit. For example, in a study with housewives about detergents, the male facilitator convincingly explained he knew very little about washing beyond that you had to separate colored stuff from white stuff.

If participants in your session know each other, or show a strong dislike of each other, it's wise to subtly direct them to sit apart, otherwise such pairs may disrupt the activities of others, or branch off in separate directions not connected to the group.

Similarly, as a facilitator you will have to encourage some participants to speak up, ask them about parts of what they made that they did not explain yet, and cut off divergent conversations which stray too far from the topic of interest.

Hint#: Don't be too afraid of silences, and fill them by talking yourself. A silence can force participants to think deeply about a topic.

A lot of the skill in facilitating lies in anticipating group behavior and being proactive. One trick is to observe the participants while they make with the toolkit and determine which one of the participants would be likely to have an inspiring and informative story to present, then start the presentation round with that person.

Hint#: If you ask for a volunteer to go first in presenting their collage, for example, you usually get an enthusiastic and engaging first presentation.

The first presenter often sets the mood for those who follow, so your life is much easier if you avoid asking the overly shy person to go first. On the other hand, varying the order in later presentations is also important: it's not nice to always be just after a very long-winded presenter, or always be the last.

During the presentations, try to have the presenter address the group instead of presenting to the facilitator. If you hold up their collage while they present, you can direct the presenter toward the group, the presenter has his or her hands free for pointing out things, and your body language in holding the paper can subtly encourage or discourage elaborations of a certain part. During the presentation, try to pick up one or two points on which you can ask a question, should the presenter fall silent. Facilitating is a skill that takes practice. If you are very concerned about your skills as a facilitator or you expect to be doing a lot of facilitating (or moderating as it is often called), you may want to read more about it. *Moderating to the Max* (Bystedt et al., 2003) is a good place to begin.

Plan for some time or informal event after the session if possible, such as a lunch or drinks break. This has two advantages. One is that the facilitator can use it as an excuse for cutting short an elaboration ("let's return to that over lunch"). The second is that the informal event is often a source of very valuable data. Once freed of the responsibilities of the formal session, participants often have all kinds of things bubbling over which they want to bring to the table; often remarks from this informal part belong to the most important pieces in later analysis.

FACILITATING ONE-ON-ONE INTERVIEWS

Whether you are conducting the interview in the participant's home (or workplace) or in a neutral setting (such as in a research facility), the first step is to try to establish a positive relationship with him or her. Keep the initial conversation friendly and informal. Then, just as you would do in a group session, you will need to let the participant know about the nature of the interview and what to expect in terms of documentation. You will ask them to sign a release form with regard to the documentation. It is also best to let them know about how long the interview will take.

If you are conducting the interview in their home (or workplace), you will want to let the participant decide where they want to have the interview. You might ask them to show you around the main part of their house (or workplace) if they seem so inclined. Remember that you are a guest in their home (or office) so follow their lead.

Be prepared by knowing the topics you are to discuss so that you need only to make minimal reference to your session guide. The one-on-one interview will be most fruitful if it feels more like a conversation to the participant than it does like an interview. You may want to have a shortened version of the session guide so that you can refer to it very quickly during the interview. You do not need to cover the topics in the same order in every interview. Let the respondent guide the conversation to some degree. For example, if they move naturally to a topic that you had planned to cover later in the session, let them talk about it as it fits naturally in the conversation. You can use the shortened version of the session guide to keep track of which topics have been covered and which are still left to cover.

You may also want to prioritize the list of topics so that you are sure to cover the highest priority topics.

DOCUMENT THE DATA

In fielding generative design research, it is best to realize that you cannot rely on memory or even on taking good notes. There is simply far too much to see and to hear, even in one session. The following are guidelines for documenting field data.

Document redundantly. Use both audio and video documentation. Bring two audio recorders just in case. Take many photographs.

Label diligently. Each recording should be labeled with a name, location and a date before you move on to the next session.

Download all the files as soon as possible and back them up on a secure server immediately.

Get transcripts for the audio recordings. There are many companies who offer this as a service now. It is well worth the cost since you will get a word-for-word account of the session for later analysis. With digital audio recording, it is possible to upload audio files right after the session and get the transcriptions back the next day if arrangements for this kind of service have been made ahead of time.

Why all this emphasis on documentation? In conducting generative design research, you will obtain large amounts of messy and in-depth information. You may want to analyze it from several angles. And you may not know exactly how you will analyze the data until you are in the middle of the analysis process. So by redundantly recording everything, you will be prepared for anything. Keep in mind that just because you recorded the data does not mean that you have to analyze everything you document.

Hint#: *When labeling the data it is best to assume that someone else will be analyzing it. Under this assumption you will need to label the data well enough that someone else will be able to find what they are looking for and be able to analyze it without your being there.*

What if you don't get permission to document the sessions as described above? Start by asking for all the documentation that you wish to have, explaining why it is needed. Then compromise.

Hint#: *Don't worry if you do not get permission to video-record. Audio recording together with photography works very well.*

HOW TO HANDLE SPECIAL SITUATIONS AND COMPLICATIONS
Accidents will happen. It is best to try to foresee everything that could go wrong and to plan for that. This can be difficult for the beginner to anticipate. Here are some situations to consider, along with suggestions for avoiding or dealing with them. These situations have all occurred while fielding generative design research.

You get to an in-home session with a family who has a toddler and a baby. They have agreed to have a babysitter for the children during the session. When you arrive you learn that the babysitter cancelled. Luckily, you have three members on the research team (just in case). One of you agrees to entertain the children and the session takes place as scheduled.

The flight is cancelled and you will not get to the research facility in time for the workshops that have been scheduled and there is not enough time to call people to reschedule. To avoid this situation, never book the last flight to your destination. Be sure there is at least one later flight that will still get you there on time.

The airline loses your luggage. Never check in your research materials (except scissors, of course). Check your suitcase with clothes instead. It will be easier to purchase a new shirt than to replace your research materials. Plan ahead if you plan to send your materials by mail or an express service. Leave enough time to make more should they get lost.

There is an unexpected detour on your route. You are driving in an unfamiliar city and need to let the participant know that you will be late. Be sure you have phone numbers and email addresses for every participant. Travel with your own GPS device or a smart phone with GPS capabilities.

The conversation/discussion evokes a very strong emotional response from the participant. Be sure the participant is OK before proceeding. You do not need to finish the session. Do not leave them until someone they know is present.

Internet access is down and you were relying on it to show a YouTube clip during the session. Store the clip ahead of time on at least two devices (e.g., laptop and USB drive).

The research facility does not follow through on the audio recording when the session unexpectedly runs for over the two hour estimate. Have two audio recorders running at all times.

The video-recorder stops working. Always have a backup plan with regard to equipment. Assume that something will break or that the batteries will run out of power in the audio recorder.

One of the participants decided to bring his boss, or a colleague, who has not been sensitized. This can happen if word gets around at the client's company and suddenly you have a guest who wants to join because he already knows so much about the subject. Try to avoid this. People who have not been sensitized can be quite disruptive, even more so if they feel in a position to steer the direction of the discussion to what they think is important. Be proactive. Have a plan or several alternative plans for removing this type of person from the group. Perhaps they can be given an observation/note taking role.

REUSING AND STANDARDIZING TOOLKITS AND SESSION PLANS

In the pressures of design research practice, especially commercial, you will ask yourself – or be asked by your client – why you should invest all the time in creating the toolkit, and whether a standard toolkit cannot be used. It obviously saves money to do so. But there are several drawbacks to it: (1) the toolkit is too general, and does not contain enough triggers that fit the specific topic, (2) the team does not benefit from the insight and preparation gained from making the toolkit; the making process also serves to sensitize them, (3) if the facilitator is not familiar with the toolkit him- or herself, this shows during a session, and can easily demotivate the participants.

It certainly makes sense to reuse elements from toolkits with which the team has had experience. And to recycle sections of a session plan which went well. And it certainly makes sense to create toolkits whose components you can reuse, such as the replaceable stickers in case#4.1 or the Velcro-modeling toolkit. But be careful not to prepackage the toolkits and squeeze them into applications where they don't quite fit in order to save time and money. The tools are there to support the expression and creativity of the participants, not a machine to put people through.

SUMMING UP

In conclusion, we have described how the act of gathering data in the field can be successfully executed as long as you have taken the time and effort to plan it, pilot test it, and then conduct and document it. A lot of work goes into the one or two hour sessions with the participants. And a lot of data is generated that, once documented, can be analyzed at a number of different levels later in the process.

Some design researchers enjoy and excell at the planning and organizing part of the process. Others are just happy that someone else enjoys doing that part. But most people who find themselves doing this type of fieldwork LOVE the part where they get to meet new people and learn about their lives and their dreams for the future. Memories of these sessions with people will stay with you for many years to come.

INFORMED CONSENT SHOULD BE IN WRITING

It is advisable to fully document the design research process as this will help tremendously in the analysis stage. The small size and relative accessibility of digital recording devices for images, audio and video documentation make this increasingly practical today. But it is imperative that you get the informed consent of the participants before using cameras, audio-recorders or video-recorders to document them or the things that they make. Guidelines for and attitudes about obtaining permission for documenting the research vary in different parts of the world. So it is best to err on the side of caution and get permission (ideally in writing) before beginning the research.

If your work is being conducted in a university setting, please be sure to check to see what guidelines and/ or regulations have already been put into place to avoid ethical problems in the conduct of research with human subjects. A link to the guidelines in use in the US is given above.

Contributor

Liz Sanders

Founder

MakeTools, LLC

Columbus, Ohio USA

Liz@MakeTools.com

Reference

The Belmont Report: Ethical Principles and Guidelines For The Protection Of Human Subjects Of Research

http://ohsr.od.nih.gov/guidelines/ belmont.html

PHOTOGRAPH AND AUDIO TAPING RELEASE FORM
This workshop will be audio taped and photographed. These tapes and photos will be used for research purposes only. They will not be used commercially.

Please check off one or both of the statements below, then sign and date. Thanks.

_____ I allow XXXXX to audio-record and photograph this workshop session for research purposes.

_____ I allow XXXXX to use the photos in XXXXX promotional materials (articles, presentations, Web site).

Name _____
Date _____

Here is an example of a very simple informed consent form. While you are getting the participant's written consent to be recorded, it can be helpful to ask also for permission to use the documentation in presentations to be made in the future.

Contributors

Stephanie Patton

President

Spot-On Consulting

Columbus, Ohio USA

spatton@spot-on-consulting.com

Liz Sanders

Founder

MakeTools, LLC

Columbus, Ohio USA

Liz@MakeTools.com

LESSONS LEARNED ABOUT AUDIO-RECORDING IN THE FIELD

> Invest in a digital voice recorder or use a smart phone with audio recording capability.
> Be aware of how long you can record. Test this out ahead of time.
> Be aware of how long your batteries last. Test this out ahead of time.
> Carry plenty of backup batteries with you.
> Consider purchasing accessories such as amplifiers.
> Announce the participant's name, session number and date/time every time you press 'on'.
> If someone is taking notes, ask them to put time codes in their notes every 5 to 10 minutes.
> Stop and then start the audio recorder at major section changes within the session to keep the size of the audio files small and manageable.
> Practice active but silent listening when moderating. Use body language to indicate your attention to and interest in what the participant is saying. Otherwise you will have transcripts full of 'uh-huhs'.
> Move the audio recorder with you if the action shifts to another part of the room.
> Use video-documentation as the back-up for audio-documentation. You can change video files into audio files if your audio recorder fails.
> Download your audio files at the end of every day and put duplicate copies of each file on a secure server.
> Name your audio files in such a way that someone else could find the one they are looking for.

SOME QUESTIONS TO ADDRESS AS YOU CONSIDER THE USABILITY OF YOUR TOOLKITS

Generative design research works best when carried out in 'the field', e.g., in the places where people live, work, learn and play. So it is important to consider the entire life cycle of toolkits together with related components of the process such as supplies and documentation technology.

Toolkit usability reflects upon the toolkit itself at all stages in its use such as assembling it, packing it, transporting it, unpacking it, introducing its use to the participants, having it used by the participants, recycling and/or disposal of the components, packing it back up again, getting to the next session and having the components you need, and transporting the artifacts back home. Toolkit usability also considers the other essential components of the generative design research process such as supplies (scissors, markers, glue, etc.) and technology for documenting the session (audio-recorder, camera, video-camera, etc.) Usability is especially important, for example, when you are going directly from one home session to another or when you are traveling from one part of the world to another.

Contributor

Liz Sanders

Founder of Make Tools

Columbus, Ohio USA

Liz@MakeTools.com

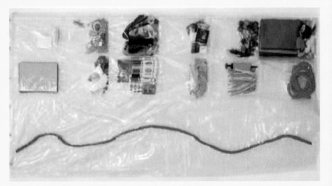

In the 2005 SCAD Design Charrette, students explored the usability of generative toolkits. Here, a shower curtain was folded, glued and slit to form pockets for the toolkit materials and supplies. The "pockets curtain" was simply unrolled to reveal the full array of toolkit components to the participants. (Savannah College of Art and Design, 2005 Charrette)

Here are some questions to address as you consider the usability of your toolkits:

- Are the toolkits organized by visit and labeled ahead of time so that you know what to bring in for each session? Can you carry everything inside in one trip?
- Is each toolkit self-contained so that you can reach for the entire toolkit at once? If the toolkit has layers, are the layers clearly marked?
- When traveling by air, what do you check with the airlines and what do you carry on board? Does it pay to ship any of the components ahead of your arrival? Is this a reliable option or not?
- Do you have several extra toolkits and supplies just in case someone else (perhaps a spouse or a friend) asks to join the session?
- Do you have the toolkits, supplies and technology organized in such a way that you can find what you need when you need it even while you are carrying on a conversation with the people you just met?
- Is your documentation technology readily accessible, labeled, pre-tested and fully charged? Do you have agreed-upon file names established ahead of time?
- Are the toolkit components organized to correspond to the steps in the discussion guide?
- Will any of the components be recycled? How? When?
- Do you have a plan for how and when clean-up will be handled?

At the end of the session, the participants were motivated to help clean up by refilling the pockets. Upon leaving, the pockets curtain was rolled up and secured with a carrying strap. Travel to the next session was quick, easy and organized. (Savannah College of Art and Design, 2005 Charrette)

A REUSABLE, MOBILE, AND FLEXIBLE TOOL-KIT FOR PARTICIPATORY USE DURING THE 'IDEA' PHASE OF DESIGN DEVELOPMENT

Considering the use and reuse of materials is no longer an after-thought for many designers in this age of "eco-consciousness". However, toolkits for many projects I have been a part of in the past have been large and somewhat wasteful in terms of the amount of materials used. 'Idea Space', which I developed for my undergraduate senior thesis at The Ohio State University, was therefore designed with reusable materials and equipment in mind.

This toolkit was designed to aid in the beginning phases of product development where there are often broad, high-level issues to consider. Designing a product for this situation requires a flexible nature that affords spur-of-the-moment discussions and meetings to happen, wherever that may be. The portable features of 'Idea Space' allows for people on the go to be able to work in a café, client's office, or wherever inspiration strikes. The repositionable canvases were designed in many sizes to facilitate both individual introspection as well as group efforts. This affords all types of people to informally and spontaneously get their thinking out and visible so that everyone can participate, give feedback, and quickly revise any ideas.

Contributor

Lindsay Kenzig

Senior Researcher

Design Central

Columbus, Ohio USA

Lindsay.Kenzig@gmail.com

Lindsay's contribution is based on her work as an Industrial Design Student.
Senior Thesis: *Idea Space*, The Ohio State University, Department of Industrial, Interior and Visual Communication Design
Committee Members: Noel Mayo and Liz Sanders, June, 2005.

'Idea Space' was designed to be an approachable and easy to use product, with preparation for the study, traveling, and documentation of artifacts; all considerations in the final design. In addition to the repositionable (sticky back) canvases, 'Idea Space' includes the following parts: a carrying container with strap, startup accessories (such as words, evocative images, and useful symbols such as arrows), writing utensils in a rolled bag, and erasing wipes. All canvases are of the same aspect ratio that most digital cameras use, to facilitate the easiest documentation possible.

Since the beginning discussions in developing an idea or product may deal with similar subject areas and strategies (such as process, methods, communication, culture, etc.), this kit provides groupings of startup accessories that can be reused over and over for different projects. Add-on kits might also be developed for different types of projects or fields, such as website development or interior design.

Idea Space

A reusable, mobile and flexible toolkit for participatory use during the "idea" phase of design development

1. carrying container
2. erasing wipes
3. writing utensils in rolled bag
4. repositional canvases
5. startup accessory tools / images
6. carrying strap

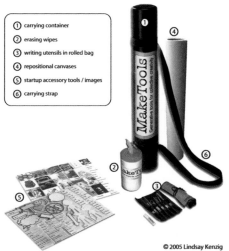

© 2005 Lindsay Kenzig

Idea Space

Packing and Organizing Components

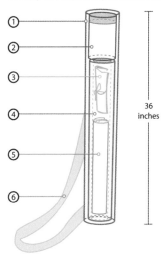

36 inches

© 2005 Lindsay Kenzig

SHOPPING FOR MATERIALS: TWO APPROACHES

Generative design research is unique in its use of a wide variety of unusual materials, making shopping necessary. We have outlined two main kinds of shopping strategies: task-oriented shopping, and opportunistic shopping.

Task-oriented shopping is best done after the research plan is complete. Once you have an understanding of the activities that participants will undergo, organizing your shopping lists is a great way to help you prepare and pack for the project at hand. Your list should include:

> toolkit materials to be used by participants (such as stickers, scissors, tape, etc.),
> materials you will need in order to prepare the toolkits (such as knife blades, print cartridges, die cutters, etc), and
> documentation and technology tools (such as camera, audio recorder, laptop, etc.).

After making your shopping list, you must determine where and how to best complete your shopping based on price, distance, lead time, labor costs, and shipping or transportation costs. For example, you may decide that while an item may cost $5 more, it is more time efficient for you to order it online. Don't underestimate the time it takes for shipping. Improvisation may be needed in certain cases. For items you use frequently, it is helpful to stock up on them to prevent future trips or shipping fees.

Contributors

Lindsay Kenzig
Senior Researcher
Design Central
Columbus, Ohio USA
Lindsay.Kenzig@gmail.com

Stephanie W. Patton
President
Spot-on Consulting
Columbus, Ohio USA
spatton@spot-on-consulting.com

A materials shopping list becomes even more useful by doubling as an organizational tool when creating materials and packaging for fieldwork.

Thrift stores and online reuse retailers are excellent places to find unusual items, those that would be expensive to buy new, or raw materials to modify. Your local waste authority may also have a reuse program with businesses, which is another source of raw or unusual materials for your creative use. For example, you might find containers to cover for the 3-D Velcro-modeling toolkit here.

Opportunistic shopping can happen at any time. For example, you may already be out shopping for something specific, but happen to stumble upon an interesting item that might be useful for some future project. Or, you may be out shopping and think "I haven't been there in a while", and stop by just to see what you can find. Another scenario is when you're in an unfamiliar city or country where other shopping choices are available. The potential windfalls gained from opportunistic shopping create a strong argument that every project team member should shop for materials or, at the very least, be aware of the materials needed for projects so that they can take advantage of the unexpected gems that they may happen upon in their everyday lives. Opportunistic shopping with a partner can be especially fruitful and is often lots of fun.

Buttons for sale in a unique display in a small store in Delft, The Netherlands. Findings like this can be a rich source of inspiration for future toolkits.

INSIGHT INTO THE EXPERIENTIAL WORLD OF AUTISTIC CHILDREN

Children with autism cannot be involved in standard 'make and say' techniques. Their limited communication skills ask for a different approach. In this project, three boys and their caregivers were involved in observations and generative techniques to provide insight into the experiential world of children with autism.

In the 'LINKX' project, I developed a language-learning toy for children with autism. The toy involved linking blocks, and helps children learn to speak names of objects in their everyday environment, a first step towards speech and communication in children with autism. To design for this special user group, insight into the experiential world of children with autism was needed. Starting with searching information on the internet, reading books, and watching documentaries, I realized the need for contact with autistic children and their caregivers. Each could in their own way provide me insight into their experiential world from a personal perspective.

Therefore, I involved three autistic boys: Beer who loves numbers and letters, Robbert who enjoys music, and Jakob who is a big fan of colors. They participated with their parents and pedagogues. Each of these participants had a different way of communicating, and required communication tools fit for their specific way. Involving the children in standard 'make and say' techniques was impossible, because of their limited communication skills. As a solution, their caregivers helped out. Observing children and their caregivers at home, school, and therapy provided understanding and empathy. At the start, the children's behavior was confronting: 'Through interaction, I experienced myself the struggles in communication for and with these children'. This first contact helped me to prepare generative sessions with caregivers and shape the 'right' questions.

Contributor

Helma van Rijn, M.Sc.

PhD candidate

Faculty of Industrial Design Engineering

Delft University of Technology

The Netherlands

h.vanrijn@tudelft.nl

Helma's contribution was based on her Master thesis: LINKX a language toy for autistic toddlers, developed in co-creation with parents and pedagogues,
Delft University of Technology, Industrial Design Engineering, ID-Department. Chair: Prof. Dr. P.J. Stappers Mentor: Mrs. Dr. Ir. C.C.M. Hummels,
January 2007.

References

Van Rijn, H., Stappers, P.J. (2007) Codesigning LINKX: A case of getting insight in a difficult-to-reach user group. *IASDR conference*, Hong Kong, November 2007.

Van Rijn, H., Stappers, P.J. (2008) The puzzling life of autistic toddlers: Design guidelines from the LINKX project. *Advances in Human Computer Interaction, special issue child and play*.

Parents participated in an individual generative session about their child's preferences and skills and their life with the child. They received a booklet with small exercises around this topic. In the session, the parent shared a lot about their child and their personal life, such as feelings, daily patterns and family routines.

Four pedagogues participated in a generative session about language-learning, and how they achieve that with the children. In contrast to parents, pedagogues kept professional distance and helped me to make sense of the theory with their stories. They described the children's language learning without referring much to real life examples. So, the different people brought out different knowledge through tools and techniques that were attuned to each person's role and communication style.

Pedagogues participated in a generative session about language-learning of children with autism, and their achievements in that.

LINKX: Linking interactive blocks makes them play a word recorded by their parent.

Parents completed booklets about their child's skills and preferences. These booklets were discussed later on.

During the project, the designer observed the children in their daily lives and tested early prototypes.

CO-DESIGN IN VIRTUAL 3D SPACE: FITTING BICYCLES ON COMMUTER TRAINS

Bicycles are denied access on certain commuter trains because they can take too much space away from pedestrians who share the light rail interior. To help solve this problem, Co-Design in Virtual Space (CoDeViS), developed by the author, was used as a tool to find effective solutions.

This tool can be used to solve design problems after an ideal customer experience has been determined. Designers can engage others in the design process to help generate ideas and reveal desires within the confines of a specific context. In this case, a commuter train interior where bicycles and people must travel together is explored. This tool can potentially be available to high numbers of participants in various parts of the world at low cost.

In this study, five adult volunteers were recruited to participate; one female and four males, college students, ages 20-23. None of the participants had any practical 3D computer modeling skill. Without training or instruction, each participant was given a compact disk with three files. Participants used approximately two hours of their free time during a one-week period to complete the exercise. The files were:

1. MS Word document that contained directions, a possible scenario, and a space to write in thoughts and answers to questions to help participants immerse themselves in the design problem.
2. Google SketchUp application (a 3D modeling application available at no cost, also download-able from Google).

Contributor

James Arnold

Industrial Design Faculty

Art Institute of Portland

Portland, Oregon, USA

jimarnolddesign@gmail.com

Jim wrote this contribution when he was a member of the faculty in Design at The Ohio State University in Columbus, Ohio USA

Reference

Arnold, J. (2008) A Case Study of Applied Co-Design in 3D Virtual Space for Facilitating Bicycle Use on Light Rail Systems. *Undisciplined!: Design Research Society Conference.* Sheffield, UK.

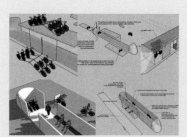

Each participant visualized their ideas by moving and placing the abstract shapes which were subsequently assigned meaning and notated using the text tool included in SketchUp.

3. SketchUp 3D model file containing a model of an empty commuter train interior and abstract shapes to use as virtual 'Velcro modeling' parts. The models had been created with minimal effort using 'Rhino' NURBS 3D CAD software and exported as a .3ds model file (SketchUp imports this and other file types).

After writing and creating 3D forms, the participants returned the files to the author through an online 'drop box.' The written and 3D modeling work was analyzed for reoccurring patterns and viable concepts. The author then created a concept, 'convertible/multi-use seating,' that embodied the most reoccurring themes/ ideas that the participants indicated in their work.

A follow-up interview with the participants revealed several things. Among the most significant was that the 3D aspect of the exercise was 'definitely' an aid in creating and expressing ideas. And the 3D modelling experience appeared to enhance the spatial and contextual awareness of the participants. Several other studies like this have confirmed these benefits of CoDeViS

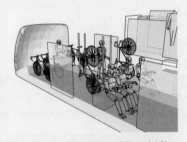

Statements and participant 3D model files inspired this resulting concept. Here, the author created a concept that embodied the design direction that most participants expressed.

The author also created these descriptive sketches to further refine the resulting design direction inspired by the participants.

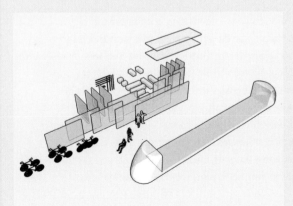

The participants were asked to install Google SketchUp on their own computer, and familiarize themselves with it. This is the SketchUp model file as it appeared when opened by participants.

FIRST IMPRESSIONS COUNT DOUBLE – PILOT TEST YOUR TOOLKITS

Toolkits need to fit the participants. A first version of a toolkit is almost never entirely right, so it is necessary to pilot-test your toolkit. Not only does this make the toolkit more effective, but the changes you will have to make already provide valuable insights, and participants who have seen the changes notice that you take them seriously.

Getting a toolkit right involves the content, the visual look and feel, as well as the tone of voice, and even small details. Here are two examples of this. In a project with greenhouse horticulturists, participants experienced what we thought was just a little spelling error in a piece of jargon (the abbreviation 'WKK' was written as 'WWK') as a sign that we had made no effort in understanding their world. For them, the WKK (meaning 'cat gas generator set') was a technology at the heart of their companies, and if we had left the error in there, it would probably have disturbed them so much that the purposes of the workbook would be defeated. We changed it immediately and planned visits to their greenhouses; this proved highly valuable for both the working relationship, and as a means to provide many leads for following up in the study.

The picture shown is a sensitizing booklet used in a contextmapping study with families. We had decided to use a single booklet for elderly, grownups and youngsters, so we could have an efficient overview of differences and similarities. The booklet was piloted with two people of each generation, one after the other. When we found that the elderly could not read the print, we scaled up the booklet. The grownups experienced this as pleasant, but the youngsters thought it was too 'old' for them. On the basis of this feedback, we worked with two versions.

The examples show that a pilot-test is an integral part of a study; it is a production check on the toolkit, but also a first contact from which you learn, and provides insights which may lead you to adjust the further steps.

Contributor

Sanne Kistemaker

User-centered Designer and Creative Director

Muzus

The Hague, The Netherlands

sanne@muzus.nl

A pilot workbook and tools for preparation, including a disposable camera, pens and stickers (from case 2 in chapter#4).

Different visual styles were used to appeal to the grownup participants (more formal) and for the youngsters (more playful).

Contributor

Bruce M. Hanington

Associate Professor and Program Chair

Industrial Design

Carnegie Mellon University

School of Design, MMCH 110

Pittsburgh, PA 15213-3890

hanington@cmu.edu

Related publications

Hanington, B. (2007) Generative Research in
Design Education, *Proceedings of the International
Association of Societies of Design Research*,
IASDR, International Conference, Hong Kong.

Hanington, B. (2010) Relevant and Rigorous:
Human-centered Research and Design Education,
Design Issues, Vol XXVI, No 3, Summer.

Credits

Luke Hagan

PILOT TESTING GAUGES KITS, TIMING, AND COMFORT FOR THE SESSION

Pilot testing is critical to gauge the appropriateness of design elements, to determine timing and flow of the session, and to ensure comfort of both facilitator and participants. In one example, a student designing a backpack had participants sort images of camping objects into a line drawing of a basic backpack form. The simple graphics were too limiting, however, so the kit was converted into an impressive full-size 3D Velcro modeling kit, with compelling results that allowed participants to construct an actual backpack, stuff it with supplies and test their ideas.

In another case, a kit with perspective renderings of product features was designed to allow janitors to configure their ideal cleaning carts, but some were unable to visually rotate 3D forms communicated in 2D, forcing the kit and participatory sessions to be revised.

INVOLVING BUSY PROFESSIONALS IN DEVELOPING NEW HEALTHCARE WORK ENVIRONMENTS

In the healthcare building industry, builders and architects seek input from the client and stakeholders, but often those who participate were selected on their hierarchical position, or their ability to express their point of view. This leaves out the essential expertise of many professionals (the end-users) on the work floor (Beekman, 2010; Kleinsmann et al., 2010). In our experience in developing new healthcare work environments, we found that involving these professionals is possible and valuable, but requires tools and techniques that match their busy work styles.

During our projects it quickly became clear that these professionals are heavily involved in the primary process of their work, and have little opportunity or desire to participate in additional sessions. Because they are used to a tight working routine, to improvisation and quick thinking and are highly focused on patient care, we adapted our way of researching and questioning to their busy schedule. We had to facilitate sessions that allow a quick in and out. Therefore we also had to adapt the tools to fit their work style.

We tried several tools and interviewing techniques, some of which worked very well. For instance, we translated hundreds of pages of thick project documentation into a few clear diagrams, and asked the staff of a rehabilitation hospital to point out what they recognized, missed, and (dis)agreed with. [Fig. 1] This resulted in a living document that can be consulted at short intervals when there is time in the work day.

We also had them participate in the analysis; to achieve efficiency we used color-coded post-its (pink for opportunities, orange for constraints) [Fig. 2]. The tools worked well, probably even better for this user group than for others, because of their ability to improvise and quickly switch to a new perspective. Another analysis tool was an online webpage which

Contributor

Quiel Beekman

User participation designer

4Building BV

Rijnsaterwoude, The Netherlands

beekman@4building.nl

References

Beekman, Q, (2010). A hospital's main asset is its people: User participation in a healthcare environment. In: Stappers, P.J. (Ed) *Designing for, with, and from user experiences.* StudioLab Press: Delft, Netherlands, p. 58-61.

Kleinsmann, M., Beekman, Q., Stappers P.J., (2010). Building hospitals using the experience of the stakeholders: How learning histories could enable the dialogue between architects and end users. In *Product Academic Issues, No. 2*, November 2010. Mybusinessmedia, Rotterdam, Netherlands, p.12-18.

Fig. 1 Pages of the Living Document and the card set used as a sensitizer preliminary to the generative user sessions of the rehabilitation hospital.

was regularly updated. Seeing their input reflected on the webpage motivated the participants because it showed that we were doing something with their input.

During a project in which we developed the requirements for a future Intensive Care Unit (ICU), we used large on-the-wall posters to which they could add by writing, drawing, pasting post-it notes or pictures; these posters hung in the corridors at the ICU ward. [Fig. 3]

The strength of these tools is not only revealing hidden information and knowledge by actively involving the professionals (the end-users) of the future building into the development process, but also creating a strong sense of ownership and responsibility in the participants. Participants appreciate that they have been heard and listened to. They were very enthusiastic about the method.

A team manager of the children's department of a rehabilitation hospital said: "Thinking in dreams instead of restrictions has proven to be a real eye-opener. Our creativity was stimulated and we discovered ourselves having much more fun compared to conventional user consultations."

"These techniques lead to a generative language and therefore a mutual understanding. The project leaders of the building development project got acquainted with our medical and organizational jargon and we end-users of the building understand the construction terminology better."

Fig. 2 Visual elements such as post-its of different colours facilitate clustering data and simplify the analysis.

Fig. 3 Mapping patient needs on the ICU department at "Het Westfriesgasthuis" at Hoorn, the Netherlands, November 2010.

MAPPING THE SOCIAL: USING GENERATIVE TECHNIQUES TO LEARN ABOUT PEOPLE'S ROLES, COMMUNITIES, AND SOCIAL VALUES

People's experiences of product and service use are inextricably linked to the social, or how people deal with each other. One way of learning about people's social practices and experiences using generative techniques is by asking people – couples, friends, colleagues, relatives – to jointly reflect on one and the same situation.

Baby care is a fundamentally social activity. In 2008, we conducted an exploratory study to learn about parents' social practices and experiences of baby care as part of a new product development project at Philips Research Europe. The aim of the project was to develop new technologies and product concepts for baby care, based on rich understanding of the lives of parents with babies aged between three and ten months old. Six couples with babies participated in our study. First we planned the study and developed a preliminary workbook and generative tools together with the project team. The workbook contained creative exercises in which the parents were asked to reflect on their routines and experiences of caring for their babies. They were, for example, asked to indicate on a timeline what their baby's day looks like, and to explain what they do to get their baby to sleep. The parents worked on the probes individually during five consecutive days.

Then we visited each couple for a generative session in their homes. During such a session, the couple explained what they had created in their probes, showed us around in their baby's bedroom, and together mapped their baby's bedtime routine on a poster, using a variety of abstract shapes and markers. Jointly reflecting on their practices of caring for their baby triggered stories about their roles, community, and social values of baby care, and how they felt about this – the social. Moreover, the couples

Contributors

Carolien Postma

Product Researcher

Philips Consumer Lifestyle

Eindhoven, The Netherlands

carolien.postma@philips.com

Elly Zwartkruis-Pelgrim

Research Scientist

Philips Research Europe

Eindhoven, The Netherlands

elly.zwartkruis-pelgrim@philips.com

This contribution was written when Carolien Postma was a Ph.D. candidate, ID-Studiolab, Delft University of Technology, Delft, The Netherlands Dissertation: Postma, C.E. (2012) *Creating Socionas - Building creative understanding of users' social experiences in new product development practice*, Delft University of Technology.

complemented, contradicted, and corrected each other's stories, providing us with insight into their social practices and experiences from two different angles. For example, when Laura (one mother) pointed out that she usually brings the baby to bed, her husband (Mark) hastened to explain that Laura tries to establish a bedtime routine by feeding the baby upstairs just before bedtime, and that he does not believe that feeding the baby upstairs will help to establish a bedtime routine. He thought it was too much trouble to feed the baby upstairs, and decided to leave this up to Laura and do some household activities instead.

Insight into the parents' social practices and experiences of baby care helped the project team to develop concepts for baby care that fit these social practices and met the needs of both parents.

The parents showed us around in their baby's bedroom, and explained why they furnished the room the way they did.

One couple considered the bedtime ritual to be a cycle that starts and ends with breastfeeding the baby. While the mother feeds the baby, the father plays together with his toddler son.

The timeline of the mother (top) fills the gaps in the timeline of the father (bottom): Today is the mother's day home, the father is at work during the day.

7DAYSINMYLIFE.COM: AN ONLINE DIARY RESEARCH TOOL

7daysinmylife.com is an online environment that mirrors physical workbooks for self-documentation as they are widely used in design research. The tool was developed to combine the authenticity and directness of these physical forms with the flexibility and accessibility of online research tools.

Workbooks for self-documentation are a great way to get to know users of a specific product or service. The downside of these, however, is that they are laborious for the research team. They have to be crafted, taken to the research participants, collected, and then disassembled for analysis. What's more, while the respondents work on their assignments, the research team has no insight in the developing content. Having done many projects involving these physical workbooks, our team set out to circumvent these disadvantages. We decided to build a closed online environment that would have the same basic functionality of physical workbooks, but with a number of advantages:

> We can create different workbooks for different clients, using the same content management system.
> The research team (including the client) can follow the progress of the workbooks and add notes and comments to them. (The participants don't see these comments since we don't want to influence their progress). Anyone who is provided with a login code can access the materials and study them, whenever they want.
> The research participants can upload images and text through their web browser, e-mail, SMS or MMS, anytime, anywhere.
> The resulting workbooks can be exported to PDF, printed out and used in analysis workshops as many times as we want.

We have used 7daysinmylife.com for many client projects and we've learned some important things:

Contributor

Erik Roscam Abbing

Founder/Owner

Zilver Innovation

Rotterdam, The Netherlands

Erik@zilverinnovation.com

References

www.7daysinmylife.com

Rowland, N. and Hagen, P. (2010) Mobile diaries, discovering daily life.

http://bit.ly/mobilediaries

Bowmast, N. (2010) Critical reflection on digital versus 'old school' diaries: http://bit.ly/ oldschooldiaries

Gaver, W., Dunne, T. and Pacenti, E. (1999) Cultural Probes. *ACM Interactions*, 6, pp. 21 – 29

A screenshot of a 7days page as it is filled in by a participant. The colored post-its are comments made by different members of the research team.

> It's a very useful tool, fun to use for participants and research team, and great to get the research team involved in the users and their lives.
> Because we have lost the contact moment we used to have when taking the workbook to the respondent, good personal phone and e-mail contact become essential in building trust. We invest a lot of time in making sure the participant feels comfortable with sharing his/her answers online.
> You have to craft the questions in the right way to invite creativity and openness in the digital environment.
> For some research topics (e.g., very private) or target groups (e.g., elderly) we have chosen to combine or replace 7daysinmylife.com with physical workbooks.

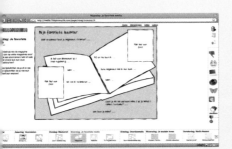

A screenshot of a typical 7days page: The participant has room to make a collage of photos and notes, and on the right he can pick icons to use. On the bottom is an overview of the questions.

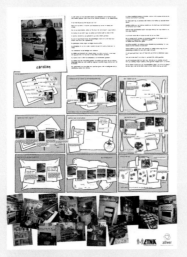

The Content Management System supports printing out the diaries and formatting them into posters that collate the diary results and the house visits or generative session results into one overview.

7daysinmylife.com results are very useful and inspiring for immersion and analysis workshops we hold with our clients

CO-DESIGN: GETTING IN TOUCH BY COOKING TOGETHER

When working with participants who are not at ease with expressing themselves on paper, or in the structured setting of an organized discussion, you have to modify your methods. Doing an activity together can create an effective setting for talking about personal matters and telling stories (as, e.g., the little talks during the washing of the dishes during a family event).

In one case study for a municipal authority of a large city, we explored the needs of homeless people from a minority group. Many of them were alcoholics and longtime unemployed, and we decided to cook a traditional meal together with them. During these activities, we talked about their daily lives, dreams, and needs. The activity also established a level of trust. Afterwards, a few of them guided us through their area, during which we exchanged stories. The explorations provided insights that formed a starting point for co-designing with the homeless.

Contributor

Sanne Kistemaker

User-centered Designer and Creative Director, Muzus

The Hague, The Netherlands

sanne@muzus.nl

CHAPTER 7
ANALYSIS:
WHAT TO DO
WITH
WHAT YOU GOT

INTRODUCTION

Many challenges are posed in analyzing qualitative data gathered through generative design research. There are no "canned" programs or methods such as those that you find for the analysis of quantitative data. The data you will be dealing with are "messy" and there often is quite a lot of it, and in different media, as well. There are many options as to how far you take the analysis of data gathered through exploratory generative research and we will cover three such options in this chapter. One option is not to analyze the data at all but to immerse yourself and the team in the raw data. We call this 'immersion for inspiration only'. At the other extreme is analysis that done with computer databases. The third option is similar to analysis with computer databases but it relies on the use of the walls in a room to organize and manipulate the data. We will this option "analysis on the wall."

In some cases, it can take you more time to analyze the data than it took for you to gather it in the field. And one of the biggest challenges that you may face is that the people who analyze the data may not be the same people who will be using the results and they will have not been involved in gathering the data.

THE CHALLENGES OF DEALING WITH QUALITATIVE DATA

The analysis of qualitative data is always an adventure of exploration, and the analysis of the qualitative data that comes from generative design research especially so. The generative research process draws simultaneously from many different methods and techniques. The sources might include any or all of the following:

> secondary research in the form of previously published work,
> ethnographic field research which may be documented by field notes of observations, or by photographs or by audio and video-recording,
> interviews that can be documented in any number of forms including field notes, audio-recording, video-recordings, word-for-word transcriptions of the audio-records, etc.
> informal conversations which may be documented in any number of forms,
> questionnaire results (some open-ended and some closed),
> photographs taken by the participants which may or may not be annotated,
> the outcomes of sensitizing assignments and workbook data such as diary entries and responses to open-ended questions or toolkit exercises which may be annotated,
> artifacts made by the participants using the generative toolkits in workbooks, sessions, or interviews,
> verbal presentations about these artifacts that have been given by the participants,
> discussions between participants during the session, as triggered by the artifacts,
> notes and reflections by the research team as entries in the project diary, and
> mindmaps and idea dumps made by the research team members in the early phases of project planning.

The form of the data is 'messy' as compared to 'neat' data, e.g., marks on a 7-point scale or a response time measured in milliseconds. Qualitative data varies along these dimensions:

> method of data collection
> content
> topics addressed
> format or medium of delivery
> level of detail
> level of interpretation (e.g., interpreted vs. raw)
> visual or verbal
> generic vs. anecdotal
> subjective vs. objective

The messiness of generative data means that the activity of figuring out what the data means will not be simple or fast, nor will it be easy to prescribe how it should be done in advance of its collection. Dealing with this type of data is a skill that comes with training, experience, and reflection. It is not a fixed and rigid procedure. But some patterns have emerged in our collective experiences that we will share in order to help you determine what to do with what you've got.

How is the analysis of data from generative design research the same or different from the analysis of data from a traditional user-centered approach? Both rely on qualitative analysis and the overall process of analysis flows from the same principles. (For an overview of qualitative research methodologies, see Miles & Huberman, 1994; Lincoln & Guba, 1989). But the variety of data that is collected in generative design research can be vastly different, as can be seen in Table#7.1. The generative toolkits, in particular, introduce new types of data into the mix. We will spend more time describing what to do with the 'what people make' category of data since other sources that describe the analysis of 'what people say' and 'what people do' data are available elsewhere.

WHAT PEOPLE	USER-CENTERED DESIGN RESEARCH	GENERATIVE DESIGN RESEARCH
Say	Transcripts Questionnaire data Interview notes	Transcripts Questionnaire data Interview notes
Do	Photos Videotapes Observation notes	Photos Videotapes Observation notes
Make		Image collages Cognitive maps 3-D models Workbook data of many forms Transcripts of stories told about the artifacts Annotated photographs from the participants Observations of people's behavior during the workshops

Figure#7.1 A comparison of the data that comes from traditional user-centered vs generative design research

CAPTURING: STORING, ORDERING, AND LABELING

The first step, whatever your plan for analysis, is to prepare the data for further use and to make sure you don't lose track of anything, Label every piece of data with the following items of information:

> **who** found/took/observed/recorded or heard it?
> **where** was it found/taken/observed/recorded or heard?
> **when** was it found/taken/observed/recorded or heard? This includes time and date as well as any other contextual information that seems important or interesting at the time.
> **participant name** (or code, in the case that participant names are not allowed).

Hint#: If insights or ideas pop up during the data capturing stage, be sure to document them as well.

It is possible that you will not need all this information later, but if you do need it, you will have it. It is not a good idea to assume that you will be able to remember such details once the fieldwork phase has ended. Typically, at the end of a session, a researcher may feel inspired and in touch with what was observed or said, but this overview and awareness will fade rapidly, especially if other sessions are to follow. Therefore, it is important to capture the information as soon as it is produced, and also to write down those early insights as soon as possible.

Hint#: Spot-check your work when documenting data. Ask someone else to compare your notes, transcripts or data entry to the raw data. They don't need to double check every item but they do need to check a random sampling.

When you are working with messy data, it is important that all the members of the team follow the same data collection procedures and documentation methods. Having consistency in how the data is collected and documented will make the analysis of this data much easier to manage. Introducing inconsistencies through idiosyncratic documentation can add extra time and tension in the analysis effort. And it may lead to errors. Instead, prepare the data for easy, effective, and efficient use. This may involve transcribing (parts of) what was said during sessions from the video recordings, printing and copying photo material, workbooks, field notes in a way that fits your method of analysis, e.g., on cards, post-its, or in a database on your computer.

THE AIMS OF ANALYSIS

Analyzing literally means 'picking apart', and typically involves interpreting the data, making comparisons to theories and to other data, searching for patterns and determining how well they fit, generalizing findings to a broader scope, and finding evidence to support your conclusions. In explaining the process of analysis, and positioning all these activities, we found it helpful to frame them in a variation of the DIKW scheme (the letters D, I, K, W, standing for Data, Information, Knowledge, and Wisdom) (Ackoff, 1989), which distinguishes levels of sense-making. Getting these levels straight can help avoid common confusions between data, interpretations, theories, etc. Theories typically contain principles and patterns, sometimes laws, and are applicable to many situations. Theories are aimed for general validity, e.g., the theory that people normally have two arms is meant to be true not just for me or you, but for all people in the world (excepting the unfortunate who suffered accidents). Then there is evidence, collected in laboratory experiments or in the field. It may be a photo showing five people, each having two arms. But it also shows that two of these people have a mustache (which may be irrelevant to the theory of having two arms). How evidence and theory are connected is a matter of debate and the philosophy of science.

Figure#7.2 shows a simple model, based on Ackoff's DIKW scheme. The value of this model is that it can help us structure and explain how to deal with data gathering and analysis. It shows three layers within the 'research box', labeled *data*, *information*, and *knowledge*. There is a layer called *phenomenon* below the box, and one layered *wisdom* above it. We will discuss them in the typical order of analysis, i.e., from bottom to top.

The *phenomenon* is something that happens in the world, e.g., someone having a phone conversation with a work colleague. Making sense of the phenomenon is the object of the study, but something that we cannot really catch. What we can catch and keep is *data*. Data can take the form of photos, video or audio recordings, for example.

Data can also be notes, and things people make or leave behind (a shaver and hairs). Data is different from the evidence in that it has been *selected*, maybe *recorded*, by the researcher, and therefore reflects what he or she deemed important (e.g., no x-rays were made of the person having the phone conversation; the photo has been taken from an informative direction). The researcher may have just collected the data (as in observation); he or she may also have evoked it (by asking an interview question, or asking the participant to photograph himself while he shaved). Data is typically on a physical carrier such as a camera, and can be stored and retrieved. It may be digital data, which means that it can be easily copied.

The important distinction between *data* and *information*, in that the latter is *interpreted* by the researcher or the research team. The same piece of data may lead to different interpretations. One photo may be interpreted as 'photo with bright lights', 'photo of early morning activity', 'photo of someone making a phone call' or 'photo of our participant posing for us' or 'photo of our participant showing how she wants to be seen professionally'. All these interpretations may be valid, and come from the same data. It is important to realize that the data itself has no meaning.

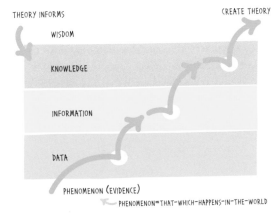

Figure#7.2 A simple model to guide analysis, based on Ackoff's DIKW scheme

Meaning is actively chosen by the researcher, through interpretation. Whereas data is typically physical and has many aspects, interpretations are symbolic (often verbal), and are often chosen within a classification framework.

Although different pieces of data cannot be exactly the same, pieces of information, being symbols, can be the same. Because of this, patterns can be sought in the interpretations, and formal methods of symbol manipulation, e.g., methods like sorting and counting, can be performed by people or computers. (It can be noted that although using computers in analysis is often referred to as 'data processing', it is actually 'information processing' in the terms of the DIKW scheme.)

These patterns are theories, and that is what happens on the level of *knowledge*. Knowledge is generalized, abstracted from the individual data and information bits about which it is made and, if we succeed in making a successful theory, it can predict further events, and further data that can be extracted from the evidence.

The activities of research are twofold: one is gathering data, the other is analyzing it. Analyzing involves building information, then layering knowledge on top of the data, in the hope this gives us an understanding about other pieces of evidence we have not yet seen. Much of the formal training of researchers is to give them understanding and skill in managing this process: getting usable data into the research system, and working it up to knowledge.

The layer above the research box kicks in when we want to do something with the knowledge. Its name, *wisdom* (maybe not a fortunate choice, because it has many connotations), indicates it goes beyond knowledge, and is outside of the level of theory. On the wisdom level lie the decisions on how to deal with the knowledge that was gained. Knowledge by necessity is an abstracted and partial view. Knowledge is a reduction of reality. That is its strength, but also its limitation. At the wisdom level, we must be aware of these strengths and limitations. At the wisdom level we make the choice to use a theory or not use it, here we decide what to do if one of our theories conflicts with another one.

In Figure#7.2, we depicted both wisdom and phenomenon (evidence) outside the 'doing research' box that contains data, information, and knowledge. One reason is because it is in the box that analysis resides, the second is because this is the space where methods and techniques are relatively well-defined. By necessity, wisdom and evidence do not fall within this box.

The levels themselves are easily recognizable in the procedures of analyzing qualitative data: interpreting the data into information, and finding patterns in that information. But they are not just successive stages in some coffee-making procedure where the end-product is drunk and the intermediate steps hidden in a black box. A lot of insight is gained in going through the steps (again, forms of tacit knowledge operate here), and making this insight explicit is a challenge. Deep understanding involves being able to move between these levels of abstract knowledge, interpreted information, and concrete data.

In communicating findings (Chapter#8), it is important to rely on all levels in the DIKW scheme. For example, you may choose to communicate findings using quotes (data) and interpretations of the quotes (information) as well as the general rules that are operating in the given situation (knowledge).

LEVEL	CONTAINS	...WHICH CAN BE...	..AND TURNED TO...	BY...
wisdom				
knowledge	theories, patterns		wisdom	using the knowledge
information	interpreted symbols, categories	compared, grouped	knowledge	finding patterns
data	selected materialized stuff	stored and retrieved	information	choosing interpretations
phenomenon (evidence)	stuff and events in the world		data	selecting, recording

Table#7.3 Operations in the DIKW scheme

ORDERING IN GROUPS OR HIERARCHIES

Raw data can be interpreted into information in many different ways. Some ways depend on what aspect the researcher is studying (e.g., in a study into communication methods, interpreting the photo of the woman making a phone call as 'photo with bright lights' may not be relevant). But there is another degree of freedom in interpreting which is relevant to design: the level of abstraction. That same photo can be interpreted as a woman that is "holding a phone", "having a conversation", "postponing a business meeting", "maintaining a business relation", "fulfilling her social obligations", to "functioning in society". So which one is the correct interpretation? The answer is that there is no single correct interpretation. All these are descriptions of the same event, and refer to the same part of the phenomenon, but at a different level of abstraction. What level is best can only be decided in the light of the purposes for which the study is conducted.

It may be valuable not to choose just one level of interpretation, but to organize the different levels and look at the relations between them. The levels in an abstraction hierarchy are related by 'laddering', by asking the questions 'why' to move up and 'how' to move down. They form a 'means-ends hierarchy'. See Figure#7.4. The answer to "why is she holding the phone" can be "to have a conversation". The answer "why does she have a conversation" can be "to postpone a business meeting" and so on. And in reverse, the question "How does she move the business meeting" is answered as "by having a conversation."

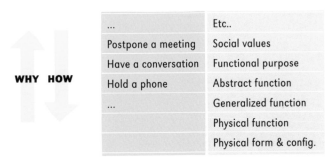

WHY HOW

...	Etc..
Postpone a meeting	Social values
Have a conversation	Functional purpose
Hold a phone	Abstract function
...	Generalized function
	Physical function
	Physical form & config.

Figure#7.4 An abstraction hierarchy orders interpretations in levels of means-ends relationships

An abstraction hierarchy can help in at least two ways. First, it can help to bring separate interpretations from different pieces of data onto the same level of abstraction, and thereby make it easier to recognize and describe patterns (i.e., prepare for the move to the knowledge level).

Second, it can point to alternative means for an end (and alternative ends that can be reached by a means). The list in Figure#7.4 invites the designer to consider "What alternative means are there to have a conversation", and the answer might be "to send a text message" or "to visit in person". Similarly at the lowest level a letter, a messenger, or a carrier pigeon may replace the phone as a means of having a conversation. And in the other direction, "What other purposes do conversations have beside postponing meetings". These may be "ask for availability", or maybe "inform of an opportunity".

In these ways, abstraction hierarchies help the search for alternative solutions. The theory of abstraction hierarchies has been developed in the area of complex control systems, such as airplane cockpits and powerplants, but it works well for down-to-earth applications as well. For an example and more background, see Peter Jones' contribution on page#230. In design research, on the other hand, our interests lie beyond the present, because we want to make use of the levels of insight in order to move toward the future, for which the new solutions (e.g., product, service,...) will be designed.

The left-hand side in Figure#7.5 represents gathering data and analyzing it. The right-hand side represents conceptualization. What connects them is what we call 'bridging'. The connection can also involve a separate step that we call 'communicating', if research and conceptualization are conducted separately. But the steps can also be mixed to a high degree. In the flow of this book, we describe the case where they are conducted separately because it allows us to introduce certain terms and models, and because it happens often. We will return to bridging in Chapter#10.

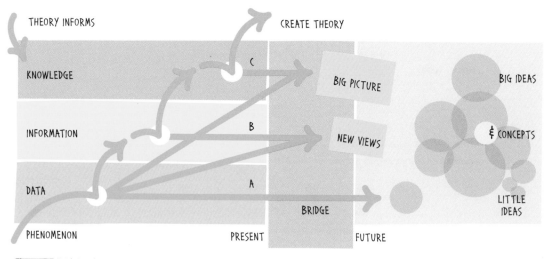

Figure#7.5 Bridging from research to design involves a shift from understanding the present situation to constructing possible futures.

MOVING FROM RESEARCH TOWARD DESIGN

The DIKW scheme of analyzing data is typical of theory formation in science, and is focused on describing and explaining what happens in the present (or what happened in the past). Data from the field study enters in at the lowest level on the left hand side, as 'raw data'. In analysis, the data is taken to increasingly higher levels of abstraction, first by interpreting it (yielding 'information'), then by relating the information into categories, frequencies, and other patterns, theories, and models (called 'knowledge'), and possibly further.

The journey from gathering to conceptualization differs from project to project. It can be very brief, or involve intensive methodical searches for patterns and interpretations. When the users of the insights are not the same people as the researchers, the journey may rely heavily on communication. Such bridges are needed to help in making the transition across the 'gap' between research and design. Many people are more comfortable on one side or the other of the gap. But there is tremendous value in having people collaborate with others when they are working on their less comfortable side. In fact, this collaboration is necessary to effectively bridge the gap between research (on the left) and design (on the right).

There are various levels at which bridging can take place. It can be done straight from the raw data, leading to little ideas shown as small bubbles on the right (Figure#7.6a). We call this crossing the bridge at the data level. For example this can be straightforward suggestions by users which fit the product that is designed, e.g., adding a mute button to a music playing device. On the other hand, when the bridge is crossed at the information level, ideas that emerge through interpretation and abstraction usually are bigger, less superficial ideas. For instance, you might realize that people only want the music playing device when they are travelling. Finally when crossing the bridge at the knowledge level, a theory is developed, and this can lead to a 'big picture', which can form the basis for new ideas which are more radical, fundamental, and/or substantial. An example might be realizing that it is a service and not a product that is needed.

When analyzing to the higher levels of abstraction the insights can be more generalizable (i.e., valid beyond the sampled data, or the participants) but at the same time more abstract (i.e., disconnected from experience). This may cause the researcher to lose touch with what is actually going on. So the most intensive forms of analysis should also carry the more holistic 'touch and feel' of the lower levels along with the big insights. As a whole, the picture would then become as is shown in Figure#7.6, with transfer occurring not just at one of the levels, but all of them simultaneously, so that ideas and insights are both generalizable and experiential.

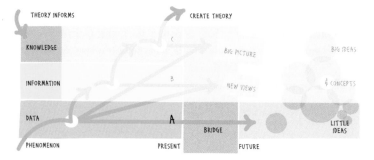

A. Crossing the bridge at the data level - immersion for inspiration only

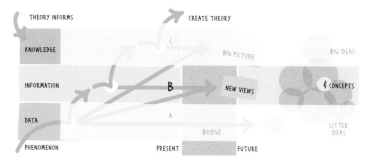

B. Crossing the bridge at the information level - on the wall analysis

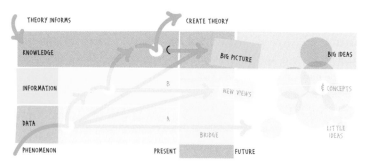

C. Crossing the bridge at the knowledge level - with a database analysis

Figure#7.6 Bridging at several levels of the DIKW scheme. (a) at the data level, (b) at the information level, (c) at the knowledge level.

CHOOSING A PATH

In this chapter we describe three prototypical paths for doing the analysis: Path A: Immersion for inspiration only, Path B: Light analysis that is done 'on the wall' and Path C: Heavy analysis that is done 'in a database'.

	PATH A: INSPIRATION ONLY	PATH B: ON THE WALL	PATH C: WITH A DATABASE
research expertise needed	good for beginners	good for beginners	highly skilled research team
number of participants	less than 10 people	less than 10 people	10 or more people
set-up required	set up room with raw data	summarize data, then set up room with raw data and summarized data	enter all raw data into a spreadsheet
format	immersive visual display of data	immersive visual display of data and summaries	data is 'hidden' in spread-sheets
analytic power	for inspiration only	limited analysis and for inspiration	highly efficient and thorough analysis
time and cost	the least time consuming	time consuming and it may not be efficient	time consuming but the most efficient
major drawback	may miss important insights	may miss important insights	may miss the opportunity for inspiration

Table#7.7 The three prototypical paths of analysis are compared

Table #7.7 compares the three paths along a number of criteria. Each path will be described in some detail, but there are actually an infinite number of paths in between the prototypical paths that arise from how the team decides to address the following factors :

> Final deliverables that were expected or promised?
> Establishing empathy between the end-users and the client?
> Getting concept designs for immediate use?
> Design concepts or only understanding of the phenomenon?
> Identification of opportunities for new products and services?
> A new framework for thinking/acting?

Who is conducting the research? Who is helping and who is watching?

> Designers?
> Teachers?
> Researchers?
> Supervisors?
> Clients?

What kinds of resources and constraints are available?

> Time
> People
> Money
> Previous research findings
> Solution capabilities of the client such as technology, sales channels, etc.

What is the prior history/experience of the team members involved? What is each team member's personal history? What previous relationships have the team members had with one another? Are they:

> Researchers with years of experience?
> People learning to be researchers?
> Strangers who are working together for the first time?
> Former team members?
> Students and instructors/supervisors?

The above list of considerations reveals how varied the paths of inquiry can become. All these factors influence what you can do, how you do it and how long it will take. Clearly, as you gain experience, you can take on more and more complex situations.

The four cases in Part#2 covered all three of the prototypical path types:

> Case 1: The student exercise describes Analysis Path A or immersion for inspiration only.
> Case 2: The senior project describes Analysis Path B or 'on the wall analysis'.
> Case 3: Integration is another example of Analysis Path B, but this time it is done as a team.
> Case 4: Large-scale international uses both Analysis Paths B and C.

We'll describe each path in detail starting with Path A: Immersion for Inspiration Only.

PATH A: IMMERSION FOR INSPIRATION ONLY

In this path, you expose the design team to the raw data without substantially selecting, interpreting, or organizing it. Immersion for inspiration only takes the form of an 'inspiration event', a prepared and facilitated session in which the team reviews the data, samples it, and draws its own conclusions. Depending on the size of the whole project, such an event can take from half a day to a series of events planned over several weeks.

WHY DO IMMERSION?

Why would you want to use generative data primarily for the purpose of inspiration when there is so much more that can be learned when the data is more systematically analyzed? There are at least five situations for which immersion for inspiration is the best answer.

First, it is a good way to learn about generative design research. Researchers or teams that are just beginning to explore the use of generative design research may want to learn how to use such data to inspire the design process before learning how to more thoroughly analyze this type of data.

Second, this path makes sense when the primary end goal is to use the artifacts and data of the research process to quickly inspire design development teams. Extremely rich and evocative data emerges from the use of generative tools that have been informed by ethnographic practices. When displayed appropriately, this data provides a fruitful context for providing relevant inspirational design spaces for creative people or teams.

Third, the immersion path has shown itself to be a good way to convince a first-time and possibly skeptical client about the potential of generative tools and methods. Analysis for inspiration is not as costly (in terms of both time and money) as analyzing the data more completely, so this can be a cost-effective way of gaining the opportunity to involve a client in the generative design research process for the first time. It may happen that the client will see the value in further analysis once the richness of the data becomes apparent. So it is important that thorough documentation is done at the start of the process in order to support any level of analysis.

Fourth, an inspiration event might be appropriate if the team members on the client side have many years of experience and already possess a deep theoretical understanding of the domain under investigation, but want to connect these abstract insights to the contextualized experience of a specific target group.

Fifth, just confronting the design team with the raw data may be a good first step to be followed by more extensive analysis and communication. It gives the experienced researcher an opportunity to get to learn the sensitivities and blind spots of the design team that will be at the receiving end of the work.

PREPARING FOR AN INSPIRATION EVENT
Before starting, check to be sure that every piece of data that has been collected has been labeled as described earlier. Find a room or a space that can be reserved for several days. Ideally, the space is large enough for the whole team to work in at once. Inspiration events can be done with teams of up to 10-15 people. The room should have moveable furniture. Natural light is also a plus. The walls of the room are also important since the data will be exposed across all the walls. If it is not possible to pin or tape directly to the wall, it will be necessary to put up large sheets of foam core on which to post or pin the materials.

Hint#: *You may first want to put large rolls of paper up on the walls (or the foam core). That way you can post or tape to the paper, making the task of tear-down or clean-up much easier. You can simply take down the paper and roll it up to take with you.*

Put all the research data and materials up on the walls. Consider how the material is best organized and be sure to use large labels so that newcomers can quickly come up to speed on what is going on. For example, you might want to organize it by medium (e.g., photos on one wall, workbooks on another) and then by participants. Chances are that you will want to rearrange the materials, so keep that in mind when choosing how to pin or stick the materials up. You can use post-it glue so it is very quick and easy to move things around. Leave room for additional notes and cards so that team members can annotate and add ideas to the walls. Provide materials (such as sticky notes in a variety of colors and sizes) that encourage people to make annotations. It is a good idea to designate a special colored background shape for documenting and highlighting ideas or insights that will likely pop up over time. Also provide thick line markers so that the notes can be easily read from a distance. You might want to ask people to print instead of using cursive writing for improved legibility.

Invite the team members into the space to do their thinking and dreaming and ideating. Preferably, the space offers a range of seating and meetings areas (as opposed to an office room filled with a conference table). Physical activity and food are also likely to help with creative thinking, so bring some snacks and drinks. If possible, provide an environment where people can move around while they think.

Take pictures every day as new content and material emerges. This is especially important if the room is not available for a long period of time. Photographic or video-documentation of the immersion experience can be shared with others at a later point in time if it is documented well. It also helps in explaining how the insights came into being.

CONDUCTING AN INSPIRATION EVENT
In addition to making the space available for the team members to work in, it is advisable to conduct a

special event to ensure that inspirational thinking is provoked, collected and sustained. Invite all the members of the client's team who need to understand the research results and those who will be using the insights in subsequent phases. Immersive events for inspiration rely on four types of activities: immersion, role playing, storytelling and making. These activities work well together when applied in the following order.

IMMERSION FOR INSPIRATION ONLY: FOUR STEPS
1. Immerse the team in the topic that is being explored. It is best if everyone comes having completed some type of 'homework' before the event. For example, you might ask them to complete some or all of the same workbook exercises or generative toolkit exercises that were filled out by the participants in the research. This gets them familiar with the research protocol, sensitizes them for the topic, and will also help them to more clearly see how they are different from the participants.

2. Use the data to tell stories from the field. The rich (and messy) data from the generative design research process is ideal for sharing stories from the field. Selected video segments can be especially powerful forms of communication although photos with voice-overs by a narrator are also good.

3. Encourage empathy with roleplaying. Ask the research team members to enact future scenarios from the perspective of the partici- pants. Roleplaying the part of participants is not likely to appeal to all the members of the research team, so it is best to ask for volunteers to roleplay. Those who decline can then serve as audience members or as observers. You can facilitate roleplaying by offering props such as hats or other symbolic wearables. Depending on the stories, and the team's ability at roleplaying, you can also offer the use of hand puppets to encourage roleplaying.

4. Give them generative toolkits to use. Give the team members generative tools to use for making maps, models, or stories about future experiences that are inspired by the sharing of stories and roleplaying activities. Create toolkits for group use to encourage collective creativity. The intent is not to generate concepts. The intent is to come to know the research participants in many ways.

IMMERSION FOR INSPIRATION ONLY: AN EXAMPLE
Role playing, telling and making can be an effective means of providing the client team with an empathic understanding of the participants' lives.

In this example, an inspirational event took place during the data gathering phase. Many members of the client's team observed (from behind a one-way mirror) a series of twelve participatory workshops with a range of their 'customers'. The schedule was set up such that a three-hour workshop with the client team members playing the role of their customers took place after six of the customer workshops were complete.

For the immersion/inspiration workshop we invited the client team members to use the generative toolkit (in the workshop room) themselves to create concepts that expressed what they thought they were hearing from the participants. In this case, the generative toolkit consisted of an array of hundreds of items including:

> Three-dimensional components in many shapes and sizes
> Pictures
> Words
> What-if? cards (These were pre-prepared cards that spelled out future situations for consideration)

The client team members, having just watched six of the customer workshops, were very immersed in how their customers were viewing the experience domain. They had no trouble in quickly mocking up their own concepts. They presented their concepts to each other in the form of stories from the future as told through the eyes of the customers they had just spent time observing and listening to. They had a lot of fun in the process and the research team gained some incredible insights into the mindsets of the client team members, in particular, what they found to be the 'new' ideas. The entire three-hour client immersion/inspiration workshop was video-taped so that later analysis of it was possible.

DOCUMENTING THE INSPIRATION EVENT
Be sure to document the event with photography, video-recording and audio-recording. Keep in mind that you may not use all this documentation later. In fact, you may never use it. But you will have it just in case. For example, a new team member may find the video-recording of the inspiration event to be invaluable as a way to get up to speed on the project. And, of course, most people will enjoy seeing themselves in retrospect, reliving the event at a later point in time.

What comes out of an inspiration event? In this path to analysis, many insights may remain tacit, under the surface. Some insights can be made explicit, but typically the outcomes of this path are not explicit or generalized conclusions, but rather a sense of 'reality check'. The event gives the team members a chance to connect to the richness of the research participants' lives around the topic of study. Inspiration, in the form of many small ideas related to the topic of study, is also quite likely.

HEY, DIDN'T I READ THIS BEFORE?
In reading the description of the inspiration event, you may recognize many elements from the generative sessions with users: there is sensitizing, an inspiring workspace and tool elements, and a lot of freedom for people to determine the direction that the event will take. At the same time, they work with toolkits and techniques which are prepared to let them live through past events and make connections, involving creative actions, reflection, and visualization. A main difference will be the data the design team starts with (generated from the session), and the goals set for the meeting (aimed toward the needs of the design team). In fact, the generative sessions and inspiration events may even be merged in some situations as the previous example shows.

PATH B: ANALYSIS ON THE WALL

True analysis follows two paths: light analysis that can be conducted on the wall and heavy analysis that requires the use of a database. This section describes Path B: analysis on the wall, i.e., light analysis. Heavy analysis follows in the next section.

We call it light analysis because there is a limited amount of data to analyze and a limited range of movement through the DIKW analysis hierarchy (see page#200-202). For light analysis you will need raw data, paper, sticky notes and walls on which to post these materials. Light analysis for a medium-sized project can usually take place in one or two intensive sessions lasting about a day each.

WHY DO ANALYSIS ON THE WALL?

If your client is looking for relevant innovation and opportunities to pursue as new business ventures, then you need to analyze the data to realize what you have learned. The additional resources required to do so are generally offset by the value of what is returned. The real value in analyzing on the wall is that it can provide information and inspiration simultaneously.

Analysis on the wall is best when your sample size is small, such as 6 or 7 participants. Or if you are comparing two groups with only 4 or 5 people in a group, you will be able to effectively do analysis on the wall as well.

Hint#: _Don't do analysis on the wall with data from more than 10 participants._

Analysis on the wall can be handled by a lone researcher but the ability to get the most out of a data set is much higher when a team of researchers is analyzing the data together.

Analysis on the wall is the best way to learn about how to analyze the "messy" data that is collected in the generative design research process. By putting it on the wall, all the research team members can participate in analysis and insight identification. Light analysis on the wall can also be very useful as a preparation for analysis using computer databases. In this section we describe light analysis with a focus on analyzing the outcome of a collage-making exercise by six participants. In reality, other types of data might also need to be addressed. The data consists of:

Figure#7.8 Materials used in analysis on the wall. From top to bottom: cards with quotes and interpretations, clustered cards and other notes on the wall. The last photo shows the team working through analysis on the wall.

> Six sensitizing workbooks and six collages,
> Transcripts of the collage presentations and discussion from the workshop and
> Photos and video of the workshop.

PREPARING FOR ANALYSIS ON THE WALL

The set-up of field data for analysis on the wall is similar to the set-up that was described in the set up for inspiration above. There is, however, some additional preparation. For example, transcripts of all the presentations and discussions need to be generated before the workshop. All the materials are prepared and posted on the wall, and you have collected a supply of pens, markers, post-its, large sheets of paper and recording devices (e.g., video and photo).

Before the workshop all members of the research team will have read the transcripts and marked interesting quotes. They will also have been asked to copy the 20 or so most important quotes from the transcripts, together with an interpretation in their own words, onto small cards. They will have also marked each card with their personal color, so it becomes easy to track whose card is whose.

If specific themes have been established for the research, it may be good to prepare labeled 'theme' sheets on which relevant quotes and observations can be posted or "parked". It is good to have a 'spare parking lot' to place those things which someone feels can be important but cannot yet be placed on the theme sheets. Expect that new themes will emerge during the analysis itself so be sure to have extra sheets available.

Hint#: Analysis on the wall requires diligence and rigor. You are actually using the wall as though it were a large spreadsheet. It is critical that you label each data point before it goes up on the wall.

CONDUCTING THE ANALYSIS ON THE WALL WORKSHOP

In several ways, the workshop to analyze data on the wall is similar to a generative session: ideally, team members have been sensitized and arrive with something that is prepared, e.g., a workbook, a set of cards with quotes and interpretations, etc.

After the initial get-to-know each other round, the workshop begins with a briefing by the facilitator who describes what is to be achieved during the workshop. This introduction brings the goals of the study into focus, and helps the team to guide their time and activities. Then, each member briefly discusses his or her main findings from the homework, calling out one or two 'most striking insights or themes'.

These first insights may give a start to add new theme cards, and all members can add their cards to the themes, placing left-over cards on 'parking lot' sheets. Team members then pair up in groups of two or three. All the insights in each category are structured by one group each. In addition, one group studies the 'parking lot' sheets to see if more categories are needed. When all groups are finished, a quick round is made where the findings for each category are summarized by one member of the group who structured it. It is important that these interpretations are clearly marked in writing, because after a while these insights fade from the team's memory. For that reason it is recommended to always make a record (audio and video) of the analysis session, so that key insights and associated data can be retrieved.

Then, the groups join up to discuss their feelings about the categorization, and to go over the materials (e.g., workbooks and collages) that the participants have produced. It may be worthwhile to make a summary about insights from each participant in the same way as the themes; this will help in later construction of personas and scenarios.

When the discussion winds down, it is good to bring up the original mindmaps of preconceptions that were made at the beginning of the study, and to see (i) if these provide leads for insights which were missed in making the cards, and (ii) which unexpected new areas have popped up or turned out to be richer or more important than had been expected earlier.

Finally, try to construct an integral visual summary in the form of a diagram or model, and discuss this in the group. Again, making a formal presentation of the visual summary on video can be a valuable part of the documentation of the session. An on-the-wall analysis session that takes place over two days can have two rounds, where the first day is spent on harvesting the most telling quotes and establishing themes, and the second day is devoted to creating elaborate stories about each of the themes.

WHAT HAPPENS WHEN YOU DECIDE TO ANALYZE ON THE WALL AND YOU HAVE TOO MUCH DATA?
This is an analysis disaster waiting to happen. In one such situation, generative design research data from 24 in-home visits across three geographical regions in the US was collaboratively analyzed on the wall by a team of 18 people. A room big enough for all the data and the entire analysis team was only available intermittently so the location of the analysis meetings changed every week. Background sheets of paper were put on the wall so that the ongoing analysis could be rolled up and moved between sessions. The analysis team was an interdisciplinary group of people most of whom had not had previous field research experience. Post-it notes fell off the rolled paper between weekly sessions and because

the data items had not been appropriately labeled due to inexperience, no one knew who collected the data point, where it went or what it meant. The lead researcher had bad dreams about falling post-it notes. The analysis took about ten times longer than anticipated and went over the estimated budget. It was not possible to draw conclusions about differences between the geographic regions, nor was it possible to look at the data from multiple perspectives. Conclusions were ultimately reached, but ideas and insights were lost along the way. This is a case where analysis in a database would have been a much better approach.

ANALYSING A TOOLKIT IN ANALYSIS ON THE WALL

Analysis of toolkits when working on the wall is typically a qualitative process, with team members reviewing, discussing and making notes about the collages or maps and the associated transcripts of the presentations about them. Still, some quantitative methods can be used on the wall. For instance, in the case presented in section#4.1, the research team made a matrix of all trigger words and images versus the collages in which they were used. Counting revealed that almost everybody used the 'no smoking' sign, indicating that smoking (or not smoking) was an important issue for the participants. Such a quantitative focus can lead the team into further analysis. A quantitative focus can also be useful when reporting findings to clients with a quantitative mindset, who find some attention to quantitative aspects reassuring.

More formal structuring can also help in making the toolkit material easier to review, and to facilitate comparison between participants. An example of more formal structuring are the foldout workbooks in the contribution by Hsu on page#233. Here all the workbooks of participants are placed on the wall in long strips one above the other, so the rows allow quick comparison within a participant, whereas the columns facilitate comparing answers to one assignment across participants.

Finally, it is important to keep track of which pieces of data were often referred to, or experienced as most striking. These are likely to be the ones you will need in communicating results afterwards.

REPORTING ON THE ANALYSIS ON THE WALL SESSION

After the analysis session is over, one or two members of the team should be responsible for the results. These would include a one page summary of the process of analyzing, and one page of themes that may include, for example, general conclusions and main insights. For each theme, the report gives a description of the meaning of the theme, the main observations and conclusions, and a set of main quotes and their interpretations. There can also be a descriptive summary of the participants along with this.

PATH C: ANALYSIS WITH A DATABASE

More thorough or 'heavy' analysis becomes necessary when your sample size is larger than 10 to 12 participants and when you are interested in making comparisons between groups. Heavy analysis is also recommended when there is an abundance of data to be analyzed. For example, if the raw data does not fit on the walls of a room that is big enough for 6 people to work in, then it is advisable to go to analysis using a database. Like analysis on the wall, analysis with a database can be handled by a lone researcher but the ability to get the most out of a data set is much higher when a team of researchers is working together.

WHY DO ANALYSIS WITH A DATABASE?

Analysis on the wall is flexible, inspirational, tangible, and social. But it does not scale up well due largely to the limitations people have as information processors. When data from more than 6 participants are being analyzed, or when the participants were selected to vary on multiple demographics, or when there is just too much data, working with formal tools, e.g., software, starts to pay off as a means to divide, conquer, and reconnect. A database such as Excel enables quick sorting and resorting of data as different types of findings and insights reveal themselves through different perspectives taken on the data. A database also serves as an efficient and effective means of storing and organizing the data in a form that is conveniently delivered to the client.

A disadvantage in analysis with a database is that it hides the richness of the data inside the computer. It is advisable for beginners to start learning about generative data analysis by doing it on the wall and moving later to the database method. Similarly, everyone on the analysis team will benefit from having large paper print-outs of what is housed in the database to put on the walls.

	PATH B: ANALYSIS ON THE WALL	PATH C: ANALYSIS WITH A DATABASE
Immersion into the richness of the data	★★★	★
Sorting and filtering capability		★★★★
Capability for organizing	★	★★★★
Sharing with others	★★★ local sharing only	★★★ remote sharing works, too
Speed of analysis	★★★	★★★
Scalability		★★★★
Open ended	★★★	★

Table#7.9 A comparison of Path B: Analysis on the wall and Path C: Analysis with a database

Various software applications can be used for this type of analysis. Qualitative data analysis packages such as NVivo and ATLAS.ti are designed specifically for this type of analysis. These applications take some time to master and the coding of data items is quite intensive and time consuming. For those who spend most of their time analyzing qualitative data, these applications make sense. However, for those people who do not spend most of their time analyzing data, Excel can be used quite effectively.

Table#7.9 compares analysis on the wall and analysis with a database. Because their strengths are so different, it is clear that a combination of analysis on the wall and analysis with a database is the preferred situation. This is the path that the GDT team took on the large-scale international project described in Case#4.4.

The first step in analysis with a database is to establish the team, their roles and the timeline. Analysis with a database is best done with a team of 3 to 4 analyzers. That way each analyst can focus on a specific segment of the data, e.g., workbook data, transcripts, etc. As they enter and later analyze the data, they become intimate with the content and the details of their segment. Regularly scheduled meetings between the analyzers help ensure that the connections between the different parts of the data are made. It is also important to establish a device for collecting ideas and insights so that ideas that pop up during the intensive data entry phase are not lost.

The second step is to prepare the data. You will need to get transcriptions made from the audio-recordings of each session. As we mentioned previously, there are outside firms that provide this service and most of them use digital transmission today so your location for fielding should not be an issue. The cost of transcribing data is well worth the result. You will get a word for word documentation of the session which can then be analyzed at a number of different levels. Establish a file-naming convention for your files and stick to it. Imagine that your client would want to access the data once the project is over and you are not there to answer. What kind of information will need to be available in the file name to ensure that they can find the piece of data they are looking for? Photograph all the artifacts of the generative design research process such as collages, maps, Velcro-models, etc. Then name all of the field photos, artifact photos, videofiles and audiofiles using the file-naming convention.

Hint#: Make sure that the quotes (like all other things) are labeled with who said them, when and where, so you can always retrieve the context in which they were made.

The third step is to set up the database(s). Most of the data you will have collected can be put into a spreadsheet or database. You will need to set up separate tabs for different types of information such as textual, numerical, close-ended, toolkit data, etc. Each page should have participant information so that you can sort and/or filter any of the data by participant characteristics.

The fourth step in this type of analysis is to fill up the database(s). You will enter all the workbook data (except the photos) and the data from the various generative toolkits. You may decide to enter the transcripts, or segments from the transcripts, as well.

The fifth step is to print out the organized data for review. Clean up the transcripts. Reformat the database pages for easy reading and annotating. For example, make headers to mark the beginning of section/exercise changes and create a table of contents. Make a file that puts the photograph of each artifact together with the portion of the transcript that has the participant describing the meaning of the artifact. The more visual and visible you can make the data, the better you can analyze it, especially if you are working collaboratively.

CONDUCTING AN ANALYSIS WITH A DATABASE
Review and annotate all the data and start to look for patterns. Once the data have been recorded, organized and printed out for review, the analytical process can take place. Different forms of data require different types of analysis. You will need to read and annotate the transcripts. While you are doing so, make notes about possible themes, ideas and/or insights. Note questions that you may be able to answer using other parts of the data set.

Review the photographs taken during the fieldwork. Use the sorting capability of photographic databases such as Picasa to look at the photos from a number of different perspectives, e.g., demographically, by theme etc.

Sort and print the textual data from the workbooks. Highlight and annotate as you go and look for patterns that may become evident now that you can see how all the participants have answered each question. Count and graph the numerical workbook data. Make visual summaries of the results of the generative exercises, as in Figure#7.10. Excel has many options to choose from such as bar charts and spider graphs. See 'Analyzing a toolkit with a database' for more details.

Meet daily to discuss preliminary insights and hypotheses about the data. Sharing your insights with other members of the analysis team may lead to new questions to ask of the data. You may find that you need to sort the data in alternative ways and then print it out again. You could find that exploration of the data in this way reveals alternative ways of grouping the participants that are more useful for later stages of design conceptualization.

Analysis with a database will not address everything. Analyzing rich and messy data using database functionality is an area where further research and exploration is needed. You could actually spend months of time on a heavy analysis. But the timeframe in practice will not accommodate that level of exploration and investigation. The academic environment may be one in which the opportunity for this type of exploration exists. Another area of opportunity is in exploring ways to use new information technologies to facilitate or to speed up the analysis process.

ANALYZING A TOOLKIT WITH A DATABASE
We are spending more time describing toolkit analysis since it is not likely to be covered elsewhere. The description in this section covers only one toolkit in isolation. In reality, the toolkit will be related to the analysis of other toolkits and other types of data.

Table#7.11 shows a small piece of a spreadsheet that has been used to analyze collage data. The names of all the collage items are on the rows following the first few rows of identifying information. The names of all the participants are on the columns. Both word and image items are included. The photos have been named so that easy reference can be made to then. Each time the participant uses a particular word or image on their collage, a mark is made in the corresponding cell. The marks can be coded to indicate how the item was used on the collage. For example, the '1' means the item was chosen and placed above the line while the '-1' means the chosen item fell below the line. Getting a frequency count on each item is easy to do with the "count if" function in Excel. It

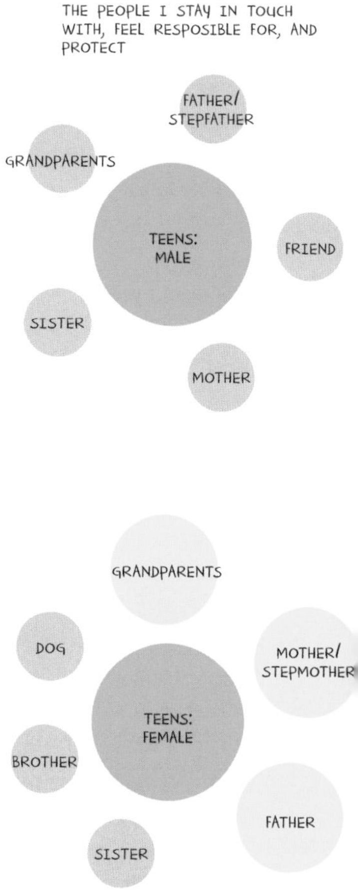

Figure#7.10 Visual summaries of generative exercises can help to reveal the meaning in the data. Here it is easy to see how the communication circles of teenage boys and girls differ.

is important to include potential sorting variables (e.g., city, segment, etc.) on the spreadsheet to enable quick sorting. In this sample, you will need to transpose (i.e., transform the spreadsheet so the rows become the columns) the spreadsheet before sorting since sorting can be done on columns but not on rows. With Excel it is then easy to get summary statistics on the data.

Table#7.11 The advantage of analyzing with a database is that you can more easily resort and link data items, which are stored in one place; the disadvantage is that most computer interfaces work mostly with words and symbols, and provide less support for visual thinking.

NAME	ROXANNE	JAN	MICHELLE	BROOKE
City	Col	Col	Col	Col
Segment	MT	CL	CL	CL
Current stuff	AS	CH	CH	CHU
Other Stuff	?	AS	AS	AS
Whose team?	x	3	1	2
Which Day?	x	M	T	M
Absorbent	1	0	0	1
Aloe	0	0	0	0
Cheap	0	1	0	0
Chemicals	0	0	0	0
Clean	0	0	0	0
Cloth like	0	-1	0	-1
Comfortable	0	0	0	0
Cottony	0	0	0	-1
Cutesy	0	0	1	0
Design	0	0	0	0
Dirty	0	0	0	0
Durable	0	0	-1	1
Expensive	0	0	0	0

DOCUMENTATION OF ANALYSIS WITH A DATABASE

A major advantage of analysis using computer databases is that it results in a rigorous and thorough documentation of the data. This makes the delivery of this data to the client quite efficient in the end. You can simply burn a CD or a DVD with all the data files. If you have done a good job of naming and organizing files, the client should be able to search and retrieve data they are interested in inspecting further.

But it is likely that you will also need to deliver a paper document. It is important to understand what the client organization (or the instructor) is expecting with regard to the paper documentation since so many different forms of it can be developed from the kind of data/information/ knowledge and insights that we are talking about here. Ask your client for documents from recently completed, successful research projects to get a better feel for those expectations.

HELPFUL HINTS FOR ANALYSIS WITH A DATABASE

It is not possible in one book to describe all the ways that generative data can be fully analyzed. Here are a few hints that we hope will be helpful as you explore ways of using databases to help in the analysis of rich and messy data.

Separate observations, interpretations, implications, conclusions and ideas. Analysis can be a creative process, in which different types of insights come bubbling up. Some of them will have a place at the time they are generated, others need to be noted, documented and saved. Premature conclusions can bias data analysis, leading to missed insights and opportunities. This can particularly be the case with creative people such as designers who are eager to get into the conceptualization phase. So be aware of when a statement is 'raw data', or an interpretation by a team member, or a loose idea, or a general conclusion arrived at by the team. You might want to use color-coding to keep these categories of ideas separate.

Encourage intuitive leaps. But verify them later. As the research team members move up the levels of analysis, encourage intuitive leaps and document them as they occur. It is impossible to prevent creative people from making such leaps. Encourage the leaps but tag them accordingly. Then put them aside as the analysis progresses. Verify the intuitive leaps later on.

HELPFUL HINTS FOR ALL LEVELS OF ANALYSIS

All three paths of analysis have in common the goal of moving data about experience up the levels of the

DIKW hierarchy and bridging over to design. Here are some hints derived from practice that may help.

Design your analysis tools. Contrary to what many may think, analyzing data can be inspiring and enjoyable. There are some things you can do to help to make it so for others. Just as you devote attention to the making of workbooks or collage toolkits, you should devote attention to the research materials. These quality considerations, which are so natural when applied to workbooks and toolkits (and for presentation of the end results) are also valid for the tools we make for analysis. For example, in immersion for inspiration, the thematic areas for hanging sticky notes and quote cards can be given clear visual boundaries, and a good collection of colored markers or symbol stickers can invite the team to produce colorful annotations.

In analysis on the wall, you can improve the readability of textual material and labels on the wall before the analysis takes place. For example, a transcript of a discussion need not be a dull, telex-like printout. The transcript can be formatted to enhance readability and empathy, the latter by including photos and names for the people appearing and objects discussed. Sufficient space should be given to encourage annotation on first reading.

In analysis with a database, you can format the spreadsheets so that they are easy to review and to annotate. Be sure to provide background information about each participant on every page so that the reader does not have to reference back to earlier pages for participant information.

Take advantage of collective thinking/action. Use a team of people from different backgrounds to conduct analysis if at all possible. Let people focus in on the components they are most familiar with, but let them work in pairs for discussing their findings. Having a partner to talk to can help you to formulate rich insights with less chance to get stuck in familiar patterns of thought. In the analysis with a database pathway, meet at least once a day with other team members to share discoveries, surprises and insights. More perspectives on the problem space can help to identify insights, to generate possibilities and to see opportunities.

Work from both ends simultaneously. Some people thrive on getting the details perfect while others are driven to see the big picture. It may take some time and a variety of experiences for these patterns to be recognized. Encourage the use of both modes.

Hint#: *Encourage the use of personality and working style inventories by members of the research team. This way of knowing oneself can be very useful in collaborative settings. Encourage people to play on their strengths while they work with each other.*

Use triangulation. Triangulation refers to looking at a phenomenon from multiple perspectives. There are a number of types of triangulation. For example, several members of the research team can study the same data. This is called *investigator triangulation*. Several sources can be checked for evidence of the same finding. This is *data triangulation*. For example, you might review the workbooks for corroboration of insights found in the discussion transcripts. Or several methods can used to study the phenomenon. This is *methods triangulation*, which is exemplified in the use the "What people say, do and make" approach. Triangulation raises confidence in the reliability of the results, both through confirmation (two perspectives yielding the same result) and confrontation (a result is sharpened or reformulated when two perspectives disagree).

Use quantitative analysis skills also. The key to analyzing qualitative data is to find the connecting threads and contradictory segments. Expertise in quantitative analysis does not provide much background in making sense of the mountain of generative data but it may be very helpful in generating summaries of the data.

Explore various ways of categorizing. At the knowledge level, you will be ordering, categorizing and organizing information. This can be done with different types of schemes that are either ready-made or custom-made for the study or a domain. A general one is Aristotle's advice to writers (ask 'who, where, what, why, with whom, when,...') This is good for beginners and for those who do not categorize intuitively. But the custom- made varieties that emerge in the course of the analysis are often far more powerful and lead to greater insights.

Be aware of where you are on the layers of analysis. Make clear where you are in the DIKW levels: is it selected data, interpreted information, or (established) knowledge? Does it apply to all participants (and beyond) or is it unique to a single participant?

Catch ideas, insights and connections on the fly. Ideas and insights tend to pop up from the very beginning of generative design research projects, but it is best if attention toward them is postponed until after analysis has been done. Dwelling on ideas too soon may lead to biases in data analysis or premature conclusions. So it is best to prepare a repository to catch and keep the ideas, concepts and insights. When they are written on cards, it can be worthwhile to 'stamp' them with event, time, date and author, just as any other piece of data in the study. Be sure to provide for both short term and longer term idea repositories. For example, a short term repository might be a 'parking place' from a working session. A longer term repository might be a researcher's project diary that is kept during the whole project as a collection device for insights and ideas.

Be ready to be surprised. Don't try to predict the outcome of the analysis. And don't use prescriptive categorization schemes unless it is your first time analyzing this type of data. Be open to the patterns that will reveal themselves if you have documented and organized your data well.

WHAT DO YOU HAVE AT THE END OF ANALYSIS?
At the end of analysis you will already have begun to bridge the gap between research (which is about the current situation) and design (which is about what the future could be or could hold) via the generation and collection of ideas, concepts and insights that pop up along the way. The quality of these ideas will vary, however, depending upon the level of analysis in which they emerged. If little or no analysis has been done, the ideas can run the risk of being somewhat superficial. The farther up in the DIKW analysis scheme you go, the more likely it is that more ideas and that bigger, more significant ideas will emerge along the way. But the real value of a thorough analysis is in crossing the research/design gap at a higher level of knowledge, enabling the identification and communication of a 'big picture' or framework. The big picture or framework connects backward to the data, and serves to organize it in a way that reveals previously unseen patterns and structures. The big picture or framework also points forward to the future, and serves to suggest or provoke new ways of thinking about the design problem. We will talk more about the creation of the big picture and how it can provoke new ways of thinking in the chapter called Communication.

Contributor

John Youger

Director of Consumer Insights

WD Partners

Dublin, Ohio USA

john.youger@wdpartners.com

Credit

This work was completed by John Youger as an independent consultant together with: Corona (Client - New garden tool line) and Priority Designs (Partner - Design and Engineering)

TIPS FOR NEW TEAMS IN GETTING STARTED WITH MESSY DATA

Ambiguity throughout the analysis phase is a big hurdle for new teams to overcome when coming out of the field. Deciding where to start is often a daunting task. Seasoned teams more comfortable with this question quickly document and bucket thoughts and observations.

A new team can benefit by starting first with structuring findings around participants or tools used in the field. Placing photos of participants or completed generative tools on the wall provide a starting point for the team. It provides a location for observations and thoughts to be posted and gets the analysis ball rolling. It also arranges content into the beginnings of participant snapshots or eventual personas depending on your deliverable. As the team gets more comfortable, you can begin transitioning into capturing themes present across participants and tools. Identify themes with different colored cards or put entirely new categories on another wall.

The initial structure for analysis is based on the participants and the tools used in the field.

This is a close-up showing some of the participants.

Later in the analysis process, new themes emerge.

STATEMENT CARDS HELP TO MOVE UP LEVELS IN THE DIKW SCHEME

In moving up the layers from data to information and knowledge, two steps must be taken: interpretation and pattern finding. Statement cards are a format we developed for teaching these steps. They help to make the interpretation and pattern finding steps explicit. The statement cards also help teams to do these steps more collaboratively and efficiently.

A statement card contains three fields: a quote (small font), a paraphrase (large font), and researcher ID (color band). When analyzing a transcript, each member of the research team selects interesting passages, and for each passage copies the text to the quote field. They then interpret the quote and write a paraphrase (in his or her own words) in the form of a statement that reveals why the passage is relevant. Finally, he or she fills the color band with their signature color.

The cards are then printed, and brought to the analysis session, where the research team studies each other's cards, discusses the interpretations, and tries to group the cards that have related interpretations into categories or themes. The design of the cards helps make this process efficient: because of the color band, it is easy to see who made the interpretation and ask him or her for further explanation; it also helps to see who contributed most to which categories, which helps in having one-on-one discussions about the categories and themes that arise. Because the paraphrases are in the language of the research team, it is easier to compare the cards and find patterns. Students often have trouble in making the paraphrase a statement, not just a label indicating a topic ('he shaves every morning' vs 'frequency'). However, because the original quotes are retained with the paraphrases, it is easy to refine the formulation by referring back to the source, and discussing the interpretations within the team.

Contributor

Pieter Jan Stappers

Professor

Faculty of Industrial Design Engineering

Delft University of Technology

The Netherlands

p.j.stappers@tudelft.nl

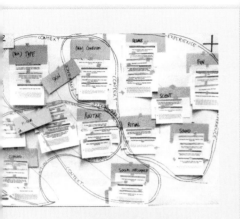

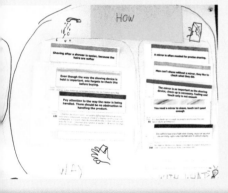

Having the cards printed and all in the same format and size, rather than hand-written, makes them easier to read. Moreover, each member has committed to the information level by explicitly formulating the paraphrase. Of course, this interpretation may change during the discussions, but it gives the team a clear starting position to move into the analysis.

Such a formalized method may be experienced as restrictive, but works well as a first learning exercise. We have found that our students often repeat the method in this form or a variant (e.g., adding statement cards with photos of artifacts instead of quotes) as they continue learning about generative design research.

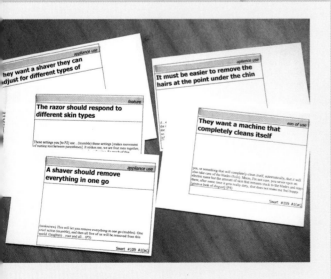

PREPARING FOR ANALYSIS, FROM PROJECT PLANNING THROUGH REPORTING

A research study was conducted to understand the full context of the home-buying process for new homebuyers. The goal was provide a rich, in-context description of the home-buying experience, determine how a redesigned client web site could better support the entire home buying process, and thus, bolster the client's brand positioning and customer service offering.

The home buying process is by nature a complex one, filled with numerous, important milestones and practical steps, and layered with the emotional rises and falls of any big, life-changing decision. At the pre-planning stage, and harnessed with only our own personal experiences of buying homes, the research team nonetheless understood this complex nature and knew the project data set would become unwieldy (like many qualitative data sets can) if not planned meticulously.

As is the case with many projects in today's business climate, the home-buying project was tight on time. Our data set would be large: 3 markets, 27 interviews, and 12 visual diaries, including photos and hours of videotape, with an analysis timeline of just 2 weeks. To prepare for this bottleneck, and instead of planning for analysis as a discreet step to happen only after fieldwork was complete, we implemented a project process that integrated analysis (or at least prepping for analysis) into each step of the project – from project planning through report writing. This would in a way extend the 2-week analysis stage and allow us to enter the two weeks of analysis with insights already organized.

The project planning started off with a hypothesis about the home buying process – a process model that depicted the steps people take when buying a home. This process model helped to frame everything from the key areas of inquiry, to developing a discussion guide template and visual diaries, to

Contributor

Karen Scanlan

Independent Consultant

Chicago, Illinois USA

karenscanlan@gmail.com

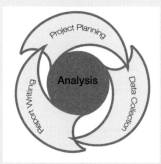

Instead of planning for analysis as a discreet moment in a linear project process, analysis can become part of each step in the process, making for a richer and more time effective outcome.

Framing the areas of inquiry within an initial process model helps organize and ready relevant data for quick entry into a database.

database development for aggregating the fieldwork data, and finally, for helping to organize the 2-week analysis session. And though we allowed for our tools to be "retooled" if necessary as the project progressed, having a cohesive toolkit enabled an organized approach and anticipation for analysis based on quality, speed and depth of inquiry.

As with any large qualitative data set, the organization, search and recovery of data was to be of critical importance. For this, a database tool allowed us to organize, compare, retrieve and output data as we proceeded through the project, and especially, as we navigated analysis sessions towards identifying actionable insights and recommendations.

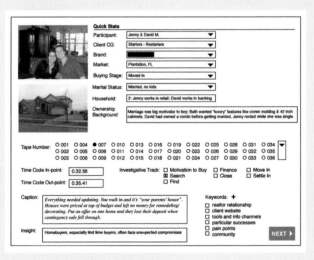

A database can serve to store, organize, retrieve, compare, analyze and help transform data into meaningful, actionable information for development.

DESIGN YOUR ANALYSIS MATERIALS TOO

Although designers are eager to invest their skills in making workbooks for participants or creating appealing communications for giving life to findings, it comes as a surprise that the materials for analysis benefit as well from making them appealing and efficient. Research does not need to be bland, impersonal, and boring! For example, when transcripts are no longer anonymous but are given an appealing form and participants are given names (possibly fictional), analysis becomes more enjoyable, empathetic, and inspiring. It pays to invest in your tools, and that goes for analysis tools and materials as much as generative tools or communication media. The photos show the difference between a plain and a personalized version of the same transcript.

Contributor

Pieter Jan Stappers

Professor

Faculty of Industrial Design Engineering

Delft University of Technology

The Netherlands

p.j.stappers@tudelft.nl

| Ernesto | Sasja | George | Leon |

23Leon: Yes, you have to do that right away, and if you leave it, it sticks tightly...

24Sasja: ...and then it's difficult to get rid of it again. I agree.

25Ernesto: I look intensely at that vortex, to make sure that all is carried out.

26Sasja: Yes..

27Lili: That's important for you too, of course, even though you shave electric. Well, of course you also have hairs.

28George: That's right, but I'm just a bit lazy in that respect, so I just leave the tap running.

29Lili: ...while you are shaving, so it is rinsed out by itself...

30George: Exactly. And when I forget, I get to hear it in the evening.

31Lili: Then you get a reprimand...

32George: Yes. My wife gets up much later than I do, so she's also much more awake (laughs) and, yes, then I get to hear that in the evening, like when we go to bed, and use the bathroom, like,... "this morning, you probably were too..." or "you didn't wear your glasses, this morning, what?" I think it's quite normal that you clean up. To me it's just normal if (mumbles).

33Lili: Are there any reactions or additions anyone got to the story that he (George) just told?

34Leon: Well, that mirror..... Yeah, you can't do without one.

35Lili: Does that hold for all of you?

36Leon: Just quick in the shower, but afterwards I STILL go to the mirror and check to make sure.

32P2: Yes. My wife gets up much later than I do, so she's also much more awake (laughs) and, yes, then I get to hear that in the evening, like when we go to bed, and use the bathroom, like,... "this morning, you probably were too..." or "you didn't wear your glasses, this morning, what?" I think it's quite normal that you clean up. To me it's just normal if (mumbles).

33F1: Are there any reactions or additions anyone got to the story that he (P2) just told?

34P3: Well, that mirror..... Yeah, you can't do without one.

35F1: Does that hold for all of you?

36P3: Just quick in the shower, but afterwards I STILL go to the mirror and check to make sure.

37P4: In the shower...I don't do that (mumbles). But for shaving dry I use a magnifying mirror.

38F1: Also...

39P4: It's just that I find that when shaving wet you always get out of the shower and the hairs are still nice and wet, and then I shave wet, but then the mirror is also clouded up, so ...

40F1: Yeah, yeah, ...

41P3: You have to spray shaving foam on it.

42F1: But then you don't see anything through it?

43P3: No, just add a little bit, it lowers the surface tension.

44F1: You also do that with swimming specs [spectacles], not? (mumbles, spit, wipe it with a newspaper) yeh yeh.

45P2: You just have to ventilate the bathroom, so it won't ...

46P4: Yes, well, just a nice hot shower, I like, I always put it really hot.

47P2: Just open the window

48P4: ...so it's really steaming in there with me

If the participants appear as people with names and photos (even if these are not the real ones; picture left) it is easier to read the transcript with empathy than if the speakers are anonymized and depersonalized (picture right)

Contributor

John Youger

Director of Consumer Insights

WD Partners

Dublin, Ohio USA

john.youger@wdpartners.com

Credit

This work was completed by John Youger as an independent consultant together with Corona (Client - New garden tool line) and Priority Designs (Partner - Design and Engineering).

TIPS FOR MANAGING DATA WHEN TEAMS CAN'T MEET

A real challenge when analyzing data is keeping teams physically together during analysis. Coordinating schedules for team members to work together can be extremely difficult.

Managed poorly, the lack of physical proximity can greatly increase time and costs to complete the analysis. The inability to effectively share thoughts across team members can potentially compromise the thoroughness and depth of understanding around the information collected.

Creating and maintaining a visible "working" high-level outline of the presentation and findings is very helpful. Highlight who is working on each part to focus everyone on his or her specific contribution. As team members review the outline, additional themes and findings can be quickly and easily added to the outline. As analysis moves into documentation, maintaining an up-to-date printout of completed and missing pages allows teams to assess the progress and flow of the presentation. Missing content can be easily spotted and added after by referring to the original outline.

The high-level outline of the presentation (on the wall) helps to keep all the team members on task during the analysis of messy data.

The outline changes as it is reviewed and used.

Later in the analysis process, the outline takes shape as the actual presentation.

ABSTRACTION HIERARCHY IN DESIGN RESEARCH

The Abstraction Hierarchy is a matrix of functions and components of a system, revealing their relationships to each other based on the functions necessary in a sociotechnical system. It is an analytical method for understanding the cognitive and process structures and opportunities in a system or work process. Based on cognitive engineering (Rasmussen, 1986) and extended by Vicente's Cognitive Work Analysis (Vicente, 1998), the method offers designers a way to quickly understand the purposes, priorities, and functions in a system. While the method has roots in engineering and systems sciences, a simpler technique drawn from the methodology (presented here) offers value in design research as an analytical tool for identifying different options for design and problem solving.

The process of creating an Abstraction Hierarchy is an analytical, step-by-step identification of functions in a problem space and decomposition of systems into parts. The cognitive engineering approach requires two passes of analysis.

1. Creating the Function Matrix

An Abstraction Hierarchy is shown, with levels of abstraction in columns and whole-part components in rows. In the example shown, the total system of healthcare is simplified (abstracted) in the leftmost column.

> Within a column, each level indicates a means relationship, a single-step higher function than the one below it, from purpose (top) to physical functions (bottom).
> The means-end coupling can be tested by determining whether the function at each level is an "end" state for the means function below it. If a Healthy Society is the function ("What"), Healthcare Provision is the "How" or means to accomplishing that function.

Contributor

Peter Jones

Innovation researcher and research innovator

Redesign, Inc. and

OCADU faculty

Toronto

peter@redesignresearch.com

References

Lintern, G. (2009). *The Foundations and pragmatics of cognitive work analysis: A systematic approach to design of large- scale information systems.* Victoria, AU: Cognitive Systems Design.

www. cognitivesystemsdesign.net

Rasmussen, J. (1986). *Information processing and human-machine interaction: An approach to cognitive engineering.* New York: North-Holland.

Vicente, K. (1999). *Cognitive Work Analysis: Towards safe, productive, and healthy computer-based work.* Mahwah, NJ: Lawrence Erlbaum Associates.

What functions does the healthcare system provide?

Whole-Part MEANS - END	Total System	Subsystem	Functional Unit	Sub-Unit	Component
Functional Purpose	Healthy Society	Regional Healthcare System	Community Health	Patient Community Health	Individual Health
Abstract Function	Healthcare Provision	Capacity to Coordinate Healthcare Resources	Complete Patient Treatment	Provision of Clinical Procedures	Self-Care for Maintaining Health
Generalized Function	Healthcare System Policies	Community Resources for Acute & Critical Care	Provide Full Care Services	Primary Health Services	Health Seeking Behaviors
Physical Function / Form	Healthcare Organizations	Hospital Networks	Local Clinics	Primary Care Physician	Health Awareness

> The upward test is to ask "Why" is this function performed in the system. Why do we need Local Clinics (bottom row)? To Provide Full Care Services. Why? To provide Complete Patient Treatment.

2. Creating a Local Example

While the complete matrix is helpful for analysis, the synthesis of design problem solving is enhanced by creating local examples that focus on a subset of activities, not the whole map. Figure 2 shows a similar matrix specialized for understanding the problem space and motivations in the current healthcare system.

Here the example shows the abstracted functions of interest to the design team. Values and Priorities have been added as a layer of abstraction between Purpose and Domain Functions. The decomposition is not a complete set of components, and most of the functions are left blank. The functions being analyzed are in bold. The activity relationships are shown by indicating a path through the functions, from A-E. A given actor in the social system traverses the functions from Health Awareness (of a symptom) to Health Seeking, through a Treatment cycle, and then Self-Care. A feedback loop is shown (not typical of most Abstraction Hierarchies) because here we show how completing the activity cycle reinforces Health Awareness and leads to better Self-Care.

The Abstraction Hierarchy is a powerful aid to analysis and synthesis in the data analysis process, particularly in transforming Information to Knowledge in the DIKW cycle. While its historical application has been in engineering in large-scale systems, the method has been found valuable in systemic and service design where human activities are re-envisioned for organizational and systemic level redesign (Lintern, 2009).

What are the Functions of Primary Care in the Healthcare System?

Whole-Part MEANS · END	Total System	Functional Unit	Component	Part "Patient"
Functional Purpose	Healthy Society	Community Health		Individual Health
Values & Priorities		Complete Patient Treatment D		Self-Care for Maintaining Health E
Domain Functions		Provide Immediate Care Services	Primary Health Services C	Health Seeking Behaviors B	+ Feedback to Awareness
Physical Functions			Primary Care Physician	Health Awareness A · Manifested Illness
Physical Objects			Office / Exam Room Equipment / Informatics	Physical Symptoms

THE ART OF THE INTERVIEW

Fundamental to all qualitative research is the research interview. There is an art to this. It is not a simple conversation; it is a carefully structured session in which the interviewer skillfully guides the participant – without asking leading questions – toward revealing tacit and latent issues about the research topic.

We created a demo video of an expert interview and ask students to analyze everything the interviewer does to elicit meaningful responses from the participant. We have also given the same interview agenda and materials to the students and asked them to duplicate the interview themselves. In this way, students understand the interview from the spectator's as well as the interviewer's point of view.

Contributor

Katherine Bennett, IDSA

Associate Professor

Art Center College of Design

Pasadena, California, USA

kbennett@artcenter.edu

Contributor

Kang-Ning Hsu

Secretary

Diabetes Association of the R.O.C

Taipei, Taiwan

hiopie@gmail.com

Kang-Ning's contribution is based on her Master's
thesis work at Delft University of Technology.
Hsu, K-N. (2007) *Contextmapping in Taiwan*,
MSc Design for Interaction, Faculty of Industrial
Design Engineering, Delft University of Technology.
Supervisory team: P.J. Stappers, O.A. van Nierop
and H. van Rijn.

UNFOLDING THINKING WITH FOLDOUT WORKBOOKS

A large amount of raw data is generated when several different methods or tools are used in generative design research. During analysis, it is helpful to spread out all different kinds of materials. However, this can take a lot of time if the materials are in the form of workbooks that need to be taken apart and copied. You can save time in analysis if you design your materials with ease of analysis in mind from the beginning.

Foldout workbooks, in which pages are not stapled but folded in a harmonica-like fashion, make it much easier to spread out large amounts of raw data to facilitate analysis on the wall. By unfolding, and then spreading out the workbooks and sticking them up on the wall it is quick and easy to gain an overview of all the data. There is no need to make copies or flip over pages. By using foldout workbooks, researchers can make the comparisons and connections more easily, thus unfolding their thinking.

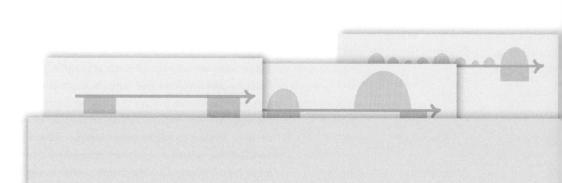

CHAPTER 8
COMMUNICATION

INTRODUCTION

In this chapter we discuss ways to communicate the results of the generative design research process. We describe these communication activities as taking place after the analysis phase and before design conceptualization since this is the typical flow of events. However, the three phases (i.e., analysis, communication and conceptualization) do not always occur as separate steps in this order. For example, analysis and design conceptualization may run in parallel on projects taking place on a very tight time frame, with communication occurring throughout the process. But this separation of the activities helps to describe what needs to happen in the process and various ways of getting it done.

Depending on the objectives of the research, the audience(s) and their role(s) in the design project, communication can take on many different forms. Each of the factors below will influence the final form that is chosen for the communication:

> What was the objective of the research?
> Where in the design development process is the communication happening?
> Who is the audience? What is their responsibility on the overall project?
> Are there multiple audiences? Will you communicate with all of them at once or in separate meetings?
> How involved has your audience been in the process? You will need a different approach for communication when the audience has been involved throughout the process vs. when they are just attending the final presentation. All these factors will have been considered in the planning phase at the start of the project, of course.

WHAT IS THE PURPOSE OF COMMUNICATION?

Before planning what to communicate and how to do so, you will want to consider whether you will be making a presentation or if you will be setting the stage for a participatory session or both. And you will need to decide what physical forms of documentation you will leave behind for future reference.

Presentation is the traditional mode of communication for research findings and the one that is most commonly used today. Presentation generally takes the form of a Powerpoint that is presented to an audience who is then invited to ask questions either during or immediately after the presentation.

Participatory sessions are often longer, more interactive and more hands-on than the traditional forms of communication/presentation. The roles of presenter and audience change to the roles of facilitator and participants. Some alternative types of communication events that are based on participatory principles have been introduced in the last few years and are being applied today in the business context. As the scope and complexity of design challenges continues to grow, we can expect to see more alternative forms of participatory and interactive sessions that bring together people from all types of backgrounds to work together.

PRESENTATION AND PARTICIPATION

There are tradeoffs to consider in the decision about whether to use presentation or participation in the communication of project results. Presentation is a more familiar approach and will usually be less expensive than the participatory approach. On the other hand, participation will generally lead to better use of the research results and better ownership of the insights and ideas. Table#8.1 describes some of the ways in which presentation and participation as forms of communication differ.

	PRESENTATION	**PARTICIPATION**
Communication goal	To impress the audience with the research findings and hope to convince them to follow the recommendations	To immerse the audience in understanding the findings and insights so that they can become collaborative partners in design ideation and/or conceptualization
Duration of the meeting	Usually one to two hours	May take several hours to one or more days
Level of formality	More formal and structured	An informal setting that is conducive for hands-on participation
Flow of content	One way flow: from research team to the audience	Once the client is immersed in the research findings, the space for open collaboration and a two-way flow of content exists
Closure	The presentation marks the end of the research phase	The participatory meeting marks the beginning of the next phase of design conceptualization

Table#8.1 Differences between presentation and participation

WHEN IS IT MOST APPROPRIATE TO USE THE PRESENTATION FORM OF COMMUNICATION?

If the client or the audience has made it clear that a presentation is expected, then it is best to meet their expectations, especially if this is a first-time engagement. Other signs that a presentation is in order include:

> When the client has not been involved in the research process by choice
> When the client's mindset is characterized by the expert mindset
> When the client has very limited time available for the meeting

The presence of any or all of these factors suggests that making a presentation may be most appropriate.

When is it most appropriate to use participation? There are several conditions that call for the consideration of using participation as the means of communication:

> When the client team has been involved throughout the research process
> When the client team approaches design with a participatory mindset
> When the client team is willing to devote the time needed to ensure a successful participatory event

Hint#: *It is important to decide up front, when making the proposal, whether you will be communicating via presentation and/or participation because this decision will impact your plan and the deliverables of the project.*

There may also be the opportunity to blend both forms of communication and to first make a presentation (usually for a larger group of people) followed by a participatory event. The participatory event may be designed for the smaller group of people who will be championing the results of the generative design research forward in the organization. This blended communication style is ideal in many respects but will certainly take the most time, effort and cost to do successfully. However, it will also yield the most return.

THREE APPROACHES TO COMMUNICATION

Presentation and participation addressed variations in the purpose or objective of the communication. The three approaches that we will discuss in this section address variations in the locus of communication. The first two approaches focus on communication occurring at the ends of the design process. The third approach focuses on communication occurring throughout the process. You can also combine elements of all three approaches. But since this is an introduction, it is best to think of the approaches as prototypical cases.

HIGH-LEVEL FINAL PRESENTATION

In the high level final presentation approach to the communication of results, nearly all of the communication takes place at the beginning and the end of the process. A presentation format, whereby the research team presents and the client listens, is used. At the beginning of the process there is likely to be a presentation of objectives, process and anticipated deliverables and at the end of the process there will be a larger presentation of findings and insights (i.e., the larger block at the end) as shown in Figure#8.2.

This approach is useful when the client/client team has not had time to be involved throughout the process. Or there may be a large number of people interested in the results of the research who have limited time for listening.

Hint#: Set aside time with the core members of the client team to preview the presentation with them. Allow time to make revisions before the final presentation.

Powerpoint (or some other 'slide' based program) can be used to communicate the main findings. Some basic guidelines for making presentations are given below.

HIGH LEVEL PRESENTATION GUIDELINES

> Start with the executive summary. The audience will be most interested in what you found, not necessarily in how you found it.
> Be brief on describing the research process but be sure to give information, such as sample size, that is critical to the application of the findings.
> Use a visual model to communicate the 'big picture' and to show the relationships between the various perspectives in the findings.
> Be sure to plan time for questions.
> It is useful to give handouts of the Powerpoint to all those attending so that they might follow along and listen instead of trying to capture everything by note taking.

Hint#: If you provide a voice-annotated Powerpoint, members of the client team can more easily share the presentation in your absence with others in their organization. Footnotes associated with each slide are also useful to ensure that the intent of the research is communicated well by others.

You may need to provide two levels of documentation. For example, you may need to prepare the high-level presentation but also provide a more complete and detailed document that provides enough information for the results of the research to move forward in the hands of the client team members.

IMMERSION-RICH EVENT AT THE END

When the communication of results is accomplished via an immersion-rich event at the end of the process, both presentation and participation are usually utilized at both ends of the process as shown in Figure#8.3.

At the beginning of the process there is a presentation of objectives, proposed process and anticipated deliverables as well as a hands-on immersion activity (i.e., the small bubble above the line) to get the client involved in the process. For example, it can be quite effective to bring a rough prototype of all the research materials to the first meeting and to engage the client in first trying out these materials and then contributing toward their refinement. At the end of the process there will be a presentation of findings and insights with a more elaborate and immersive event (i.e., the large bubble above the line) planned so that the client can experience the fieldwork without having been involved in it themselves. It is most effective when the immersion experience precedes the presentation.

Edited videotapes can be used very effectively in such immersive events. And the artifacts of the generative design process such as image collages or day-in-the-life timelines can also be very effective in the setting up of an immersive event. It is important that the participants' explanations of the generative artifacts be presented along with the artifacts if they are to be used in this way.

GUIDELINES FOR IMMERSION-RICH EVENTS

> The event should be held offsite if at all possible. In this way the audience will be more open to new ideas.
> All mobile communication devices should be turned off.
> The workshop participants need to be prepared ahead of time for this type of communication to be the most effective. Participants should be given "homework" to help prepare them for the event and to help ensure that they come with the appropriate mindset.
> It can be effective to do a preliminary activity whereby the workshop participants reveal their preconceptions about what they expect to learn before the immersion begins.
> Make the immersion-rich event as interactive and hands-on as possible.
> Encourage a casual and enjoyable atmosphere by inviting people to wear 'play clothes' and by offering good food.

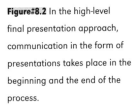

Figure#8.2 In the high-level final presentation approach, communication in the form of presentations takes place in the beginning and the end of the process.

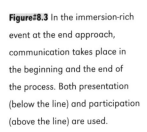

Figure#8.3 In the immersion-rich event at the end approach, communication takes place in the beginning and the end of the process. Both presentation (below the line) and participation (above the line) are used.

The workshop will probably take a full day. It can be effective to split the time into two half days. For example, start with the immersion into the data on the afternoon of the first day. The evening in between can be a very good time for the participants to get to know one another socially. The workshop can begin again in the morning of the second day with the delivery and discussion of the big picture, the insights and next steps. The intervening time between days is also good for the incubation process to occur. The morning of the second day can be used very effectively for collectively generating ideas based on the insights.

Here is another idea that we have used to immerse the participants in the data from the research experience. If you are going to be presenting the results of some generative sessions with end-users, you might invite the client team to predict what they think the results of the end-user input will be. This can be quite revealing as it tends to show a large gap in the understanding and empathy that the client team members have toward the people who were involved in the generative design research.

The immersion rich option will take more time and resources to prepare than the big presentation at the end. But the immersion of the client team members in the field experience and the collective generation of insights based on that immersion into the field experience is invaluable. If your client/client team needs to own the data and to be able to act on the findings on their own, but they have not had time to take part in the process, this is the best option.

For more information about planning and conducting participatory events, the books about *Open Space Technology* (Owen, 1997a and 1997b) and the *World Café* (Brown, Isaacs and the World Café Community, 2005) are highly recommended.

COMMUNICATION ALL ALONG

In communication all along, the client team is involved in the project at every step of the way. (See Figure#8.4) Presentations are made at key stages (i.e., the boxes below the line) and participation in the process (i.e., the bubbles above the line) occurs during any or all of the following stages:

> Project planning and the preparation of materials
> Screening and recruiting of participants
> Data collection and documentation
> Analysis and generation of the big picture/model
> Identification and development of insights
> Preparation of the final deliverables

It helps to have worked together with your client in the past before taking on the communication all along approach. And if you are using this approach with a first-time client, it is advisable to schedule a face-to-face meeting at the beginning of the process so that all the players get to know one another.

If the client cannot be involved throughout the process as a dedicated member of the team, when is the best time to bring him/her into the process? If you only have one opportunity to immerse the client in the process, it is best to bring them in when the analysis is coming together, i.e., when you are making a model of the big picture. This way they can add their internal perspective to the creation of the model and then to the identification of insights. This is likely to make the results easier for other members of the client team to understand and to move forward with. The second most opportune time to involve the client who has limited time is in the data collection stage since it is in the contextual visits where true empathy with the participants can occur.

Empathy is a form of understanding in which the empathizer attempts to understand somebody else's situation or perspective, and tries to predict how that person would experience and react to events or changes in conditions. Theories of empathic understanding and how it can be achieved were developed originally in the field of psychotherapy, with the therapist empathizing with the patient. In empathic design, the designer is empathizing with the user, trying to 'step into his or her shoes' in order to design for the user. Achieving empathy takes a process (Kouprie and Sleeswijk Visser, 2009) in which the empathizer first immerses him or herself in an understanding of someone else's life, steps into and explores that perspective, but then steps back out of that perspective into his or her own. A designer going through this process would do so in order to think of ideas, concepts or solutions. This stepping in and stepping back process distinguishes empathy with someone (i.e., stepping back) from sympathy for someone (i.e., stepping in). The empathic process is important for the ability to act, whether in design or in therapy.

Figure#8.4 In the communication all along approach, presentations (below the line) and participation (above the line) take place at all points along the process.

Communication all along can be a useful form of apprenticeship and can provide a very effective learning experience for members of the client team. The development of personas during the analysis step is another way to bring the client into the process and to generate empathy with the participants.

What do you do if your client wants to take part in the process but cannot afford the time and cost of traveling to another city or another part of the world to do so? Many new communication technologies have become or are becoming available to help communicate across long distances. The opportunities for communication all along expand with these new technologies and the ability and enthusiasm of people to take advantage of them. Ambient awareness, the state that is generated through 'incessant online contact' is a phenomenon that is being studied now as new communication technologies such as Twitter and social networks become more and more popular (Thompson, 2008). Ambient awareness is the online version of 'communication all along'.

Hint#: *Dropbox and shared documents such as Google Docs are helpful in working across distances.*

Even though you are working closely with your client, documentation of the process and the data is still very important. In fact, it is a good idea to document the process in such as way that you would be able to create a full documentary of the process at the end, if needed.

TOOLS FOR COMMUNICATING

Communicating insights from generative design studies can be viewed as a design project in itself. Depending on the needs of the design team, different channels can be chosen and used. There is always a tension between levels of abstraction (abstract generalizations versus concrete details) and a need for factual, objective statements versus getting a feeling for the topic and the experiences of the users (understanding versus empathy). Sleeswijk Visser (2009) has developed a framework, using the factors of inspiration, empathy, and engagement to guide researchers in making use of communication media to carry the findings to the design team.

Especially in the area of communicating beyond the single presentation meeting, there is a range of options that can be used to promote awareness of the project and its progress.

1. Weekly conference calls (or Webex calls) with the client team and/or other participating stakeholders to share progress.
2. Frequent emails or texts to share progress.
3. Client in residence: Members of the client team join the research team in a hands-on mentorship. This can be particularly effective during the fieldwork and the analysis.
4. Continual harvesting and sharing of ideas that emerge during fieldwork and analysis using a blog or other form of communication that allows visual input.
5. Intensive workshops on particular topics.
6. Playful teasers or reminders, such as 'messages from users' placed in the offices (near the coffee machine, in the elevator, printed on coffee mugs etc.).

DESIGNING AND MAKING COMMUNICATION TOOLS

In communicating findings, a great variety of deliverables can be made, and various expressive styles can be used. The contributions (especially pages#245-251) show some of the variety. In each case, whether it is personas, storyboards, overview diagrams, or teasers, you should consider who is the audience, what you want to achieve with the communication tool, and how it is viewed, read, or otherwise used. It is beyond the scope of this book to give how-to guidelines here, but the contributions give examples to consider. Further guidance can be found in books on communication, such as Pruitt & Adlin (2006) on personas.

DEALING WITH PRIVACY OF YOUR PARTICIPANTS

Using images and quotes of your participants presents a tension. On the one hand, you want to show them to be as real and complete as possible. On the other hand, privacy rules often require that you hide their identity. This means removing their names and other information that can pin-point them, both from transcripts and artifacts such as collages and workbooks, and anonymizing pictures. Both with names and faces, be aware that anonymizing techniques can affect the content of the communication as well, as illustrated in Figure#8.5 (We used the bottom-right form in this book, e.g., on pages#114 ,193 ,196).

RELATIONSHIPS BETWEEN APPROACHES TO ANALYSIS AND COMMUNICATION

In this chapter we have discussed three approaches to communication (high-level final presentation, immersion-rich event at the end and communication all along). And in the previous chapter we discussed three approaches to analysis (analysis for inspiration, analysis on the wall and analysis with a database). What is the relationship between these sets of approaches? When we cross communication and analysis approaches to form a matrix, as shown in Table#8.6, we get nine possible combinations. A careful consideration of each of the nine cells reveals that some combinations are more compatible than the others. The orange cells show ideal combinations. The blue cells indicate other relevant situations. The green cells indicate conditions that are not recommended to be used alone.

WHERE DO THE CASES IN PART TWO FIT IN THE ANALYSIS/COMMUNICATION MATRIX?

The cases in Part Two were selected to describe different parts of the analysis/communication matrix. The first case tells a story about a team of design students learning about generative design tools in a one-week workshop. Their challenge was to learn to use the tools, collect and analyze data and also to present their findings by the end of the week. They analyzed their data on the wall and prepared two different high-level presentations.

The second case tells a story about one student's graduation project. She carried out analysis on the wall, mostly by herself, and presented findings (including summaries of the data on the wall) at several points to her company and university mentors, before using the data herself in designing the solution. At the end, she gave a high-level presentation where her design was also presented.

The third case tells a story about a large project that relies entirely on analysis with a database. In this case, however, all three approaches to communication are utilized since the working relationship between the client and the collaborating research teams was very close and interactive throughout the project.

Petra Wilson: "I always have coffee first thing in the morning"

P3: "I always have coffee first thing in the morning"

Mary: "I always have coffee first thing in the morning"

Figure#8.5 Anonymizing names and faces affects the message. E.g., blocking out the eyes, or replacing a name by a number calls up the connotation of showing a criminal, or turns the speaker into an object rather than a person. (Image from Sleeswijk Visser et al., 2007)

The fourth case tells a story about a large research project that relies primarily on analysis with a database, but also utilized analysis on the wall for the photographic data. Communication in this case is a combination of immersion (but primarily relegated to day one), followed by a high-level presentation.

	IMMERSION FOR INSPIRATION ONLY	ANALYSIS ON THE WALL	ANALYSIS WITH A DATABASE
Communication all along		4.2	4.3
Immersion rich event		4.4	4.3, 4.4
High-level final presentation		4.1, 4.2, 4.4	4.3, 4.4

Table#8.6 Comparison of the communication and analysis approaches. The orange cells show ideal combinations. The blue cells indicate other useful opportunities, while the green cells indicate conditions that are not recommended to be used on their own. The numbers refer to the cases in Chapter#4.

FINAL THOUGHTS

Communication of generative design research results does not follow a prescribed plan or formula. The creation of a plan for communicating will depend upon the people involved, the content to be delivered, the timing, the budget, etc. It is best to approach this stage with an open mindset each time in order to make the most of the situation based on past experience, the current context and future aspirations.

Be sure to stay aware of new online communication tools and networks and discuss ways to improve communication in the future. For example, gestural interfaces and large displays, which are now becoming more reasonably priced, can provide an immersive and interactive medium of communication.

It is best to decide on how to communicate findings while you are still in the planning stage, because it helps in gathering material for the final presentation. If, for instance, you planned to present a movie at the end, you could have participants shoot video as part of the sensitizing exercises.

Contributor

Marco C. De Polo

Innovation Lead

Roche Incubator, a division of Roche Diagnostics

South San Francisco, California USA

marco.de_polo@roche.com

References

Bolt, M. (2004) *Pursuing Human Strength: A Positive Psychology Guide*, Chapter 2 Empathy: Worth Publishers, New York.

Merholz, P., Schauer, B., Wilkens, T., and Verba, D. (2008) *Subject to Change: Creating Great Products and Services for an Uncertain World.* O'Reilly Media.

FOSTER EMPATHY THROUGH CONTINUOUS RESEARCH IMMERSION

After being immersed into the rich content of generative design research one of the challenges is to foster the empathy that has been gained and thus ensure that ideas and concepts are continuously informed by the research. The further back the research, the more likely it is that personal experiences and preferences inform the design instead. To avoid designing what we want (vs. what people need), fostering empathy through continuous immersion can be an effective guiding principle.

> Create visibility: use posters about the users for easy access to research information and thus keep an open dialogue between teams and the research
> Become a user: immerse yourself by using products and services to experience the user's point of view
> Never stop observing: do occasional field trips to observe people's behaviors, environments and interactions
> Stay true to people's needs and always ask: Who are we designing for? What are people trying to achieve/avoid?

Create visibility by providing easy access to research information to open up the dialogue between the design teams and the research.

Experience the user's point of view by using products and services that they would use. Document and share these experiences.

A STRATEGY AND TOOLS FOR DRIVING CHANGE

Human-centered tools were employed by the Medical University of South Carolina Medical Center (MUSC) leaders to identify and prioritize needed changes in practice and process in preparation for the successful opening of their new facility. A one-day retreat was conducted to focus on the future and establish a plan for action.

It had been a couple of years since the original planning work was completed and progress on the construction of the new hospital was progressing faster than anticipated. The group needed to immerse themselves in previous plans and concepts to refresh their memories and prepare a clear strategy to quickly and successfully transition staff and develop process-es for the new building. MUSC leadership across all hospital disciplines gathered to develop the structure that would assist them in decreasing the complexities of organizational and operational change.

A strategy for action and materials for interaction were developed in advance of the session to facilitate the day. Issues listings, personas, and future scenarios were crafted specifically for MUSC reflecting their staff, patients, desired culture, and future operational intent.

Culturally and clinically relevant stories were read to the group reflecting patient, family and staff journeys. These scenarios stimulated conversation and idea generation. The team quickly began to identify both barriers to successful operations of their new facility and opportunities for change. These enhancements were unlikely to have been discovered if departments had discussed their future planning in isolation.

Contributors

Carol Cosler, MBA
Project Manager
RH Transition & Occupancy Planning
at Nationwide Children's Hospital
700 Children's Drive
Columbus, Ohio USA 43205
carol.cosler@nationwidechildrens.org

Janet L. Beck RN, MBA
Liaison for Ambulatory Ventures
Mount Carmel Health System
Columbus, Ohio USA
jbeck3@mchs.com

Carol and Janet's contribution was written when they were working at Mithoff Healthcare Consulting in Columbus, Ohio USA.

Creative and innovative leaders from all clinical and operational disciplines at MUSC came together to visualize and strategize for their future.

Teams immersed themselves in previous work through reviewing and discussing graphics, documents, and pictures.

Personas were developed to reflect typical patients, physicians, nurses, and families. The personas were then used as characters in stories about journeys across the healthcare continuum.

Teams collaborated in a hands-on e!ort to sort and prioritize the issues as they grew to understand their needs.

Simple tools of cards and markers were used to capture thoughts as they were generated. These cards were immediately taped to walls in 'bucketed' categories to make manageable the exhaustive list of over a thousand issues. The bucketed issues were reviewed and multi-option voting prioritized to give the team a place to start as a launching pad for moving forward.

Using simple tools, the team was able to clearly identify complex issues, categorize them and then break the categories down into manageable steps. The strategy and tools used were embraced by MUSC and utilized independently by many internal disciplines to vet additional ideas and to assist the move past the inevitable roadblocks.

"This methodology quickly connected staffs to real-life patient scenarios that drove change for our care delivery in the new hospital."
Marilyn J. Schaffner, PhD, RN, CGRN, Administrator Clinical Services and Chief Nursing Executive MUSC Medical Center, Charleston SC.

Over 1,000 cards with issues and needs were prioritized through a simple voting exercise. The number of dots on each card reflected consensus on priorities and defined where the work should star.

COMMUNICATION TOOLS

The outcomes of generative sessions are rich and diverse. They are characterized by individual stories that are fragmented, incomplete, and full of anecdotes and diverse material. After analysis, there are also abstractions, occurring themes, and interpretation layers such as feelings, routines, values, meanings and even latent needs and dreams in the information.

When communicating the results of generative design sessions, tools are needed that support a multidisciplinary design team to explore, get an understanding of the participants and feel inspired by the results. Showing only the raw data is too much, too diverse and not structured.

But when showing only the conclusions (i.e., the abstractions), the richness of the data is lost. New communication tools are being developed to communicate the results of contextmapping studies to multidisciplinary teams, e.g., the personal cardset and action posters.

The personal cardset can be used interactively. Design teams can use the cardset in a number of ways. They can organize, select, and read in detail what each participant said. The participants are presented as real people, which stimulates empathy for the participants.

The action posters are less interactive than the personal cardset. This tool was used by a multidisciplinary team (8 members) during an idea generation workshop. The posters are unfinished and are made of plastic. During the workshop these posters were completed with interpretations and first insights by the team themselves. In this way the final results are created by the team. A sense of shared ownership stimulates team members to be involved.

Contributor
Froukje Sleeswijk Visser
Assistant Professor
Delft University of Technology
Faculty of Industrial Design Engineering,
Delft, The Netherlands
f.sleeswijkvisser@tudelft.nl

and

Director of ContextQueen
Rotterdam, The Netherlands

Froukje's contribution is based on her PhD work.
Sleeswijk Visser, F (2009) *Bringing the everyday life of people into design.* Doctoral thesis, Delft University of Technology, Faculty of Industrial Design Engineering.

References

Sleeswijk Visser, F., Stappers, P.J. (2007) Who includes user experiences in large companies? *International Conference on Inclusive Design*, Royal College of Art, London, UK, April 2007, 1-5.

Sleeswijk Visser, F., van der Lugt, R., Stappers, P.J. (2007) Sharing user experiences in the product innovation process: Participatory design needs participatory communication. *Journal of Creativity and Innovation Management,* 16(1), 2007, 35-45.

This personal cardset represents eight individual participants by a card with a name and photo of each. On the front side some typical quotes and a few interpretations are shown. On the backside the entire narrative of each participant is written down.

The card set in use by different teams of designers. Some designers tend to look for overview, while others prefer to explore a few cards in detail.

MAKING AND TELLING: HOW PEOPLE USE VISUAL MEANS FOR COMMUNICATION AND COLLABORATION IN MULTIDISCIPLINARY TEAMS

I have explored and analyzed how people from design, engineering and business disciplines create and utilize visual means in working collaboratively at the beginning stages of a design project. This research has revealed the emergence of two equally important basic dimensions in the use of visual means: visual means that are used to generate visual representations (making) and visual means used to generate discussion and feedback (telling). I analyzed eighteen multidisciplinary design project scenarios from the very first moment teams were assigned to work on a design problem until the moment when the design team was ready to provide the initial solutions or recommendations to the client. In general, all stakeholders interacted through three common communication activities: defining perceived needs, generating ideas/opportunities and presenting solutions. Visual means for communication and collaboration utilized by discipline and communication activity were also identified. In every case, visual means proved to be valuable thinking and communication assets.

In sum, making and telling are two equally important dimensions of communication embedded in the same visual means, depending on the eye of the beholder and/or the activity that they support. For example, a logo proposal mounted on cardboard is 'made' by a designer and it serves to 'tell' an idea to the client, usually by a marketing professional. The logo proposal is the same visual means and can be 'written' (making) and 'read' (telling) in different ways and by different people.

Another example is a sketch, which not only supports the mind-hand interaction but also serves to communicate an idea for feedback and to spark the idea generation process. Furthermore, the idea represented in the sketch will change with each 'teller' and with each

Contributor

Mercè Graell

Cocreation Strategy Consultant

dnx | Designit

Barcelona, Spain

and

Owner of Visualteamwork

Barcelona, Spain

merce@visualteamwork.com

Mercè's contribution is based on her Master's Thesis done while she was a graduate student in Design at The Ohio State University.
Graell-Colas, M. (2009) "Exploring visual means for communication and collaboration in multidisciplinary teams: an interpretation and implementation for design education" Department of Design, The Ohio State University, Committee members: Carolina Gill (Adviser), Elizabeth B.-N. Sanders and Wayne Carlson

Related papers

Graell-Colas, M. and Gill, C. (2008). "Multidisciplinary Team Communications through Visual Representations". *Proceedings of the 10th International Conference on Engineering and Product Design Education*, Barcelona, Spain, pp. 555-560

Graell-Colas, M. (2010). "Visual Means for Collaboration Across Disciplines." 2010 Design Research Society (DRS) *International Conference Design & Complexity,* Montreal July 2010 'telling'. For instance, designers and engineers made sketches and models. They used them to support the idea generation process and as aids for the individual and collective analysis of insights. The visual representations generated from this process assisted team members in communicating amongst themselves, and with each other. Business managers, on the other hand, utilized the products of the previous process to support their verbal communication exchange and generate discussion, feedback and additional dialogue. Understanding how the different disciplines make visual representations and how they interpret them for telling purposes, becomes, then, an integrated skill relevant to all parties.

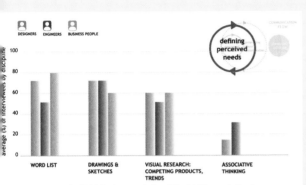

visual means identified during the communication activity of defining perceived needs

visual means identified during the communication activity of generating ideas

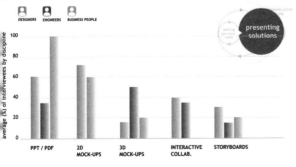

visual means identified during the communication activity of presenting solutions

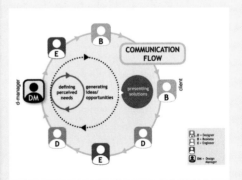

The three general communication activities identified in the communication process of eighteen multidisciplinary design project scenarios from the design, engineering and business disciplines.

DIALOGIC DESIGN AND SOCIAL DESIGN PRACTICE

Dialogic design is a practice of structuring collective language and non-verbal discourse to enact design processes. It is both a practice of integrating collective speech and sketching into design discourse, and a methodology for rigorous collective problem solving.

Design practitioners have adapted participatory workshops into the entire spectrum of design projects, from Ideation through Definition to Delivery. A significant proportion of design practice involves communication and argumentation, and most workshop methods involve some degree of planned facilitation. With the growth and acceptance of co-creative practices, leading processes are explicitly facilitating dialogic approaches to articulating design rationale and enabling more collective expression of ideation and argument. This trend has seen the growth of facilitated design processes based on non-directive methodologies (Open Space, World Café), and more structured facilitated approaches such as Appreciative Inquiry.

The role of dialogue and collective wisdom in design research remains underdeveloped, as research is viewed as a process of data collection and engagement in the user's world. Yet a range of dialogic methods can be employed in both the research field encounter (workshops with users onsite) and in presentation and knowledge translation (engaging the collective client team with the products of research).

The first figure presents a comprehensive range of well-defined dialogic methods used in design practice. These are organized from the most Open and Generative (Brainstorming, which employs dozens of techniques) to the most Structured and Strategic (Structured Dialogic Design, which is based on Generic Design Science). Solutions are based on the selection of appropriate methods for a situation. Selection is based on the type of engagement, the design

Contributor

Peter Jones

Innovation researcher and research innovator

Redesign, Inc. and

OCADU faculty

Toronto

peter@redesignresearch.com

References

Basadur, M. (1995), *The power of innovation.* Financial Times/ Prentice Hall.

Christakis, A.N. & Bausch, K.C. (2006). How people harness their collective wisdom and power to construct the future in co-laboratories of democracy. Greenwich, CN: *Information Age.*

Cooperrider, DL and Whitney, D. (2005). *Appreciative Inquiry: A positive revolution in change.* Berrett-Koehler Publishers.

Harrison, O. (2008). *Open Space Technology: A user's guide.* Berrett-Koehler Publishers.

Weisbord, M and Janoff, S. (2010). *Future Search: Getting the whole system in the room for vision, commitment, and action.* Berrett-Koehler Publishers

outputs created, and the relationship of methods to each other. References for all of these can be found on the web and in supporting citations.

The Scope of Dialogic Practices in Design

Each method in the map will follow a different process, but a common design language can be generalized from their process logic. A common process followed by many of the methods is the design language of Divergence > Emergence > Convergence. The second figure illustrates the primary social design language following the general pattern of Divergence > Convergence, found in Appreciative Inquiry, Structured Dialogic Design, and Basadur's Simplex.

A common design language is seen in dialogic practices in design. The rationale for the language pattern is based on the exploration of a field of possible choices (generative) followed by an emerging or bridging process, followed by a phase of social discrimination, decision, converging on selections (evaluative). This pattern has been codified in some processes, especially the Basadur Simplex, where each of the 8 phases in a complete process are facilitated with at least one Divergence- Convergence cycle. Social design practices are enabled by the facilitation of dialogue, structured to both ensure fair and open contribution and to produce design outcomes from a collective group of stakeholders.

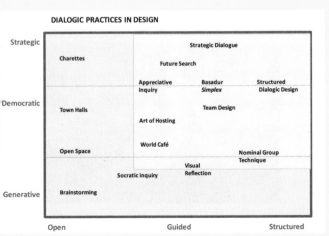

DIALOGIC PRACTICES IN DESIGN

HOW THE RESULTS HAVE AFFECTED
ORGANIZATIONS THROUGH WORK CULTURE

Centraal Beheer Achmea, one of the largest insurance companies in the Netherlands, turned to generative techniques to find out what's really on our customers' minds, because they realized insurance products are not.

A series of contextmapping studies was carried out with a client group, small entrepreneurs, to find out what drives them and what's keeping them awake at night. A range of stakeholders from within the company was engaged in the studies, to get a better grip of what was found out. The results were communicated in an organizational development program, through presentations, reports and a set of personas (also shown as people on the wall) designed to give a feeling for the target group. The program involved a change in work culture for sales staff and administrators, who service customers by phone.

Usually these people don't get to meet their customers in person. The lively anecdotes, quotes and pictures from the study helped employees to empathize with their customers. As a result, the dialogue between sales staff and clients improved from everyone's point of view.

Contributor
Annet Hennink
Concept & Proposition Developer
Centraal Beheer Achmea
Apeldoorn, the Netherlands
annethennink@gmail.com

CHAPTER 9
CONCEPTUALIZATION

INTRODUCTION

In this chapter we separate conceptualization (the generation and development of ideas, concepts, and solutions) from analysis of the research data and findings so that we can focus on the process of conceptualizing. We will put them back together again in the final chapter because in practice they benefit from each other's influence, and can be intertwined.

Conceptualization is where new ideas, concepts and solutions are made, and it has long been recognized as a core part of designing. A variety of tools and techniques for conceptualization have been developed in the design disciplines, such as methods for creativity, generating and filtering ideas, making combinations between elements and finding what fits. Also, the different design disciplines have developed their own ways to describe and visualize ideas. In the past decade, especially in interaction design and service design, there has been a growth in techniques to conceptualize not just the idea as a product, but a range of techniques have appeared to conceptualize the way people's lives can be affected by design, for example, sketching out a story of how people might live, and using that story to develop a vision on new products and services. These new techniques focus on experiences in the form of future scenarios and are aimed at fitting the richness and variety of insights that can be gained with generative design tools and techniques.

In this chapter we do not present a comprehensive list of conceptualization techniques. There are books about conceptualization and creativity (e.g., Buxton, 2007), and dozens of techniques that can be used. Here we focus on techniques linked to the say/do/make activities from the data gathering, but aimed at sketching future use scenarios through telling, making, and enacting. Central to our discussion is the development of a 'big picture', a framework for connecting the design opportunity space back to the data and for moving the ideas forward into future embodiments and scenarios.

CONCEPTUALIZATION IS ON THE OTHER SIDE OF THE ANALYSIS SPACE

We used the left hand side of the analysis space model in Chapter#7 to describe and discuss the process of analyzing the data collected in the generative design research process. We use the same model here to describe and discuss the conceptualization process. But our focus will now be on the right hand side of the model as seen in the diagram below.

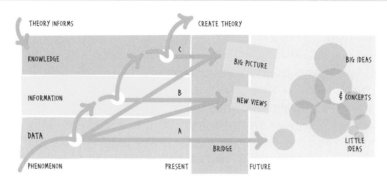

Figure#9.1 The analysis and conceptualization space model

As we described earlier in the analysis chapter, ideas and insights can pop up at any time during data collection or during the analysis process. Even raw data can lead to small ideas. In fact, low levels of the analysis hierarchy are more prone to providing inspiration for ideas than are the higher levels which are more likely to provide information, knowledge and, hopefully, insight. As we discussed in the Communication Chapter, that is why you need to provide both raw data and the big picture in communicating results of the generative design research process. You need to be grounded in the current situation and to feel empathy with people in their everyday lives in order to move forward in the design development process. And you will need this grounding to effectively share your understanding with others who will use it in their understanding to move forward in the design development process.

WHAT IS CONCEPTUALIZATION FOR?

The goal of conceptualization is to end up with one or more relevant concepts (i.e., proposals for future products, interactions, or use scenarios) that fit the insights from the research as well as other constraints that may be present (e.g., solutions to fit the client's place in the market). In doing that, we make use of both smaller and larger ideas. Ideas can be as small and fragmentary as 'users want to do this when they're mobile', 'solar power could suffice', or 'this would fit at 5:00 PM moments'. A concept is a much larger idea that is a proposal for 'the whole thing'. But a concept need not be complete (e.g., no precise cost or manufacturing calculations are yet made), as it will likely be further developed by other stakeholders in the process.

There are a number of inputs to conceptualization including:
> Ideas from the data
> Photos from the field
> Insights from the analysis
> Constraints regarding the possible solutions that can be made, etc.

During the conceptualization process, it helps to make things visible so that everyone on the team can see what it going on and can work together. The language of visualizing should be such that everybody on the team (that is likely to include people with different backgrounds) can follow, reflect on and contribute to the conceptualization process. One form of visualization is simply using post-its on the wall for capturing, collecting and organizing ideas. These post-its can describe ideas, opportunities and/or solutions. Post-its are useful because they can easily be moved and rearranged. Conceptualization is a place for new ideas to emerge as the movement and juxtaposition of initial ideas into larger "containers" is discussed and decided. Having the ideas on the wall helps the team to stay aware of the progress, and to point at ideas and combinations of ideas. Sometimes the post-its on the wall support the process, keeping track of decisions and complexity, but convey less of the content of the ideas. Later as the ideas, concepts and solutions are sketched or embodied, it becomes possible to post the content on the wall and work on it as well.

PLAYING IN THE DESIGN OPPORTUNITY SPACE
Once the space for conceptualization has been established (at least in preliminary form), it is time to further explore the design opportunity space. The generative tools can be very effective in this conceptualization process. For example, the design team might use 3D Velcro modeling to begin to explore very rough product concepts that will later give shape to future products or scenarios. Or they might start out by using improvisation to test out some of the initial ideas about future experience. To further sketch out the potential for using generative design thinking in the conceptualization space, it is useful to refer back to the diagram introduced in the first chapter that described how the design domains are in the midst of a radical transformation.

The diagram shows that design was, until recently, primarily concerned with the making of 'stuff'. In fact, the design domains around which many universities today organize their curricula still rely on these traditional boundaries of design. The traditional fields of design education are characterized by the type of stuff that designers learn to make (e.g., product design, interior space design, graphic design, architecture, etc.). Prototypes made during the design process come in the form of possible future products or spaces or buildings. The languages that designers learn in school are of this variety and are specialized for the creating of form. For example, traditional embodiments for making stuff include sketches, drawings, prototypes, and models to represent the product. And quite often, the stuff is shown without people or the environment in which it would be used.

art, documentaries, timelines of experience and experience prototyping. In the new design domains there is the need for telling stories about how people live and how they wish they could live in the future. Stories can provide a context for the imagination. Everyone can make, tell, and understand stories. And visualization techniques that enable storytelling such as props, storyboards or video, can help to create a shared and holistic level on which people from different backgrounds can communicate.

We see the use of stories in the recent trend toward using personas and future scenarios in the design development process. This design tool grew out of the interaction design field, was adapted by industrial designers and is now being adapted in interior space design. The development of personas and future scenarios can be applied in traditional ways or with a participatory mindset. For example, product designers can make up these stories and use them to inspire their designing of stuff. This fits with the more traditional ways of designing. Or the stories can come directly from the people who will be served through design. This is a more participatory way of using this design tool.

OLD > THE TRADITIONAL DESIGN DISCIPLINES	NEW > THE EMERGING DESIGN DISCIPLINES				
	design for experience	design for service	design for innovation	design for transformation	design for sustainability
visual communication design					
industrial design					
interior space design					
architecture					
interaction design					

Table#9.2 Shows that changes in design education are underway

The education of designers is now moving from a preoccupation with the making of stuff to a preoccupation with making stuff for people in the context of their lives. So with the newer design domains on the right-hand side of the chart, there is the need for alternative forms of conceptualization beyond stuff. Alternative embodiments are needed both for describing and enacting experience, with tools such as stories, future scenarios, narratives, performance

Figure#9.3 shows a model that can be used for playing in the design opportunity space to generate ideas, concepts and solutions. It is an iterative model of enacting, making and telling that describes activities for conceptualization in design opportunity spaces. It is a collaborative model of co-creation that invites all the relevant stakeholders into the conceptualization process, whether they are designers or not. For example, the stakeholders might include representatives from marketing, engineering and manufacturing playing together with designers. The stakeholders might also include the people formerly known as end-users. In the discussion that follows we will address the stakeholders as members of both the research and the design teams.

The reader may have noticed that this model looks very similar to the what people say, do and make model that

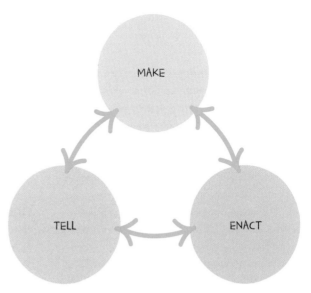

Figure#9.3 The primary action categories in the design opportunity space

was introduced in Chapter#3. It is. However, the say/do/make model describes the activities that the design/research team can use to explore and understand the experiences (past, present and future) of the people who will be served in the co-designing process. So the focus of the previously introduced model is on research, with say, do and make representing buckets for collecting the data and for organizing the findings. The enacting/making/telling model, on the other hand, describes the activities that take place during conceptualization as well as in later stages in the design development process. Here the focus is on generating and developing ideas, concepts and solutions about the future. The focus is now on design, with enacting, making and telling being the modes of play. This model combines making, telling and enacting and uses each mode to fuel the next.

In making, we use our hands to embody ideas in the form of physical artifacts. The nature of the artifact changes from early to later stages in the design process. Artifacts made early in the process are likely to describe experiences while artifacts made later in the process are more likely to resemble the objects and/or spaces.

With telling we use verbal languages to describe future scenarios of use. We might tell a story about the future or describe a future artifact. Telling alone can be difficult for people who don't have verbal access to their own tacit knowledge. It is generally easier to tell a story about a specific instantiation of something than to formulate an abstract or general assertion.

Enacting refers to the use of the body in the environment to express ideas about future experience. We also call this pretending or play-acting. Acting, improvising and performing can also be considered forms of enactment that are useful in the design process.

You can enter the enacting/making/telling model at any point, i.e., by making props or prototypes, or telling stories about the future, or by acting out ideas (enacting). And from each entry point, you can move in any direction as these examples indicate:

> First make a prototype and then use it in telling stories about how it might fit into people's future ways of living.
> First tell a story about the future and then make stuff that helps you to tell the story more effectively.
> Tell or write a story about the future and then enact it using the actual environment of use as the stage.
> First enact a future scenario and then make props to help make the enactment more real.
> Enact a future scenario and then turn it into a story.

You may find yourself going around several times. For example, you may write or tell a story about the future and then enact it. Then you could make stuff that people would need to live in the story, and enact it again. You may then find that you need to go back and rewrite the story. Based on that you can refine the prototype. And so on...

Alternative forms of embodiment for making, telling and enacting are emerging today in design practice. They are manifestations for sharing the idea with others who have a stake in the development of the idea but may not have access to the specialized language of design. As the problems that designers deal with become more complex, it has become apparent that a new design language that everyone can use is needed. The making/telling/enacting model provides for alternative forms of embodiment for all the stakeholders in the design process. By putting making together with telling and enacting, you can empower people who are not skilled in making to externalize their visualization process in other ways. Some people will respond best to stories, some to the enactments and others to the props and prototypes. By utilizing and iterating between all three, everyone who has a stake in the experience domain can contribute to the conceptualization process and to the elaboration of the design opportunity space.

THE BIG PICTURE

After you have spent time as a team 'playing' in the design opportunity space through making, telling and enacting, you will need to identify and describe the big picture. The big picture summarizes what has been learned through research, analysis and the preliminary exploration in the design opportunity space. It communicates an understanding of the current context and future situations of use. It sketches a vision for the future, and it connects to learnings from the past.

The big picture is on a more abstract level than the data/information (on the analysis side) level and is more abstract than the ideas/concepts (on the conceptualization side). (See Figure#9.1) It connects backward to the data, and serves to house and to organize it in a way that reveals previously unseen patterns and structures. Sometimes the big picture will reveal different things depending on where you are standing when looking in (or out of) it. The big picture or framework also points forward to the future, and serves to suggest or provoke new ways of thinking about the design situation or the opportunities for experience.

You can use the big picture as a way to provoke the creation of new ideas and solutions. You need to have a big picture to address innovation and future transformation. Transformation requires a long view in a large space.

There are many different forms that the big picture can take. The shape of the big picture can be a map, a plan, a matrix, a diagram, etc. Mixed forms might

e ontogeny of communication

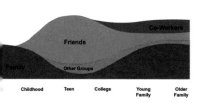

pirational Framework: Working

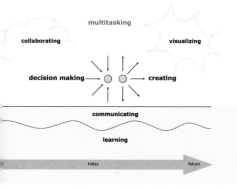

mmunication Experience Framework

Figure#9.4 Examples of big pictures from projects sponsored by industrial partners

also be used. For example, infographics might show a central image and several other perspectives.

Once the design/research team has fully explored the design opportunity space, they can facilitate the creation and expression of the big picture by using mapping toolkits to encourage thinking by making. Generative tools can help the design team explore connections and relationships and to express their intuitions about the big picture in abstract visual form.

If you have reached the level of insight/ knowledge in the analysis process, you should be able to create a simple visual representation (a big picture) of the content and the relationships within it. If you find that you are not able to summarize and visualize the design opportunity space in the form of a big picture, you are probably not done analyzing the data or exploring the design opportunity space. It should be noted, however, that the ability to see and then make a big picture is an ability that may take some time and experience to master.

Hint: *Learning how to see and express the big picture can be facilitated by highly collaborative design and research partners.*

How do you know that the big picture is working? An effective big picture has the following qualities:

> It is simple. The top layer expresses the whole idea and the visualization of it should fit on a single page.
> It is memorable. Others can take away the gist of it without having to take notes.
> It is expansive. There will be other layers of content with increasing levels of detail that are attached to the top layer.
> It contains parts from all the data. Any item of data is housed in the big picture and connected to the top layer through the intermediate layers.
> It evokes new directions in thinking. By simplifying, it reveals new ways to see.

What comes after the big picture? The big picture is an abstract summary of the design opportunity space with connections to the current context of experience as revealed through the research. It also connects to the future and provides a framework to house the most promising and most relevant ideas, concepts and solutions. The big picture should always be supported by more concrete, and generally visual, applications of concepts and solutions.

Each design discipline has its own traditional means for the expression of concepts and solutions that are available in many excellent design texts. So we will not attempt to cover them here. But we do advise that whether the concepts will ultimately take shape in the form of products, systems, spaces or services, that experiential means for embodying the concepts be delivered as well. The big picture should also be supported by communication techniques that provide experiential implications for the future. For example, this might be done using storyboards, which show a story over time, together with annotations explaining the rationale behind elements shown in the story.

Contributor

Alan Moser

Principal

Frame360

Columbus, Ohio USA

amoser@frame360.com

BUY-IN THROUGH PARTICIPATION

When an organization seeks to revolutionize itself, participation is the surest way to ensure buy-in from the top down.

Both secondary and primary research revealed that a traditional, third- generation architectural firm needed reinvention in order to endure. In an all-day workshop, the management team was first presented with the findings and implications of the research, and then participated in a 'Yin-Yang' session to reveal what the company was at its core, what it wasn't and what it aspired to be.

Throughout the afternoon the team then worked to translate that self-realization into the tenets of a brand capable of driving operational decisions well into the future. That participation led to a company-wide presentation out of the office, during which a stunning re-branding of the offices was undertaken to further reinforce management's commitment to its new direction. Project task forces comprised of cross-functional employees then pushed participation further down in the company.

This exericse identified words to describe the firm and what it aspires to be. These words are intended to work together to create the overall picture of the firm.

WE ARE	WE ARE NOT	WE ASPIRE TO BE
Local	National	National (reputation, reach, clients)
Generalists	Specialists	Experts
Informed	Intuitive	Informed Intuition
Management	Design/Technical	Design
Strategic	Problem solvers	Strategic
Relationship	Brand	Relationship
Established	Contemporary	Contemporary
Rock Solid/Excellent		Rock Solid/Excellent
Earnest	Passionate	Earnest
Seasoned	Youthful	Youthful

In this exercise participants were presented with a series of paired attributes representing aspects of what research had revealed about the company, and then asked to discuss which one of each pair most represented the 'soul' of the company.

PLAYING GAMES AND ENACTING SCENARIOS

Co-design can involve both prototyping of new future design concepts and trying out new roles, relationships and practices that follow with a new design. Here playing various design games, experimenting with tentative 'what-if-situations', and enacting scenarios in situ seem very powerful.

In a Danish project on recycling and reduction of waste, the client was Vestforbrænding, a large Danish incinerator plant owned by 19 municipalities. It was a typical fuzzy front end project with an open design agenda. A number of design consultancies teamed up with researchers from universities, public and private companies to develop concepts and explore tools and approaches for co-design processes that involve many different stakeholders. In this case, the stakeholders were both from within various parts of the waste system and users of the system as, for instance, citizens and shop owners.

The process was organized as a series of exploratory and playful co-design events. In order to find a valuable workshop format and to overcome the challenge of finding a common language and to create future visions, we used the board game metaphor as everyone had prior experiences with playing board games. In the 'new relations' design game a simple star diagram was used to identify different stakeholders and inquire into possible new roles and relationships.

Contributor

Eva Brandt

Associate Professor

Center for Design Research

The Danish Design School

ebr@dkds.dk

References

Halse, J., Brandt, E., Clark, B. and Binder, T. (Ed) (2010). *Rehearsing the Future*. The Danish Design School Press.

Brandt, E. Messeter, J. and Binder, T. (2008). Formatting Design Dialogues – Games and Participation. *CoDesign. vol 4*(1), March 2008. pp. 51-64. Taylor & Francis.

Marked on a game board as a star of relations, different stakeholders are identified. Their relationships are elaborated on by using pictures from the fieldwork and handwritten comments.

The following common activity used the results of the new relations game as a starting point for crafting stories. Examples of new roles and relations were very concretely explored through imagining and elaborating on tentative 'what-if-situations'. For instance, we explored. "What if waste collectors were heroes of recycling?" The stories were created as small doll scenarios where the participants staged and acted out their visions using dolls in front of the video camera. From being in a design studio environment, the next co-design events took place in the various contexts where the tentative new designs and relations were to be played out in the imagined futures. This time the participants played themselves in full-scale video scenarios where they improvised and acted out using simple props to illustrate and explore future possibilities.

Using design games, stories and scenarios are all very playful and experimental tools that engage the participants in co-design activities. The approaches make ideas, concepts and visions concrete and hereby accessible and negotiable for relevant people in the design process. In this way co-design is rehearsing the future.

Developing and illustrating design concepts as doll scenarios is a powerful next step from 'talking about possibilities' to being concrete by 'stepping into and exploring various as-if-situations'.

When enacting full-scale scenarios in situ, people are improvising fully immersed and thus experimenting with rehearsing the future.

THREE GAMES FOR NEGOTIATING THE VALUES, ACTORS, ACTIVITIES AND SPATIAL ARRANGEMENTS AT A UNIVERSITY SETTING

Three generative, playful co-design workshops were organised to discuss, vision and prototype Design Factory, a new center for education and research at Aalto University. The workshops also served as a collaborative stage for interaction among different stakeholders such as professors, students and researchers from three partnering schools.

Three universities, Helsinki School of Economics, Helsinki University of Technology and University of Art and Design Helsinki were merged to become Aalto University in the beginning of 2010. The objective of the merger is to build an innovative environment for strong multidisciplinary education and research. One of Aalto University's key projects is Design Factory (DF) that aims at joining people and activities from different departments of the new university. DF focuses in product development education and research, including teamwork and meeting places, proto workshops and various forms of collaboration with companies, too. The workshops were organized as the planning was still in progress and students and other potential users were eager to contribute to the development.

The first workshop focused on setting a common vision of the core spirits and values of DF, the second workshop focused on people and practices, i.e., collaboratively identifying the key actors, the activities and work cultures. The third workshop focused on brainstorming spatial solutions. It aimed at planning, concretizing and prioritizing the activities identified in the previous workshop in the actual setting of the DF.

Supporting dynamics is essential when people with diverse backgrounds and interests are involved in the design process. The three workshops were designed based on the event-driven design games approach. They combined elements from board games such as

Contributor

Tuuli Mattelmäki , DA

Senior Researcher

Academic Community Director

Aalto University, School of Art and Design

Helsinki, Finland

Tuuli.mattelmaki@aalto.fi

Kirsikka Vaajakallio, MA

Researcher and doctoral student

Aalto University, School of Art and Design

Helsinki, Finland

kirsikka.vaajakallio@aalto.fi

Reference

Brandt, E. (2006) Designing Exploratory Design Games: A Framework for Participation in Participatory Design? In *Proceedings of The Participatory Design Conference 2006,* ACM Press, Italy.

Playful tools were used to negotiate the needs and characteristics of the actors in Design Factory. Students in creative teamwork expressed different hopes than the researchers.

game rules, turn-taking, game board, and playing cards. Each workshop was an event for reflection and the outcomes were transferred, e.g., through the customized game materials, to the next event. As an example, a 'value game' was developed to share diverse opinions and to support reaching a consensus of the core values of DF. The players defined their opinions, e.g., through placing playing cards presenting different characters from Donald Duck to Dalai Lama on the game board.

After our intervention, we noticed that much of the learning and ideation took place also in the process of designing the material for each of the events. For this reason, involving the key stakeholders, such as decision makers, to participate in designing the co-design events could be useful.

The players placed the cards that represented their expectations of Design Factory values and spirit on the game board. Finally, they had to select and rephrase three core values.

Spatial arrangements were approached through the themes identified in the previous workshop. The blueprints of the building were used as the game board.

CO-DESIGNING A 'STOREFRONT WEB SITE' WITH ARTISTS IN CAJAMARCA, PERU

This research studied the collaborative process of creating a Web site with a group of indigenous artists in Cajamarca, Peru. The main objective was for the group of artists to sell their handicrafts outside Peru to an international market. The findings were used to inform non-governmental organizations, policy-makers and grass-roots developers how to work from the bottom-up to build sustainable cultural, social and economic development initiatives.

The plan was to conduct fifteen sessions in fourteen weeks with nine artists in the Northern Andes of Peru. Each session was carefully crafted before the researcher traveled to Peru. Fifteen topics addressing experiences and communities, Web analysis, color, education for customers, cooperative mission/vision, and more served as prompts within a co-learning process where artists learned about Web technologies and the Internet while the researcher collected information from the artists about their traditions, culture, products and art-making processes. The goal was to find out how the artists wanted or did not want to be represented on their Web site and how they envisioned this site. In the end, the artists would benefit by receiving a Web site where they could sell their products and educate consumers about who they are.

Sessions consisted of observing, interviewing and surveying, and 'making' images. Artists were provided with white, dry-erase boards, markers, colored paper, glue, two-sided tape, scissors, rulers, images of themselves and their products, and Web site pieces such as buttons, toolbars, logos, and headers. These toolkits were given to artists in each session so that they could 'make' mock-up Web pages.

A poster of that day's session was created and hung on the wall at each subsequent session as a way to

Contributor

Amanda S. Alexander

Assistant Professor of Art Education

Edinboro University of Pennsylvania

Edinboro, PA, USA

aalexander@edinboro.edu

At the time this contribution was written, Amanda was a Ph.D. Candidate in the Department of Art Education at The Ohio State University in Columbus, Ohio USA.

Reference

Alexander, A. (2010). *Collaboratively Developing a Web site with Artists in Cajamarca, Peru: A Participatory Action Research Study*, The Ohio State University, Department of Art Education. Committee members included Dr. James Sanders, Dr. Patricia Stuhr, Dr. Karen Hutzel and Maria Palazzi.

With toolkits ready, Gaspar (Peruvian artist) and I wait for the other participants to arrive. Previous session posters hang on the walls behind us.

show artists their progress and motivate them to reach their self-determined ending goal - the design of a cooperatively-created sales Web site.

Throughout the data collection period, the plan changed several times. Unforeseen circumstances such as artists' schedules, Peruvian holidays, and unexpected new topics emerged through the process resulting in three additional sessions and merging three previously planned sessions with others. In the end, fifteen sessions became fourteen.

After data was collected, a Web prototype was created and sent back to the artists for suggestions, comments and/or changes. Additionally, the prototype was sent with an online survey to Web users asking for feedback on the design and usability of the Web site. After tweaking the Web site based on feedback from the artists and Web users, a final version of the site was created: the Colors and Creations Web site, **www.cajamarcacyc.com.**

All nine participants using their white, dry-erase boards and supplies to discuss and "make" Web mock-ups pertaining to their experiences and communities.

Example of resulting Web mock-ups from Peruvian artist participants.

Andrea makes her mock-up Web page regarding history, traditions and culture.

A glimpse of the wonderful products that the artists in Peru are making.

REDEFINING A BRAND, SHIFTING A CULTURE

A regional bank providing retail and commercial services through more than 300 banking offices in six states brought in a new CEO to refocus and energize the business in the minds of both associates and customers. The first steps were to redefine, clearly articulate and then visualize the new brand position. A series of participatory workshops with diverse associates – management and staff with corporate and frontline responsibilities – were conducted to identify strengths and weaknesses, aspirations and a realistic vision for the future.

Through collaging and storytelling, teams of associates brought the brand positioning to life. The results were interpreted by a design team, reviewed and refined by associates, and ultimately transformed into a single brand 'look and feel collage' that would serve as a cornerstone for development of a communications strategy, brand guidelines and applications as diverse as marketing materials, website, and retail environments. Participants in the process of creation became advocates for change across all areas of the business – defining and supporting behavior changes that made the new vision a reality.

Contributor

Jaimie Alexander

Principal

Frame360

Columbus, Ohio USA

jalexander@frame360.com

CHAPTER 10
BRIDGING

INTRODUCTION

In previous chapters we discussed analysis, communication, and conceptualization as separate steps in the design research process, where communication was seen as the interface between the research findings and the design team. Separating the steps helped us to paint a simpler and clearer picture, and point out some of the things that are done in each step. But life is not often so simple, and in practice the steps are often merged in a variety of ways.

In this final chapter we bring analysis and conceptualization back together. We begin with a discussion of why it has been so difficult to bridge the gap between research and design (and between analysis and conceptualization). We then offer suggestions for how and when the bridge can be built and how it can be maintained. Finally, we describe the future transformations that are imminent when working in the generative design space with a co-creative mindset.

WHERE ARE THE GAPS?

In Chapter#7 we discussed the analysis of research data. In Chapter#9 we discussed conceptualization in the design process. In between, in Chapter#8, communication appeared as an interface between the two, siphoning final conclusions from research into starting points for design. Now we bring analysis and conceptualization back together and look at the disconnects or gaps that are likely to be present as we attempt to bridge them (i.e., join them). There are a number of different, but related, gaps to discuss in this final chapter:
> The gap between the user and the designer
> The gap between the researcher and the designer
> The gap between research and design which can lead to the gap between analysis and conceptualization

Designers are well aware that there is a gap between the user and the designer. Designers are designing for others, but they cannot know in advance what the 'user' would think, say or do. Applied social scientists and other types of researchers have come into the picture to provide information and insight about people. They can serve as the representative or advocate for the 'user'. This has helped to narrow the gap between the user and the designer to some extent. For example, applied ethnography has been recognized as providing knowledge about people, context and experience that can be useful in the design process. And applied cognitive psychology can help in understanding people's cognitive abilities and limitations.

And so with the entry of the researchers into the design landscape, the gap between the designer and the user is made smaller because the researchers advocate for the user. But there is now even more talk about the gap between research and design (and between researchers and designers). The gap is often the source of conflict, misunderstandings and sometimes even a lack of respect. The gap can be due to differences between researchers and designers in:

> skill sets between disciplines or areas of expertise,
> culture and values,
> roles and (perceived) responsibilities,
> (perceived) ownership over parts of the process
> specialized languages,
> boundaries, edges and domains of the unique disciplines, and
> mindsets and egos of the people involved.

In part, the gaps between research (researchers) and design (designers) are caused by the differences in the education and mindset between people trained to be designers and people trained to be researchers. This is exemplified in the chart in Figure#10.1 (from Sanders, 2005) that describes two distinct approaches to exploratory activities in the fuzzy front end of the design development process, i.e., the activities that take place in order to identify the relevant ideas. On the left-hand side is the information-driven approach that is favored by those coming from a research-led perspective such as people trained as social science researchers.

On the right-hand side is the inspiration-driven approach that is favored by those coming from a design-led perspective that would include people trained as or having expertise as designers. Clearly, there are advantages to both perspectives. However, the differences are often the source of conflicting views and arguments over which is the "best way" to innovate rather than being seen as essential components of a larger domain to be explored. This situation is starting to change recently with the publication of books such as *The Design of Business* (Martin, R. 2009).

FOR INFORMING	IDEA	FOR INSPIRING
Conducted by researchers and applied social scientists		Explored and applied by designers
Borrows from the scientific method		Is discovering its own tenets of what is good research
Values reliability, validity and rigor		Values relevance, generativity and evocativeness
Builds upon investigation, analysis and planning		Built through anticipatory thinking, ambiguity and surprise
Relies on extrapolation from the past as a was to move into the future		Draws primarily from the future, using imagination as the basis for expression

Figure#10.1 Differences between research conducted for informing and research conducted for inspiring.

But the gaps between research (researchers) and design (designers) are also reinforced by the tendency of organizations to house researchers and designers in different groups and often in different parts of the company. And as front end design and innovation teams become even more interdisciplinary, mini-gaps between people across additional disciplines become apparent. All these gaps are, in large part, symptoms of the expert mindset that each discipline imparts to its constituents. People feel the need to defend their expertise since they may be misunderstood or not even listened to in cross-disciplinary settings.

Generative design tools and methods can help to bridge all three types of gaps. They are a powerful way to provide information as well as insight since they enable 'users' and other stakeholders to become integral players in the design process. The tools facilitate mutual understanding through a shared medium in which everyone can bring in their own experience and expertise. The mindset of generative design thinking leads to new ways to bridge the gap between research and design (and between analysis and conceptualization). In fact, the generative design mindset reveals who the real experts are when we talk about designing for future experience. The real experts are the people we are attempting to serve through the design process. With this shift in mindset, we can invite future 'users' into the front end of the design process and move toward designing with them, not just for them.

A participatory mindset can break down other disciplinary and/or cultural boundaries. The generative design tools and methods put everyone on the same playing field and support a shared language. This enables researchers, designers, engineers, and business people, for example, to collaborate and co-create in the front end of the innovation and design process.

WHERE AND WHEN DOES BRIDGING HAPPEN?

A very simple view of the path from research/analysis to design/conceptualization is shown at the top of Figure#10.2. Note that the path moves from concrete layers (e.g., data) through more and more abstract layers (e.g., information, knowledge and insight) and then back again to more concrete layers. But this is really too simple a view. In reality, there is an

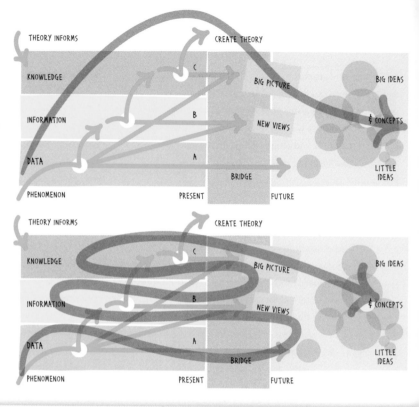

Figure#10.2 The conceptual path between research and design is shown on the top. The path between research and design as it happens in practice is shown on the bottom.

interplay between analysis and conceptualization that is quite beneficial and even necessary to the design process. Simple ideas may emerge directly from the data layer and then these ideas may reveal new views at the information layer. This more circuitous path is shown in the lower part of the figure. (Figure#10.2).

The circuitous path between research and design has great advantages. Building the bridge between research and design is the most effective when it can start at the beginning of the research process, not at the end of the research process. In this way, the process of analysis can influence the formation of ideas on the conceptual side. Similarly, the generation and exploration of ideas on the conceptual side can influence the analysis process. For example, a new idea may lead to new ways of asking questions of (i.e., analyzing) the data. Generative design research results in very rich data sets that invite and benefit greatly from many levels of analysis.

WHO IS BRIDGING THE GAPS?

There are at least three situations that describe what is going on and who is involved in the bridging process.

1. The researchers and designers are specialized in their own disciplines and are working on separate teams. They use various forms of communication to bridge the gap.

2. The researchers and designers are specialized in their disciplines and are on separate teams but there is a 'bridge' person (or people) whose responsibility it is to make effective connections between research and design.

3. One person or a small group of people are responsible for both research and design. This is often the case in small companies and for student projects as described in Cases 1 and 2.

The most challenging situations with regard to bridging the gap are the first two situations that have separate people for design and research. However, the size of the gap will be lessened to the extent that mutual respect exists between the players. If we look back at the four cases in chapter#4, we find a growing separation between research and design as we move from the smaller cases to the largest case. In the exercise of the student group (case#4.1), for example, there was no real design phase. The case included only research activities with the aim of finding design-relevant insights. In the one-semester graduation project (case#4.2) there was a longer process including both research and design with the participants being re-involved at several iterations. In this project the researcher and the designer were the same person. In medium sized case with BlueBoat (case#4.3), the design team from the company was directly involved throughout the entire research process. Only in the big international case (case#4.4) was there a strong separation between research and design and the teams involved in each. And there we see a much larger investment in communication to bridge the gap.

WHAT ARE THE WAYS WE CAN BRIDGE THE GAPS?

The time and effort for bridge building can vary greatly depending upon which approach has been taken for communication (see Chapter#8 on Communication).

1. *Communication all along:* In this approach, the bridge is being constructed via the communication between team members and other stakeholders throughout the entire process. This is the preferred situation as far as bridge building is concerned but it can be the most cost and time-intensive as well.

2. *Immersion-rich event at the end:* Here, the bridge is raised at the end of the process in a short, intensive effort with many people involved. Some people may not make it across the gap, but for those who do, this can be the most cost

and time- effective of the approaches. This is the approach that we see frequently in practice.

3. *High-level presentation at the end:* In this approach, the bridge may only be accessible to those who already have a solid grounding in the experience domain under investigation. This is certainly the most challenging of the three situations and it is the most likely approach to be used with first-time clients. It can be difficult to convince a client that an immersion-rich event needs to take place at the end of an intensive research process until they have had a chance to experience the generative design process once before.

To the extent that the client team members are not immersed in the everyday experiences of the people being served through design, there is the danger of their not understanding the opportunities and solutions delivered. This situation can happen across all three of the approaches. So it will be necessary to give them the opportunity to immerse themselves in the data in order for them to understand the context of use and the potential user's situation in an empathic way. Some of the ways to do this include the following:

> The sharing of selected video clips can be very useful as an empathy-generating exercise.

> The development of personas can be a very good way of providing understanding of and empathy with 'users'.

> Extending the persona concept and developing future scenarios based on the personas can also be a good immersive technique.

> Asking the client to predict what the results of using generative tools with the potential users will reveal by having the client team members use the generative tools themselves can be especially effective. This technique can have a big impact when the predictions don't match the results since the client will be confronted with their need to learn more about the people they are trying to serve.

You may have noticed that the same generative design language is being used both on the research side (with what people say, do and make) and on the design side (with telling, making, and enacting). On the research side we are investigating what people say, what people do and what people make in order to understand their past, present and future experiences. On the design side we are playing in the design opportunity space with the same tools and methods, i.e., we are making props and prototypes, telling future stories and enacting future scenarios in order to seed and to fill the design space with both "stories" and "stuff".

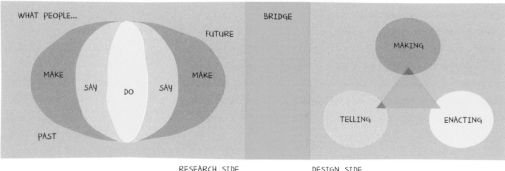

Figure#10.3 Generative tools and methods are the bridge between research and design.

So we have a common language that can be used by designers and by non-designers to remember, ideate and communicate experiential matters. The common language of the generative tools and methods is the bridge across the gap between research and design. It is a design language that works in the fuzzy front end of the design process, where we are attempting to understand and to empathize with the people who ultimately will benefit from our efforts as researchers and designers. And it is also a language for the conceptualization of future stuff and stories.

TRANSFORMATION AND CULTURAL CHANGE

To the extent that we learn how to bridge the gaps, bringing design and research closer together, we can see the emergence of a co-creative culture that has room and tools for all the stakeholders in the design development process. Figure#10.4 shows the relationship of the generative tools to the much larger context of cultural change. It shows that for tools to be effective, other contextual layers are needed. 'Tools' is only the first step in the transformation toward a co-creative culture. Tools need to be applied via relevant methods that are often nested within more inclusive methodologies. The mindset with which the tools are applied is crucial. In co-creation, you need to be working with the mindset that all people are creative and that they are able to produce creative things when given the tools and the stage on which to practice or perform. For example, we have seen good tools/ methods fail in the hands of a person who did not actually believe that the people he gave the tools to would be creative with them. In order for a co-creative culture to work, the tools need to be applied via methods/methodologies and with the right mindset by a number of people within the community or organization.

The emerging co-creative mindset, together with generative tools and a stage for their application, will build the bridges and close the gaps between designer and user, between researcher and designer and between design and research.

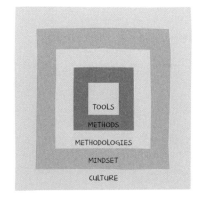

Figure#10.4 There are many contextual layers involved in cultural change.

SO WHAT DOES THE GENERATIVE DESIGN RESEARCH PROCESS REALLY LOOK LIKE?

In Part 3 we have covered all the steps that are involved in the generative design research process:

> Making the plan
> Gathering data in the field
> Analysis
> Communication
> Conceptualization
> Bridging

We described it as a linear and ordered process in order to explain it in a way that would make sense and to give the beginners among you a path to follow. But that is probably not how it will work in practice. To show you how it really works, we will end with this series of diagrams that show a transformation from a simple linear process (the basic sequence) to the messier reality that we see in the co-creation process of generative design research.

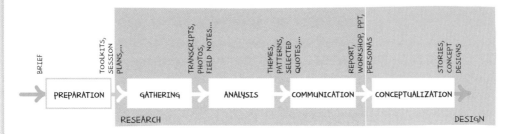

Figure#10.5 The basic sequence.

In the basic sequence, there is a one-directional flow of activities, like wagons on a train. Each activity is completed before the next one starts, and there are clear deliverables at every stage. Most of the steps relate to the research process, and design is added as a last wagon on the train. To give us more room to add relations, let's tilt the linear process into a cascade as shown in Figure#10.6.

The sequence shown in the cascade is the main temporal order of activities, but already in the logic of the activities, there are several links that point backward as is shown in Figure#10.7.

In the preparation step, plans are made, and setting up the plan requires knowing what all the later steps will need from each other. In order to make a good plan you need to know what you are planning before you can plan it. Obviously it will take some time and experience before you can make a comprehensive plan that includes activities, deliverables, role, timing, cost, etc.

But then, as we discussed in this chapter, activities in one step can have their roots in a much earlier step, and insights gained in later steps can motivate new iterations. Figure#10.8 shows a few of the relations that may become relevant.

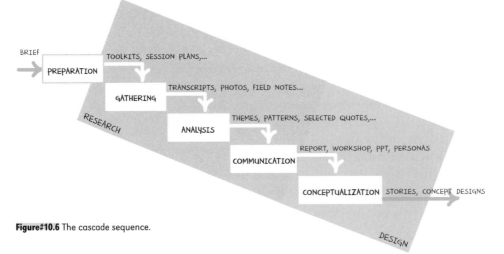

Figure#10.6 The cascade sequence.

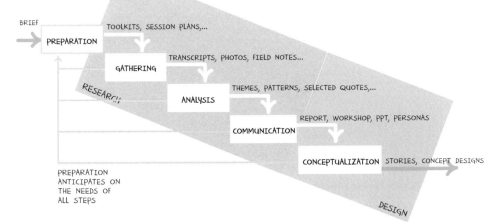

Figure#10.7 In practice, preparation requires knowing about all subsequent stages.

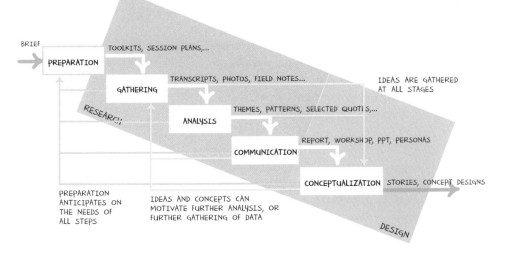

Figure#10.8 In practice, the links point forward and backward and the interdependencies are complex.

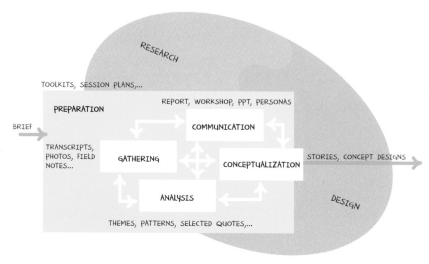

Figure#10.9 The actual execution of the generative design research process may look like this. (compare Figure#10.5).

Then finally, as Figure#10.9 shows, in co-designing, the different steps become much less separated, and activities of gathering, analyzing, idea-generating, communicating and bridging can occur in rapid succession or in intermingled sequences. It can get very messy and not really linear after all.

So the generative design research process is dynamic and very complex in practice. How do you write a proposal, with clear man-hour estimates for a fuzzy process that you have not executed before? How do you know what your deliverables will be or how long the project will take when your task is to explore in the fuzzy front end? How do you plan for a highly fluctuating process, and how do you make sure that, e.g., insights are developed to sufficient depth and the team doesn't fixate on a first, superficial idea?

The answer to this is as simple as it may seem evasive: practice, experi-ence, and getting the feel for it. For beginners it is best to gain practice with the steps in separation and in a pre-determined order in order to get a grip on the variety of activities, roles, responsibilities, etc. involved. As your experience grows you will learn how to adapt the linear model to make the most out of the situation and the challenges you are facing. We recommend learning-by-doing as the best means of improving your expertise as a generative design researcher. The cases and the many contributions from people in the field all over the world that we have included in this book will hopefully provide you with information to propel you forward as well as with inspiration to fuel your journey.

Contributor

Arnold Wasserman

Chairman

The Idea Factory

Singapore

Partner

Collective Invention

San Francisco, California USA

http://arnoldwasserman.com

http://www.collectiveinvention.com

Setting up a temporary charrette space

Working in one pod of the charrette space

VISUAL THINKING AND THE CULTURE OF THE CHARRETTE: THE CHARRETTE SPACE

In our client work as innovation consultants, we treat the physical space of the charrette as a generative artifact. We organize it as a walk-through map of the end-to-end workshop process; as a full- scale template for the steps in the process and as a visual metaphor for the theme of the project.

Charrettes take place in a space exclusively dedicated to a specific project for the entire duration of that project. To walk into the charrette space is to be instantly surrounded by and immersed in the entire, un-compressed history of the project. Neatness and tidiness do not dominate here. Continuity of argumentation, persistence of information, shared meaning, visibility, creative stimulation, and surprising interrelationships of dissimilar parts count for everything. These are the lifeblood of the kind of generative ideation that leads to innovation.

The level and type of fitting-out of the space varies according to the subject and purpose of the project. In one instance, participants may walk into a highly detailed thematic theatre set. In another, the space may be all bare white, waiting to be "dressed" by the participants as they work.

You never can have too much wall space. Providing your own vertical surfaces solves the problem of standard meeting room limitations. Moreover, as with any performance space, even a minimally transformed room shifts participants' psychological stance; it says: "what goes on here will be different from what you are accustomed to." The charrette becomes a mini-theatre in which the participants enact the narrative of the project.

We have found that it is a good idea not to completely pre-finish the "stage setting." When we enlist participants to help build out the final working environment, they experience group bonding, become proprietary about "their" charrette pod and quickly internalize the structure and flow of the coming days' activities as they build out the space for it.

VISUAL THINKING AND THE CULTURE OF THE CHARRETTE

The two key features of charrette culture are visual ideation and the generative nature of the physical space. There are many different forms of visualization that can be used to support and to stimulate the generation of ideas and boundary-testing thinking.

In the charrette, visual idea generation is done in rapid iterations, proceeding from the roughest early concepts to successively more refined versions. All working materials are put up on the walls, giving everybody the same shared view of the content as it emerges and the same shared history trail of the collective body of thought as it grows. Everybody feels free to annotate, re-arrange, cluster and re-organize the material. The effect is like viewing a visual, neural-network map of the collective mind of the project team. This stimulates spontaneous "synaptic cross-linking" of previously unrelated ideas and pattern-recognition of larger gestalts.

Visualization is not confined to representational drawings. It includes diagrams, maps, process flow-charts, icons, brainstormed phrases and key words. What is important is to generate as rich a field as possible of data-items and to keep them all visually displayed all the time. Visualization also includes the construction of three-dimensional physical models.

Finally, visualization can include enactment: that is; bringing to life the potential users of an idea being developed. This can be done by playing the role or imagining a scenario story of a hypothetical potential user.

Within the intensive and immersive context of the charrette, visual representation stimulates out-of-the-box, boundary-testing thinking. Designers do not think of visual ideation as the documentation of a thought after the thought is already completed – it is rather thought brought into being by the act of visualization.

Contributor

Arnold Wasserman

Chairman

The Idea Factory

Singapore

Partner

Collective Invention

San Francisco, California USA

http://arnoldwasserman.com

http://www.collectiveinvention.com

A temporary visualization space for collaboration

A designer will customarily "draw something to see what I think." Some visual or tactile image - a doodle, a mark, even just randomly handling an object – gives rise to a new thought, which leads to the next image, then to the next thought, and so on, in a succession of image-prototypes and thought-hypotheses chaining continuously forward.

Recent research in the neuroscience of creativity confirms the designer's empirical experience that visualization acts as a ratcheting accelerator of thought. Because it proceeds iteratively from crude preliminary gropings toward ever higher-fidelity clarity, some designers call this process "progressive approximation". The designer's rapidly iterative, parallel- processing, visually-mediated way of working is in sharp contrast to the conventional mode of organizational discourse, which tends to be linear, sequential and verbally mediated.

A more permanent and highly flexible team collaboration space that can change rapidly from small teams working on a great variety of generative tasks to sizable groups working on presentations.

Enactment as a form of experiential visualization can be done with sandplay, a technique that borrows from Jungian therapy.

MATERIALS ARE PERFORMING DIFFERENT 'ROLES' IN SITUATIONS OF CO-DESIGNING

The concept of MakeTools has continuously inspired my work since I started working with user-centered and later participatory/ co-design approaches about a decade ago. Yet, my viewpoint is slightly different: Engaging 'with' various people - or stakeholders - throughout a co-design project, also means continuously engaging 'with' different materials. Metaphorically, materials are performing different 'roles' in situations of co-designing.

The focus in this book is primarily on the tangible working materials of toolkits. The 'trigger set' (which I call 'design materials') and 'backgrounds or bases' (which I refer to as physical 'formats') of a toolkit are, for example, composed of different tangible materials, and they clearly play very important and different 'roles' in situations of co-designing. However, inspired by various 'socio-material' perspectives I will also encourage broadening the view on 'materials' during a co-design workshop. Consider the various materials as 'socio-material' participants performing in the specific situation.

The material setting of the event - like wall-space and the size and mobility of tables - plays a role in how the tangible working materials can be explored collaboratively. In addition to the materials engaged in priming, the (im)material invitation to the workshop, for example, including a description of the topic and a description of how people are intended to participate - can be a part of playing the role of getting people in the mood (or what I call frame) for creative exploration. Along with what is said, (im)material visual guideline slides or print-outs play a role in warming- up and staging how to practically engage the triggering design materials and base-formats in the explorative co-design situation. Lastly, the (im)material agenda - often also emailed beforehand and present in print at the event - plays a role in structuring the time available for exploring and engaging with the tangible materials.

Contributor

Mette Agger Eriksen

Program Coordinator of International Interaction Design Master

Malmö University

Art & Communication (K3)

Malmö, Sweden

mette.agger@mah.se

and

The Danish Centre of Design Research

The Danish Design School

Copenhagen, Denmark

Mette's contribution is based on her PhD thesis in Interaction Design from Malmö University, Sweden.

Eriksen, M.A. (2011) *Material Matters in Co-designing*. Malmö University, Dept. of Culture and Society, Field of Interaction Design, K3, Malmö University, Sweden. Tutors: Pelle Ehn & Thomas Binder.

References

Eriksen, Mette Agger (2009) Engaging Design Materials, Formats and Framings in Specific, Situated Co-Designing - A Micro-Material Perspective. *NORDES 2009*. www.nordes.org

When preparing for and engaging in co-designing, I suggest not only to consider the important tangible working materials (triggering-design materials and base-formats) of a unit toolkit. Additionally, I suggest viewing various other materials as also playing different important 'roles' in and around co-design workshops and situations.

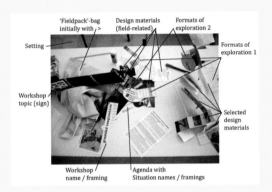

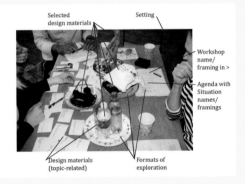

The co-designers will leave to do their own quick fieldwork during this one-day hands-on conference-workshop of exploring 'Grounded Imagination' in relation to the topic of tourist memories (in Santorini - June 2002). To immerse the co-designers in the topic and to prepare them for going out, we introduced new materials - performing different 'roles'. First, the workshop name-tags, the topic signs and printed agendas set the scene. Second, the 'Fieldpack' unfolded the rich collection of previously gathered field-related design materials. Third, the different formats of exploration (1 then 2) performed the 'roles' of structuring and provoking a process of selecting, organizing and naming important issues with the design materials.

'Things on the way' (e.g., old plastic bottles, T-shirts, electronics, etc., for re-cycling or waste-handling) were brought along by the different stakeholders. They triggered stories while collaboratively cooking and organizing them with poetic, topic-related cards on the plate-format - provided by the organizers. All materials had entered the table at the same time. Later the plates - with the work of other groups - set a larger candle-lit 'cake-table' of waste-related issues. This situation happened during the kick-off workshop of a two years user-driven design-anthropological-innovation-project with a case on waste-handling (in Copenhagen - April 2008).

PARTICIPATORY DESIGN METHODS IN CHI AND CSCW

There are many participatory design methods in Human Computer Interaction (CHI) and Computer Supported Cooperative Work (CSCW). Here is one way of finding your way through them.

Participatory design methods offer enhanced communication between users (professional workers, lay workers, hobbyists, children, recreationalists, spiritualists, etc.) and the software professionals who create systems for them (designers, developers, analysts, marketers, testers, etc.).

This communication can be made richer through the use of "third space" or "hybridity" concepts (Bhabha, 1994). In brief, a third space is the undefined territory between two known domains – owned by neither domain, and open to interpretation and dialogue among people who call each domain "home" (Muller and Druin, in press). The use of a third space can be a crucial equalizer among people with different backgrounds, especially if they come from domains with unequal power, because the neutral and ambiguous hybrid space does not reflect existing power differences, and provides a space for negotiation of meanings and creation of powerful new ideas (Krupat, 1992).

Contributors

Michael Muller

Research Staff Member and IBM Master Inventor

IBM Research

Cambridge, MA, USA

michael_muller@us.ibm.com

Allison Druin

Associate Dean for Research

College of Information Studies

Director, Human-Computer Interaction Lab

2117 Hornbake South Wing

University of Maryland

College Park, MD 20742 USA

allisond@umiacs.umd.edu

References

Bhabha, H.K. (1994). *The location of culture.* London: Routledge.

Krupat, A. (1992). *Ethnocriticism: Ethnography, history, literature.* Berkeley: University of California Press.

Muller, M.J., & Druin, A. (in press). Participatory design: The third space in HCI. In J. Jacko (ed.), *The Human-Computer Interaction Handbook* 3rd Edition. Mahway NJ USA: Erlbaum. (For an earlier version of this chapter, see the Handbook 2nd edition, edited by J. Jacko and A. Sears, 2007)

Using concepts from third space theory, we have analyzed participatory design methods into four high-level categories:

> **Spaces and places**, in which users are brought away from their workplaces or home environments, and software professionals are brought away from their laboratories and office. Examples include Future Workshops, Starting (or Search) Conferences, and Strategic Design Workshops.

> **Narrative structures**, in which users create documentaries of their work and/or lives. Examples include stories and storytelling, CARD and other storyboarding methods with workers and/or children, collaborative photodocumentaries, collaborative videodocumentaries, and workplace drama enactments.

> **Games**, in which users and software people engage in an atmosphere of play to create new ways of describing work and other activities, and new technologies. Examples include Carpentopoly, Layout Kit, CARD, Icon Design Game, and multimedia collage-like collaborations such as User Game and Landscape Game.

> **Constructions**, in which users and software people collaboratively design and construct the concepts for new technologies, often using low-tech materials to facilitate equal abilities by users and professionals to express and critique ideas. Examples include creation of new language concepts to capture the users' perspectives, co-creating evocative descriptive artifacts (e.g., Strategic Design Workshops), co- creating specification-oriented artifacts (e.g., PICTIVE and other paper-prototyping approaches), and collaborative software prototyping.

For details, and for an extension to other forms of participatory work (e.g., participatory analysis, participatory evaluation) see Muller and Druin (in press).

EPILOGUE

INTRODUCTION

In the seven years that it has taken to write this book (i.e., we worked on it in our 'spare' time and across two continents), the world has changed. This final chapter describes the starting situation, the current situation and then poses some possibilities and implications that generative design thinking may have for the future.

THE STARTING SITUATION

In the early 2000's, the mindset, tools and techniques of generative design thinking were being utilized primarily in the product design and development arena, particularly in the U.S. This was a time of rampant consumerism and large, progressive corporations were eager to differentiate themselves and their products from the competition. Generative design thinking was seen as a means to relevant innovation and companies such as Microsoft, Motorola and Procter & Gamble were willing to try it out. During this same time period, the contextmapping approach was introduced to students at TUDelft and grew rapidly in the following years. For example the first class in contextmapping was held in 2003 and had 30 students. Five years later this had grown to over 200 students. The diverse contributions to this book made by people all over the world reveals the spread of generative design thinking as well.

TODAY

Since then, rampant consumerism has reached the flipping point and a significant financial recession broke in the winter of 2008-2009. Companies found themselves needing to make more relevant and sustainable decisions about new product development. They realized that the product is just one of the components in the design of services that they offer to their customers. Thus, organizations are faced with larger scale and more complex challenges. It is not just about innovation and the next new thing anymore. Understanding what *not* to make has finally become more important then 'creating' wants and needs. The stakes are higher and the challenges are bigger now.

Co-creation has become a household word, and the emergence of a participatory mindset has come with it. People now expect to have a say in what the marketplace offers and how it is communicated to them. The new communication tools enable them to enter the conversation and to connect globally and in real time with others who share the same interests and/or passions.

The application of design thinking is moving beyond the design and development of new products toward designing for experience and service. This move is also manifesting in the application of design thinking to more complex social issues at larger levels of scale, such as obesity in school children. Smart organizations are adapting to the change. Former product design and development consultancies are now using design thinking to address issues such as improving healthcare experiences, insurance, public transportation, future education, etc.

Everyone wants to be a designer. Members of the business community are finally realizing that they are lacking in the skills needed for the new world. Leading business schools now offer courses in design thinking. At other business schools, MBA students are demanding that they learn about design thinking and the faculty are scrambling to respond.

THE FUTURE

The value of design thinking is just now beginning to be explored and the consequences felt. The potential for *generative* design thinking which invites all relevant stakeholders into the fuzzy front end of the design process to collectively imagine and express future experiences is even more significant. Generative design thinking requires a different mindset, a participatory mindset that ensures that all stakeholders have an equal voice in what the future holds for them. The use of visually driven toolkits that are the hallmark of generative design thinking will lead to the emergence of new forms of visual literacy that all people can use. Generative design thinking puts tools for communication and creativity in the hands of the people who will benefit directly from the results of this process. This way of designing will ultimately result in more useful, desirable and sustainable ways of living, working and playing for people. Generative design thinking will result in shared responsibility and ownership for the future human condition. The implications of new levels of conviviality and cultural sustainability are just now beginning to be explored.

EXTERNAL CONTRIBUTORS

Amanda Alexander is an Assistant Professor in Art Education at Edinboro University of Pennsylvania where she is continuing her research with the artists in Cajamarca, Peru, teaching undergraduate and graduate courses in art education, and working to develop a nonprofit organization in the U.S. for the Peruvian artists. She is looking forward to initiating and teaching courses in cultural policy and arts administration where she will interweave her experiences with Peruvian artists and knowledge on building sustainable cultural, social and economic development, new product prototyping and human factors.
aalexander@edinboro.edu, asalexan@hotmail.com **Page 268**

Jaimie Alexander, principal and co-founder of Frame360, is responsible for strategic development, client relationship management, and creative expression. Jaimie's training in communication design and her years of experience leading brand strategy programs have resulted in understanding how information is received and understood from a consumer perspective. Her role includes leading teams of strategists, expressionists and researchers through Frame360's business and market analysis process called MAP™ (Market Alignment Process). Many of the programs Jaimie has been involved in over the past 25 years have set the standard for positioning brands, reinvigorating corporate cultures and establishing clear market communications that result in product/brand loyalty and tangible business growth.
jalexander@frame360.com **Page 270**

Jim Arnold has worked professionally as an industrial designer in the recreational boat and health care industries and has managed the design activity for numerous successful products from concept to production. His involvement in the design process at these companies as design staff and design management capacities, contributed to high sales growth and industry leadership. Areas of expertise include: new product innovation, design visualization, virtual product development, new product prototyping and human factors. He currently serves as industrial design faculty at the Art Institute of Portland, Oregon, USA.
jimarnolddesign@gmail.com **Page 186**

Janet Beck has over 35 years of experience in varied health care roles. Her previous experience has focused on redesign of work processes and planning for patient care delivery. She enjoys the challenge of "out of the box" thinking and promotion of team solutions to continue high quality care. Ms. Beck utilizes her strong communication skills and team synergy to create positive client results.
jbeck3@mchs.com **Page 246**

Quiel Beekman was educated as a Strategic Product Designer at Delft University of Technology (DUT), the Netherlands. During her graduation project she researched whether the tools and techniques used to involve end-users in the designing process, as taught at DUT, where also applicable within the healthcare housing industry. She developed a method based on Contextmapping. Since 2009 she has workeds as a project leader at 4Building, a housing advisory company. She is specialized in user participation during the housing development process.
beekman@4building.nl, a.q.beekman@gmail.com **Page 190**

Katherine Bennett has been a member of the Art Center faculty since 1988 in research, strategy, information architecture, design development and design/technology history, specializing in understanding the user experience to discover design opportunities. An active member of the Industrial Designers Society of America (IDSA), she has served as vice president of education, on the Board of Directors, as western district education representative, and Chapter Chair. Katherine has worked with Henry Dreyfuss Associates, Hauser, the Mega/Erg think tank, Saul Bass Associates, and Don Chadwick, designing laboratory and business equipment, tableware, gas stations, furniture, and consumer products. Clients included Herman Miller, Avery Dennison, WMF AG, and Johnson Controls.
kbennett@artcenter.edu **Pages 94, 137, 232**

Boris Bezirtzis is designing and conducting qualitative research methods that inspire the development process of innovative software applications. The research and design tools he applies include participatory design approaches, ethnographic research methods as well as visual validation methods that utilize storyboards, paper prototypes, or interactive prototypes. These methods drive a Design Thinking approach that articulates the possible and inspires the potential by balancing human desirability, technical feasibility and business viability. He is also teaching Design Thinking at SAP.
borisbez@gmail.com **Page 84**

Eva Brandt, Ph.D., is an Associate Professor at The Danish Design School. As a researcher Eva strives to achieve an ever greater

understanding of design processes. What is it that designers do when they design, and how can design work be facilitated by the development of design approaches, etc? Her research is closely associated with practice and is typically carried out in cooperation with companies, design agencies and/or partners from the public sector.
ebr@dkds.dk **Page 264**

Trudy Cherok: Working 15 years professionally as a multidisciplinary designer, my training and experiences blend design, research and writing through practice in visual communication design, product design, environmental graphic design and interior design & environments. My approach is holistic; it entails reaching in: digging deep, reaching out: digging deeper. My ethos is human centered and my goal is to become a part of the thinking, action and orchestration of transformative design; design with a greater purpose in mind.
trudy.cherok@earthlink.net **Page 140**

Catey Corl has been conducting generative research and building creative strategies for collecting relevant information about people's experiences for the past nine years. During this time, she has been busy traveling the world conducting interviews and workshops, on topics ranging from healthcare to potato chips. Catey holds a degree in Visual Communication Design from The Ohio State University. She uses her design skills to creatively gather information, organize complex data, interpret the results, and then share the information in a way that can be easily internalized and acted upon by design and business teams. Catey is currently part of the User Experience Team at Nationwide, in Columbus Ohio, where she uses her experience in participatory, generative methodologies to inform and inspire relevant designs.
catey.corl@gmail.com **Page 13**

Carol Cossler: Project manager leading the efforts related to the transition and occupancy planning for the currently under construction 293 bed replacement hospital at Nationwide Children's Hospital in Columbus, Ohio. This new patient tower, combined with completed back fill strategies, will bring the full 2012 buildout to a total 465 beds. This eighteen (18) month effort involves project oversight and management, project planning and detailed schedule/work plan, future operating plan development with integration across services, and transition support to include future state vision and performance metrics, resource strategy and staffing plan, training strategy and orientation schedules, communication and plan integration with marketing strategy, transition budget, and overall strategy for patient and staff move.
carol.cosler@nationwidechildrens.org **Page 246**

Christine De Lille is a PhD candidate at the Delft University of Technology, the Netherlands. Her PhD research focuses on User-Centered Design in Small-to-Medium sized Enterprises (SMEs). Her experience lies in methods for user involvement in the fuzzy front end especially in time-pressure and budget driven projects as for example in SMEs. Christine obtained a master's degree in Design for interaction from Delft University of Technology in 2007. In 2012 Christines hopes to finish her PhD and in April 2012 she started with a Post Doc on Design Thinking as enabler for change in organizations.
c.s.h.delille@tudelft.nl www.christinedelille.be **Page 138**

Marco De Polo leads the User Experience Design group at the Roche Incubator. After years of gaining expertise in all phases of the product development process with the successful global product launch of Roche Diabetes Care in Switzerland, he has been establishing the Front End Innovation expertise at the Roche Incubator in California. He drives innovation by discovering opportunities, designing and evaluating prototypes with real people in their natural environment through an exploratory, iterative, human-centered design process. By integrating applied behavioral psychology into the design process, Marco and his team are now implementing and evaluating solutions that will eventually change the way people adopt sustainable health behaviors.
depolo@me.com, marco.de_polo@roche.com **Page 245**

Dr. Allison Druin is the Associate Dean for Research in the University of Maryland's College of Information Studies. She is also the Director of the Human-Computer Interaction Lab (HCIL) where she leads participatory design research teams of children and adults to create new educational technologies for children. She is the author or editor of four books published from 1996-2009. And she is a monthly technology radio correspondent for National Public Radio's WAMU.
allisond@umiacs.umd.edu **Page 286**

Mette Agger Eriksen: Through practical, experimental design research, I am exploring co-designing processes and how these relate to and differ from traditional design practices, for example materially – in which I combine material culture studies, performance studies and actor-network theory perspectives in my analysis of examples of co-design situations from five different participatory, IT and methodology-oriented design research projects. The aim is to contribute with a co-design material ecology for both understanding and staging co-design situations. Currently, these experiences are combined with my background as an industrial designer from an architecture school and my interest in sustainable, service design perspectives, in my coordination and teaching of interaction design master students.
mette.agger@mah.se **Page 284**

Erik A. Evensen is a designer, illustrator, and graphic novelist. He holds an M.F.A. in Design from The Ohio State University, a B.A. from the University of New Hampshire, and studied at the School of the Museum of Fine Arts in Boston. He is the owner and principal of Evensen Creative, a creative studio and consulting firm in Bemidji, MN, USA. He has taught at The Ohio State University, Bemidji State

EXTERNAL CONTRIBUTORS

University, the Art Institute of Pittsburgh, and in the Maine Community College system. *You can find Erik on the web at www.erik-evensen. com, or www.evensencreative.com.* **Page 80**

Lois Frankel is an Associate Professor and past Director at the School of Industrial Design at Carleton University, Ottawa, Canada. She is also a PhD student at Concordia University, with the generous support of a Doctoral Fellowship from SSHRC (the Social Sciences and Humanities Research Council). The focus of her work is simplifying the relationship between people and wearable computing products. In particular, she is interested in generative methods for designing wearable computing devices and/or clothing that bring older people and designers together in the early stages of the design process.
Lois_frankel@carleton.ca **Page 92**

Jen Gellis: I have a background in occupational therapy and a graduate degree in design. Working as an occupational therapist at Sunny Hill Health Centre for Children, I collaborate with children, families, technicians, engineers and healthcare providers to design and enable solutions for positioning and mobility. I have also worked on independent design projects and am a volunteer board member for the Design for Development Society. I am passionate about inclusive and human-centered design, global health, design for social impact and the use of creative design methods with children.
jengellis@gmail.com **Page 82**

Mercè Graell is currently exploring integrative languages using 2D and 3D artifacts to empower people's creativity through generative design thinking and a co-creation mindset. MFA in Design Education by The Ohio State University, US, her areas of expertise are participatory design research and co-creation strategies with users; creative thinking for effective communication and collaboration in multidisciplinary teams; and interdisciplinary curricula development. Currently, she teaches at Elisava Escola Superior de Disseny, Universitat Politècnica de Catalunya and at the Istituto Europeo di Design, in Barcelona, Spain, and at the Human Centered Innovation Institute h2i in Madrid, Spain. She is the owner of visualteamwork and a co-creation strategy consultant at dnx/Designit.
merce@visualteamwork.com **Page 250**

Bruce Hanington is an Associate Professor and Program Chair of Industrial Design in the School of Design at Carnegie Mellon University. His research and teaching encompasses the personal, social, and cultural context of product design and interpretation, the meaning of form, human factors and ethnographic and participatory research methods. He has consulted on design projects with GE Appliances and Johnson and Johnson. His work has been published in *Design Issues, The Design Journal,* and *Interactions,* with chapters in *Designing Inclusive Futures,* and *Design and Emotion: The Experience of Everyday Things.* His co-authored book with Bella Martin is *Universal Methods*

of Design: 100 Ways to Research Complex Problems, Develop Innovative Ideas and Design Effective Solutions
hanington@cmu.edu **Pages 34, 189**

Annet Hennink: As a Concept & Proposition Developer at Centraal Beheer Achmea (a large insurance company), I translate the company's strategy, market trends and user needs into innovative and distinctive concepts or propositions. The customer is central during the whole development process. I use and test the latest user-driven methods such as personas, service design and co-creation. The 'Concept & Proposition Development Department' is the linking pin between the commercial departments and business lines. I manage concept or proposition development projects, which are all multidisciplinary (e.g., with Sales, IT, Legal, Marketing, etc.).
annethennink@gmail.com **Page 254**

Kang-Ning Hsu: I'm living in Taipei and work fulltime now. In my leisure time, I participate in design related activities when I am able to. TientienCircle, a group of my friends, is a team that tries to discuss our lives, our land and ourselves. It is touching to have a group of friends to talk about these issues. Three years after graduation, I'm still on the way to find balance of my work, hobby and time.
hiopie@gmail.com **Page 233**

Sofia Hussain is a PhD candidate at the Department of Engineering Design and Materials at the Norwegian University of Science and Technology (NTNU). She has a MSc. in Industrial Design. Her Masters thesis concerned design of prosthetic legs for children in Nepal. Her current research project is conducted for the International Red Cross Committee and regards participatory design with children using prosthetic legs in Cambodia. She focuses on showing how considering emotional, cultural, and social needs, along with functional and economic requirements, can lead to development of better assistive devices for people with disabilities in developing countries.
sofia@ntnu.no **Page 90**

Alëna Iouguina: I'm an industrial designer interested in sustainable human behaviour. In particular, my research lies within the application of collaborative design methods to solving environmental problems. Revealing unmet needs, uncovering new opportunities, and stimulating creative thinking can have a significant effect on reducing society's resource dependence, and users' dependence on experts to understand and modify the technology available to them.
alyona.iouguina@gmail.com **Page 92**

Marlene Ivey is a designer interested in developing innovative design methods, technologies and infrastructure to support environmental, economic and cultural sustainability. Her design practice investigates participatory approaches to designing, using creative play, visual thinking and experience scenarios to bring people together from diverse backgrounds to share knowledge and generate design vision. Her current research is footed in the Gaelic milieu where she is collaborating with the Nova Scotia Gaelic community to create An Drochaid Eadarainn (The Bridge Between Us) an interactive online social space for Gaelic language renewal and cultural restoration – a virtual cèilidh. She is currently Associate Professor at NSCAD University, Halifax, Nova Scotia, Canada and has published work in UK, Asia, Continental Europe, Canada and the USA.

mivey@nscad.ca **Page 33**

Peter Jones, Ph.D. is managing director of Redesign, an innovation research firm that reconceives value and strategy for services and systems design, through human-centred research and organizational capacity building. Redesign researches organizational, intellectual and work practices, and designs leading information resources as contexts for thinking. As a board member of the Agoras Institute, Peter promotes the practice and science of dialogic design for collaborative action on wicked, socially complex problems. Dr. Jones lives in Toronto and teaches in the Strategic Foresight and Innovation program at OCAD University. He is the author of Team Design, and Design for Care (2011). His papers and online work are found at designdialogues.com.

Pages 230, 252

Channeling the inner child in all of us, **Lindsay Kenzig** constantly asks 'Why?', striving to get to the bottom of what is most important. From shadowing customers, to observing waiting behaviors in clinics, to facilitating collaborative charettes, she is constantly looking at the world through others' perspectives. With both a design and social science background, Lindsay is uniquely qualified for design research. As a Senior Researcher at Design Central, she loves that her job allows her to constantly learn, get to know people, find out what makes them tick, and design solutions that better our world.

Lindsay.Kenzig@gmail.com **Pages 180, 182**

Amar Khanna has a background in the fields of Design Research and Participatory Design. He has worked within organizations such as SonicRim, Yahoo Inc. and Realtor.com to learn and promote innovation by co-creation and field research methods. Currently he works for the Online Computer Library Center located in Dublin, Ohio as a Senior User Experience Designer. The non-profit organization helps libraries increase access to their patrons and reduce information costs. At OCLC, his team creates the vision for communicating, and implementing the user experience on web and desktop based interfaces.

khannamar@gmail.com **Page 86**

Sanne Kistemaker has a background in Industrial Design Engineering where she developed affinity with the human factor of design. After graduating with honour, she founded the user-centered design agency

Muzus. She is specialized in conducting research to gain insight into the wishes and latent needs of people, in order to design concepts that fit the life of the envisaged end-users. In her projects, Sanne always co-creates both with users and clients to ensure that her designs fit the experience of the users as well as the portfolio of the client. Furthermore, Sanne is part-time design tutor at the faculty of Industrial Design Engineering to educate user-centered designers.

sanne@muzus.nl, www.muzus.nl **Pages 188, 196**

Preetham Kolari is a designer, researcher, ethnographer and innovation strategist at Microsoft. He is extremely passionate about bringing the human experience and design thinking perspective into the business decision making process. He leads a team of designers, writers and researchers that drive a consistent design language and user experience quality throughout the Lync product. The team is responsible for building and delivering an end-to-end experience framework while collaborating closely with the rest of the product team.

pkolari@gmail.com **Page 145**

Steven Lavender is an Associate Professor in the Integrated Systems Engineering Department and the Department of Orthopaedics at The Ohio State University. His research focuses on understanding the stresses placed on the body during occupational activities and how these stresses can be moderated through the design of targeted interventions. Of particular interest is how the occupational activities and interventions affect the back and shoulders. He has authored or co-authored over 50 peer-reviewed journal articles and several book chapters. He currently serves on the editorial board of Human Factors and the Journal of Electromyography and Kinesiology.

lavender.1@osu.edu **Page 142**

Tuuli Mattelmäki works as a senior researcher in Department of Design at Aalto School of Art and Design and as academic community director at Aalto Service Factory. She is specialized in developing explorative methods for user-centered design and co-design, design probes in particular. During her research she has done collaboration with various organizations, recently with the City of Helsinki among others. Her publications include articles on probes, empathic design and co-design. Currently she is involved in Aalto Service Factory's activities in research projects related to service design. She was awarded as the industrial designer of the year 2008 by the Association of Industrial Designers in Finland for her valuable work in design research.

Tuuli.mattelmaki@aalto.fi **Page 266**

Alan Moser, principal and managing partner of Frame360, is responsible for client relationship management and strategic development. Alan has over three decades of advertising, brand communications and interactive media experience. Through this experience he has developed a discerning eye and ear for distinctive brand and corporate qualities

EXTERNAL CONTRIBUTORS

that many companies overlook or underestimate. Working with clients in a participatory manner is a hallmark of Frame360's approach. Alan's ability to lead groups through workshops and discussions about their business is rigorous, provocative and enlightening. That combined with his focus on translating the results into strategic direction and action items enables clients to feel ownership of ideas and confidence that they can deliver on the goals and objectives they have established.
amoser@frame360.com **Page 263**

Michael Muller works as a social scientist in the Center for Social Software and the Collaborative User Experience groups of IBM Research in Cambridge, MA, USA. Recent work has focused on attention management, social metrics, online communities, social file-sharing, and user innovations in social software.
michael_muller@us.ibm.com **Pages 95, 286**

Mark Palmer is a design researcher with over twenty years experience in consulting and corporate product development. He is the founder of Geneva, a firm that provides research management and consultation to companies that want to become more focused on the user-experience. Using his training in psychology and anthropology, Mark helps companies develop world-class competencies in research and, in the process, establish new innovative product and service strategies. He has built, managed and mentored design and research teams in North America, Europe, and Asia with a consistent and effective philosophy of keeping the user at the center of the creative process.
mark@geneva-sciences.com **Page 87**

Stephanie Patton is the consumate 'people person' who has really never known a stranger; so you might as well smile right when you meet her, because she'll just needle one out of you in the end anyway. She loves to connect with people by listening, learning, mentoring, writing, describing, discussing, questioning...you get the picture. She has turned her avocation into her vocation as president of Spot-On - a consulting practice that helps organizations 'get to the point...and go places' by better understanding and communicating with their stakeholders.
Stephanie.w.patton@gmail.com **Pages 177, 182**

Carolien Postma is product researcher at Philips Consumer Lifestyle, specializing in user studies in the early stages of new product development. She previously worked for ID-Studiolab at Delft University of Technology, where she developed a user-centered design approach, Creating Socionas, as part of her Ph.D. research in industrial design. Her interests include design for user experience and design research methodology.
carolien.postma@philips.com **Page 192**

Erik Roscam Abbing is a consultant and teacher in design management, with a strong focus on bringing together the disciplines of branding, innovation and design. Having studied Industrial Design Engineering

at the Technological University of Delft and Design Management at Inholland/Nijenrode, both in the Netherlands, Erik has worked as a practicing product designer for 10 years before founding his consultancy Zilver Innovation in Rotterdam, the Netherlands. Erik consults for a variety of international clients in the product and service industries. Erik is also a part time teacher at the school of Industrial Design at the Technological University of Delft, where he develops and teaches classes related to strategic design, design thinking and branding.
Erik@zilverinnovation.com **Pages 144, 194**

Karen Scanlan has been honing her expertise in the field of qualitative research. With this, she applies a strategic approach to the understanding and analysis of real-world behavior and experiences to reveal the most compelling, resonant space for product, communication, business and branding innovation. Karen holds a BA in Psychology from the University of Illinois and a Master of Design from the Institute of Design, Illinois Institute of Technology. Her work has been featured in *The New York Times*, *Dwell* magazine and *The Journal of Consulting and Clinical Psychology*. Karen has worked for both non-profit and multi-national companies, and currently works as an independent consultant.
karenscanlan@gmail.com **Page 226**

Samantha Serrer is an industrial designer with an interest in private and public spaces. My research focuses on how users interact with, and orient themselves within, these spaces. Through interdisciplinary design practices and collaborative techniques, designers can better understand and meet the needs of users, as well as create appropriate solutions to everyday issues.
samantha.serrer@gmail.com **Page 92**

George Simons works in a blur of generative design thinking, co-creation and design to develop innovation and branding strategies. The core of his work is an ongoing passion for integrating user experiences and stories that provoke business to better understand and act upon complex issues, and generate visions of possible futures. He has held positions as Director of Advanced Concepts Research and Design at Steelcase, owner of a design and strategy consultancy - fahrenheit, a managing partner and location lead at IDEO, and a principal at nbbj architecture, forming a design research group, with Liz Sanders, focused on the human experience, effectiveness, relevance and adaptability of built environments.
georgesimons@mac.com **Page 62**

Froukje Sleeswijk Visser has a background in Industrial Design Engineering (Msc and PhD). Her PhD dissertation (2009) called 'Bringing the everyday life of people into design' discusses how user data can be useful in the explorative phase in design practice. In 2006 she started the company ContextQueen, and since 2009 she is part-time

assistant professor at the ID-StudioLab (Delft University of Technology). She is specialized in researching people's everyday experiences and uses this for idea generation of new products and services.
f.sleeswijkvisser@tudelft.nl **Pages 76, 248**

Dr. Carolyn Sommerich teaches, advises graduate students, and conducts research focused on ergonomics and occupational biomechanics, health, and safety, with special interests in the upper body and upper extremity musculoskeletal disorders; ergonomics in office, industrial, and health care settings; and ergonomic issues affecting youth and older adults. She has authored or co-authored 10 book chapters, 30 peer-reviewed journal articles and 55 conference proceedings on a range of topics concerning musculoskeletal disorders associated with overuse. Her current research involves intervention development in the areas of imaging technology and material handling in warehousing; ongoing investigation of the etiology of carpal tunnel syndrome using a novel model; and paid and unpaid caregiving.
sommerich.1@osu.edu **Page 142**

Louise St. Pierre has been teaching, researching, and writing about industrial design for 18 years, at both the University of Washington and Emily Carr University. She is co-author of Okala Ecological Design, a curriculum that helped to establish ecological teaching methods in design schools across North America. She has received numerous awards for her design work, and funding for a broad range of collaborative research projects. She writes on sustainable design, product longevity, and human-centered design. In her teaching, she works with students to explore how co-design methods can support the transition to a sustainable future.
lsp@ecuad.ca **Page 78**

Robert Strouse has a B.S. in Industrial Design from Virginia Tech and a M.F.A. in Design from The Ohio State University. He has worked in the design field for over ten years and has enjoyed creating new things alongside talented and capable people. During his undergraduate experience, one of the most influential classes he took was entitled 'Design Research'. The class started the now decade long pursuit to combine the rigor and inquiry of research with the natural creativity and craft of design. Using prototypes as tools for discovery is a powerful technique for both researchers and designers to explore, tweak and verify information about the world. Robert now works in a division of Applied Research Associates alongside Cognitive Scientists where he creates prototypes that help to investigate and support Decision Making in Hazardous Work Environments.
rstrouse@ara.com or robert.strouse@gmail.com **Page 79**

Kirsikka Vaajakallio is a design researcher and a doctoral student in School of Art and Design at the Aalto University, Finland. Her background is in industrial design and she is specialized in user-centered

design. Her research focuses on co-design processes in early stages of design projects conducted in university-industry collaboration. In particularly, she has been exploring various types of design games as framework for creative teamwork in several contexts from banking services to senior houses. Her publications include articles related to empathic design, co-design, and service design.
kirsikka.vaajakallio@aalto.fi **Page 266**

In 2007, **Helma van Rijn** graduated cum laude for the M.Sc. program Design for Interaction on LINKX, an educational toy for children with autism. After that, she started a PhD research at the ID-Studiolab of Delft University of Technology. Her research focuses on designers learning from direct contact with children with autism and their caregivers for their design process. In her studies, she explores how designers can be supported in this learning by means of developing new tools and techniques for learning from direct contact and using these in encounters between designers, children with autism, and their caregivers.
h.vanrijn@tudelft.nl **Page 184**

Arnold Wasserman is a consultant for innovation, design and strategy and a pioneer of the field of human-centered innovation. He has been head of design for NCR, Xerox and Unisys Corporations; Director of the Raymond Loewy design office in Paris and Dean of Pratt Institute of Design in New York. Named a "Master of Design" by Fast Company magazine, he serves on numerous boards and consults for numerous corporations, governments, NGO's, foundations, international organizations and consortiums and design councils. He speaks and writes frequently at venues around the world and posts about RE:Designing Everything and World 3.0 on his website at http://arnoldwasserman. com. **Pages 281, 282**

John Youger (Director of Consumer Insights - WD Partners, Dublin Ohio USA): My current professional and personal focus is understanding how and where digital (virtual) experiences intersect, compliment and supplement retail (physical) environments. The process includes a combination of constantly monitoring technology trends and understanding how and where they intuitively connect to shoppers. Ultimately this creates interactive experiences that connect shoppers to environments, products and brands. Recent clients include Fortune 500 companies like Best Buy, Wendys, ConAgra, Red Bull and Walmart.
john.youger@wdpartners.com **Pages 223, 229**

Elly Zwartkruis-Pelgrim is research scientist at Philips Research. She has a background in psychology and Human-Computer Interaction. Her work has focused on exploring user needs for specific target groups, such as the elderly and parents with babies. She is currently working on methods to enhance sleep and translating them into product propositions.
elly.zwartkruis-pelgrim@philips.com **Page 192**

REFERENCES

PREFACE

· Florida, R. (2002) *The Rise of the Creative Class. And How It's Transforming Work, Leisure and Everyday Life*, Basic Books.
· Illich, I. (1975) *Tools for Conviviality*, Harper & Row Publishers, Inc.
· Pine II, B. J., & Gilmore, J. H. (1999) *The Experience Economy*, Harvard Business School Press, Boston, Mass.
· Pink, D. (2005) *A Whole New Mind: Why Right-Brainers Will Rule the Future*, The Berkley Publishing Group, New York.

CHAPTER 1

· Avison, D., Lau, F., Myers, M., & Nielsen, P.A. (1999) Action research, *Communications of the ACM*, 42(1), 49-97.
· Bødker, S. (1996) Creating conditions for participation: Conflicts and resources in systems design, *Human Computer Interaction* 11(3), 215-236.
· Buchenau, M., & Fulton Suri, J. (2000) Experience prototyping, *Symposium on Designing Interactive Systems, Proceedings of the Conference on Designing Interactive Systems: Processes, Practices, Methods, and Techniques*, pp. 424 – 433.
· Burns, C., Dishman, E., Johnson, B., & Verplank, B. (1995) 'Informance': Min(d)ing future contexts for scenario-based interaction design, *BayCHI*, Palo Alto.
· Buxton, B. (2007) *Sketching User Experiences: Getting the Design Right and the Right Design*, Morgan Kaufmann Publishers, San Francisco.
· Chambers, R. (1994) The origins and practice of participatory rural appraisal, *World Development*, 22(7), 953-989.
· Diaz, L., Reunanen, M., & Salmi, A. (2009) Role playing and collaborative scenario design development, *International Conference on Engineering Design*, ICED '09, Stanford University.
· Dunne, A., & Raby, F. (2001) *Design Noir: The Secret Life of Electronic Objects*, Basel, Boston.
· Gaver, W., Dunne, A., & Pacenti, E. (1999) Cultural probes, *Interactions*, 6, No. 1, 21-29.
· Gilmore, T., Krantz, J., & Ramirez, R. (1986) Action based modes of inquiry and the host-researcher relationship, *Consultation*, 5(3), 160-176.
· Illich, I. (1975) see preface

· Kahneman, D. (2011) *Thinking, Fast and Slow*. Allen Lane.
· Lewin, K. (1946) Action research and minority problems, *Journal of Social Issues*, 2(4), 34-46.
· Martin, R. (2009) *The Design Of Business: Why Design Thinking Is The Next Competitive Advantage*, Harvard Business School Publishing, Boston.
· Mattelmäki, T. (2006) *Design Probes*. DA Dissertation. Helsinki: University of Art and Design Helsinki.
· Ouslasvirta, A., Kurvinen, E., & Kankainen, T. (2003) Understanding contexts by being there: Case studies in bodystorming, *Personal Ubiquitous Computing*. Springer-Verlag, London.
· Pascale, R., Sternin, J., & Sternin M. (2010) *The Power of Positive Deviance: How Unlikely Innovators Solve the World's Toughest Problems*. Harvard Business Press.
· Postma, C.E., & Stappers, P.J. (2006) A vision on social interactions as the basis for design, *CoDesign*, Vol. 2 No. 3, 139-155.
· Rittel, H., & Webber, M. (1973) Dilemmas in a general theory of planning, pp. 155–169, *Policy Sciences*, Vol. 4, Elsevier Scientific Publishing Company, Inc., Amsterdam.
· Sanders, E.B.-N. (2006) Design research in 2006, *Design Research Quarterly*, No. 1, Design Research Society, September.
· Sanders, L., & Simons, G. (2009) A social vision for value co-creation in design, *Open Source Business Resource*, December 2009. Available at http://www.osbr.ca/ojs/index.php/osbr/article/view/1012/973
· Sedaris, A. (2010) *Simple Times: Crafts for Poor People*. Grand Central Publishing, New York.
· Simsarian, K.T. (2003) Take it to the next stage: The roles of role playing in the design process, *CHI 2003: New Horizons*.
· Sleeswijk Visser, F., Stappers, P.J., van der Lugt, R., & Sanders, E.B.-N. (2005) Contextmapping: Experiences from practice, *CoDesign*, 1(2), 119-149.
· Stappers, P.J. & Sleeswijk Visser, F. (2006) Contextmapping, *GeoConnexion*, August 2006, 22-24
· Stewart, M. (2009) *Martha Stewart's Encyclopedia of Crafts: An A-to-Z Guide with Detailed Instructions and Endless Inspiration*, Martha Stewart Living Magazine.

REFERENCES

- Susman, G.I., & Evered, R.D. (1978) An assessment of the scientific merits of action research, *Administrative Science Quarterly*, Vol. 23, No.4, 582-603.
- Verganti, R. (2009) *Design-Driven Innovation: Changing the Rules of Competition by Radically Innovating what Things Mean*, Harvard Business School Publishing Corp.
- Von Hippel, E. (2005) *Democratizing Innovation*, Cambridge, MA: MIT Press.

CHAPTER 2
- Bargh, J. A., Chen, M., & Burrows, L. (1996) Automaticity of social behavior: Direct effects of trait construct and stereotype priming on action, *Journal of Personality and Social Psychology*, 71, 230-244.
- Baas, M., De Dreu, C.K.W., & Nijstad, B.A. (2008) A meta-analysis of 25 years of mood-creativity research: Hedonic tone, activation, or regulatory focus? *Psychological Bulletin*, *134*, 779-806.
- Boden, M.A. (1990) *The Creative Mind: Myths and Mechanisms*. New York: NY, Basic Books.
- Buxton, B. (2007) see chapter 1
- Buchenau, M. & Fulton Suri, J. (2000) see chapter 1
- Burns, C., Dishman, E., Johnson, B., & Verplank, B. (1995) see chapter 1
- Collins, M.A., & Loftus, E.F. (1975) A spreading-activation theory of semantic processing, *Psychological Review*, 82, 407-428.
- Csikszentmihalyi, M. (1996) *Creativity: Flow And The Psychology Of Discovery And Invention*. New York: Harper Collins.
- Diaz, L., Reunanen, M., & Salmi, A. (2009) see chapter 1
- Florida, R. (2002) see preface
- Gaver, W.W., Beaver, J., & Benford, S. (2003) Ambiguity as a resource for design, *Proceedings Of The SIGCHI Conference On Human Factors In Computing Systems*. ACM, New York.
- Gedenryd, H. (1998) *How Designers Work: Making Sense Of Authentic Cognitive Activity,* PhD Thesis, Lund University.
- Isen, A.M. (1999) On the relationship between affect and creative problem solving. In S.W. Russ (Ed.) *Affect, Creative Experience And Psychological Adjustment* (pp. 3-18). Philadelphia, PA: Bruner/Mazel.
- Khanna, A. (2008) personal communication.
- Koestler, A. (1964) *The Act of Creation*. New York: Dell.
- Martin, R. (2009) See chapter 1
- McCloud, S. (1993) *Understanding Comics: The Invisible Art*, Kitchen Sink Press.
- Meyer, K. L. (2010) *Creativity in Repurposing Textiles*. MFA Thesis in the Department of Design at The Ohio State University.
- Mintzberg, H., & Westley, F. (2001) Decision making: It's not what you think, *MIT Sloan Management Review*, Spring 2001, Volume 42, Number 3, pp.89-93.
- Nijstad, B.A., & DeDrue, C.K. (2002) Creativity and group innovation, *Applied Psychology*. 51: 400-406.
- Oulasvirta, A, Kurvinen, E., & Kankainen, T (2003) See chapter 1
- Peirce, C.S. (1878) *Writings of Charles S. Peirce*. Bloomington, IN: Indiana University Press.
- Pink, D. (2005) see preface
- Root-Bernstein, M. & R. (1999) *Sparks Of Genius: The 13 Thinking Tools Of The World's Most Creative People*. New York: Houghton Mifflin Company.
- Sanders, E.B.-N. (2002) From user-centered to participatory design approaches. In *Design and the Social Sciences*. J. Frascara (Ed.), Taylor and Francis, Books Limited.
- Sanders, E.B.-N. (2005) Information, Inspiration and Co-creation, *Proceedings of the 6th International Conference of the European Academy of Design*, University of the Arts, Bremen, Germany.
- Sawyer, R.K. (2006) *Explaining Creativity: The Science Of Human Innovation*. Oxford University Press, New York.
- Sawyer, K. (2007) *Group Genius: The Creative Power Of Collaboration*. Basic Books, New York.
- Schön, D. (1963) *The Displacement Of Concepts*. London: Tavistock.
- Simsarian, K.T. (2003) see chapter 1
- Star, S. L., & Griesemer, J. R. (1989) Institutional Ecology, 'Translations' and boundary objects: Amateurs and professionals in Berkeley's Museum of Vertebrate Zoology, 1907-1930, *Social Studies of Science* (19), 387-420.
- Sternberg, R. J., & Lubart, T. I. (1995) *Defying The Crowd: Cultivating Creativity In A Culture Of Conformity*. New York: Free Press.
- Wallas, G. (1926) *The Art of Thought*. New York: NY, Harcourt, Brace and Company.
- Wason, P. C. (1966) Reasoning in Foss, B. M. *New Horizons In Psychology*. Harmondsworth: Penguin
- Zenasni, F., Besançon, M., & Lubart , T. (2008) Creativity and tolerance of ambiguity: An empirical study, *The Journal Of Creative Behavior*, Vol. 42, No. 1.

CHAPTER 3
- Gladwell, M. (2005) *Blink: The Power Of Thinking Without Thinking*. London: Penguin.
- Gosling, S.D., Ko, S.J., Mannarelli, T., & Morris, M.A. (2002) A room with a cue: Personality judgments based on offices and bedrooms. *Journal of Personality and Social Psychology*, 82(3), Mar 2002, 379-398.
- Postma, C.E., & Stappers, P.J. (2006) see chapter 1
- Robson, C. (1993) *Real World Research: A Resource For Social Scientists And Practitioner-Researchers*. Malden, MA: Blackwell Publishers, Inc.
- Sunderland, P.L., & Denny, R.M. (2007) *Doing Anthropology In Consumer Research*, Left Coast Press.
- Wolcott, H.F. (2008) *Ethnography: A Way of Seeing*. AltaMira Press.

CHAPTER 5
- Pruitt, J., & Adlin, T. (2006) *The Persona Lifecycle: Keeping People in Mind During Product Design*. San Francisco: Morgan Kaufmann.

REFERENCES

- Scherer, F. M. (1982) "Demand-pull and technological opportunity: Scmookler revisited," *Journal of Industrial Economics*, 30, 225-37.
- Stappers, P.J., van Rijn, H., Kistemaker, S., Hennink, A., & Sleeswijk Visser, F. (2009) Designing for other people's strengths and motivations: Three cases using context, visions, and experiential prototypes. *Advanced Engineering Informatics, A Special Issue on Human-Centered Product Design and Development.* Vol. 23, 174-183.

CHAPTER 6
- Bystedt, J., Lynn, S., & Potts, D. (2003) *Moderating to the Max: A Full-Tilt Guide to Creative, Insightful Focus Groups and Depth Interviews.* Ithaca, NY: Paramount Market Publishing.
- Sleeswijk Visser, F., Stappers, P. J., van der Lugt, R., & Sanders, E. B.-N. (2005) See chapter 1

CHAPTER 7
- Ackoff, R. L. (1989) From data to wisdom, *Journal of Applied Systems Analysis,* Volume 16, 3-9.
- Lincoln, Y. S., & Guba, E. G. (1989) *Naturalistic Inquiry.* Sage Publications, London, England.
- Miles, M. B., & Huberman, A. M. (1994) *Qualitative data analysis* (2nd ed.). Thousand Oaks, CA: SAG.

CHAPTER 8
- Brown, J., Isaacs, D., & the World Café Community (2005) *The World Café: Shaping Our Futures through Conversations that Matter.* Berrett-Koehler Publishers, Inc. San Francisco.
- Kouprie, M., & Sleeswijk Visser, F. (2009) A framework for empathy in design: stepping into and out of the user's life, *Journal of Engineering Design,* 20(5) 437-448
- Owen, H. (1997) *Expanding Our Now: The Story of Open Space Technology.* Berrett-Koehler Publishers, Inc. San Francisco.
- Owen, H. (1997) *Open Space Technology: A User's Guide.* Berrett-Koehler Publishers, Inc. San Francisco.
- Pruitt, J., & Adlin, T. (2006) see chapter 5
- Sleeswijk Visser, F., & Stappers, P.J. (2007) Mind the face, *Proceedings of DPPI (Conference on Designing Pleasurable Products and Interfaces),* Helsinki, August 2007, 119-134.
- Sleeswijk Visser, F. (2009) *Bringing The Everyday Life Of People Into Design,* PhD Thesis, TU Delft. Downloadable http://www.studiolab.nl/
- Thompson, C. (2008) Brave new world of digital intimacy, *The New York Times,* September 7, 2008. www.nytimes.com

CHAPTER 9
- Buchenau, M., & Fulton Suri, J. (2000) see chapter 1
- Burns, C., Dishman, E., Johnson, B., & Verplank, B. (1995) see chapter 1
- Oulasvirta, A, Kurvinen, E., & Kankainen, T (2003) see chapter 2
- Simsarian, K.T. (2003) see chapter 1

CHAPTER 10
- Martin, R. (2009) see chapter 1
- Sanders, E.B.-N. (2005) see chapter 2

GLOSSARY

This glossary is meant to give newcomers some grip on the jargon in the field, giving informal definitions to help the reader place unfamiliar terms. But don't mistake them for precise scientific definitions that will stand up in court. For those, you will have to look in the appropriate theory (and also there find, unfortunately, that a crisp and sure definition is not often given).

abduction: logical thinking process, closely connected to creativity, in which background knowledge is connected with a problem, resulting in a new solution

abstraction: the process of making more general statements out of particular ones

academia: the academic world, e.g., universities and research institutes (as opposed to business organizations)

action research: a research methodology in which interventions are made into an existing practice, and the effects of these are assessed, typically in collaboration with all participating actors

actionable: useful in the sense of helpful for undertaking concrete actions or for making (business) decisions

advocate: somebody who is enthusiastic and active/vocal about something

aesthetic: relating to the form or beauty of an object

affective: relating to feelings and emotions

ambiguous: having multiple meanings at the same time

analyzing: making sense of research data by fitting it into a theory, or building theory onto, or out of, data

anecdote: a story from real life expressing a specific point about a topic

annotate: make notes and interpretations related to pieces of data

anonymize: hide the identity of people in a piece of research data

architecture: design discipline dealing with buildings and the built environment

artifacts: things that were made by people, e.g., photos, collages, recordings

associative thinking: thinking by means of connecting ideas to each another

attitude: readiness to act or react in a certain way

bisociation: creative process (by Koestler) in which two apparently unconnected ideas become connected, leading to new directions to be explored

booklet: small book, see workbook

brainstorm: group activity in which participants try to quickly generate many solutions for a given problem or ideas about a given topic

bridging: making the connection between research thinking and design thinking

brief: goals and objectives for the design (research) team at the beginning of the project; often this has the status of a contract between client and team

cards: pieces of cardboard or paper that each contain a chunk of information. Typically used to allow for selecting, sorting, categorizing, especially in team settings

category: a grouping of items that have something in common

cause: A is the cause of B if A occurred before B, and is the necessary explanation as to why B came about

centric: X-centered designing is a method or approach to designing, in which X is the center of attention, discussion, and criteria for success

chart: a two-dimensional graph used to provide overview and coordination

closure: bringing an event to a (satisfying or emotional) completion

cloud of ideas: a network of connected ideas, linked by associations

clustering: putting items into groups or categories

co-creation: collaborative creative action, event or artifact. Sometimes used to refer to codesign as a whole, sometimes used to refer to a single event with stakeholders

coding: assigning category codes to pieces of data

cognition: the way people think, in the broadest sense of the word 'think'

cognitive toolkit: generative toolkit, typically for expressing processes and relationships

collage toolkit: generative toolkit, typically for expressing memories and emotions

communication design: design discipline focusing on communication media, e.g., print, film

concept: see design concept

GLOSSARY

conceptualization: developing a concept design on the basis of research insights and/or other ideas

concrete: (as opposed to abstract) instantiated, clearly findable in the world

consumerism: trend in society that emphasizes people's role as passive buyers of products and services aimed at them

context: ideas or circumstances surrounding a central idea, event, or thing (i.e., called content)

contextmapping: design research approach which emphasizes user involvement through generative techniques and design team involvement with rich communication techniques

contextual inquiry: design research approach in which the researcher learns from participants by interviewing and observing them

contextualize: to connect an idea to related ideas that can be found in its context

corroboration: validating the correctness of an expectation with evidence

creative: quality of something being considered new and appropriate

creativity: the ability of seeing or making new, appropriate things

critical design: design movement that develops product concepts as a means of critical reflection and analysis of societal developments

cultural probe: design research technique in which designers send evocative materials in the form of exercises to stakeholders, and interpret what they receive back as inspirational material for design

data: (in DIKW) samples from the real world

deduction: logical thinking process, reasoning from general statements to specific statements

deliverables: items that were specified in the contract to be created and delivered by the design (research) team to the client

demographics: description of statistical properties of groups of people

design concept: idea about a possible future product or service worked out in sufficient detail on the major aspects that are being considered

designing: the activity of defining possible futures (often this is taken to include research and implementation activities)

DIKW: Ackoff's model of organizing scientific thinking in four layers: Data, Information, Knowledge, and Wisdom

discipline: area of professional expertise sharing a set of methods, knowledge, and values, e.g., dentistry, shopkeeping, psychology, design, etc.

documentation: description and explanation of method, results and interpretation of a project

documenting: ordering, storing, and labeling research data for later retrieval and analysis

doll's house kit: generative toolkit for exploring 3D spatial solutions at a small scale, e.g., in interior or retail design

dreams: ideas about possible futures which may be desirable or not

embodied: having a physical (as opposed to digital, virtual, mental) form

emergent: arising out of the process, without having been planned

emotional toolkit: generative toolkit aimed at expressing emotions

empathic design: design approach stressing the importance that the designer(s) achieve empathic understanding of the intended user(s) of a product or service

empathy: understanding another person's situation, experience, or perspective, as if it were one's own

enacting: pretending, acting out, performing, conducting a stage play, etc.

ethnography: anthropological method for intensively studying people's lives

evocative: evoking or creating associations, feelings, opinions

executive summary: short summary highlighting the essential goal, method, and findings of a report; typically used to communicate outside the team, e.g., to upper management

expectation: ideas (prejudices, beliefs, theories, hypotheses) about a future event

experience: (1) emotions associated with an event (2) first-hand knowledge

experience design: design approach in which the 'user experience' is the central focus for developing and evaluating ideas and concepts

explicit: objectively visible

facilitating: leading a group through a (creative) process, especially a session (see also moderating)

facilitator: someone who helps a process come along, e.g., in organizing and leading a generative session

factor: variable in a scientific theory or explanation, e.g., 'important factors in this choice are price, availability, and sturdiness'

fielding: collecting data in the field (as opposed to in the laboratory)

fieldwork: research activities that take place in the world, as opposed to in the laboratory

flip board: large sheets of paper, usually mounted on a tripod or on the wall, used in sessions

flowchart: diagram used in planning or design, showing logical, temporal, or causal connections between elements or phases

focus: central part of the scope of a study (i.e., the inner boundary of content)

focus group: group of people selected to represent one or more stakeholder groups, brought together for a discussion session

formal: structured according to standardized rules

fragmentary: made up of many small pieces, with no clear or complete ordering

framing: placing something in the context of an organized set of ideas (a perspective)

fundamental: general or basic

fuzzy front end: earliest phase of the product or service development process

generative: producing ideas, insights and concepts

Google scholar: search function in Google that searches databases of published (scientific) journals and books

GLOSSARY

grounded theory: approach to data analysis, in which the researcher forms new insights from the data alone, not starting from existing theories

group toolkit: generative toolkit intended for group use

hierarchy: organization in levels, with lower levels being structured via higher levels

hypothesis: statement to be falsified or confirmed in a formal experiment

idea: unit of thought, either abstract or concrete; e.g., 'home' and 'tree' are two English words referring to ideas about objects in the world

ideating: the process of generating ideas, e.g., solutions to a problem or opportunities for a context

identifying: establishing the identity of someone or something; recognizing patterns

immersing: immersing oneself in the data: exploring it with an open mind, connecting to one's experience

implications: consequences of the findings, typically with respect to the client's strategy or the product's specifications

incentive: reward (often financial) given to participants to motivate their participation in a study

incubation: incubation time: a phase in creative activity in which we do not consciously think about the topic, but let it rest

induction: logical thinking process, reasoning from multiple specific statements to a general statement

industrial design: design discipline, mostly focusing on objects created by means of mass production

infographics: communication tool, typically used to express complex theories or research findings, that combines visual and verbal elements

information: (in DIKW) the interpretation of a data item; often in the form of a symbol or word

informed consent: a person's agreement to participate in a study or experiment, where the person was thoroughly informed of the purpose and the risks involved

insight: an understanding, a research finding that was previously unknown

inspiration: something that enables and motivates someone toward acting or creating

interaction design: design discipline, focusing on the interaction between users and 'interactive ' (i.e., digital, electronic, computer) media and products

interdisciplinary: involving different disciplines

interior design: design discipline, focusing on shaping the interior spaces

intervention: an action that changes a situation, e.g., in order to (attempt to) improve or learn about that situation

interview: research technique in which the researcher discusses a topic with a participant, often on the basis of a topic checklist or set of questions

knowledge: (in DIKW) ideas at a generalizing level, e.g., theories, categories, patterns

labeling: attaching a label, name, number or code to a piece of data, in order to be able to consistently refer to it and to retrieve it

latent: hidden, existing but not accessible until later in time

lead user approach: design approach (by von Hippel) in which users who have a high level of expertise about a product (often they modify the product for their specific purposes) are identified to collaborate on development of new products or improvement of an existing one

lean manufacturing: approach to optimizing an organization toward minimizing anything that does not result in (measurable) value

literature search: searching for knowledge in academic journals, conferences, reports, and media in general

maketools: generative toolkits with which participants create artifacts

map: spatial visualization of content. It may show pitfalls and opportunities, and supporting choices of routes and targets

marketing: discipline in product development, dealing with markets, consumers, etc.

material: ingredients, such as words, photos, symbols, samples, ... used for creating a toolkit

meaning: the relevance, importance and ideas associated with an object or event

medium: a technology used for communication, e.g., print, video, audio, ...

metaphor: creative process in which one idea is imposed on another as a pattern of properties, leading to new insights

mindmap: visualization technique (by Buzan), using a spatial arrangement of related thoughts, ordered in the form of a tree with short branches linking words and images

moderating: leading a group through a (creative) process, especially a session. Unlike a facilitator, a moderator is seen as responsible for content as well as process

multidimensional scaling (MDS): statistical data analysis technique which shows the relationships between objects in a visual map. The output of MDS places similar objects closely together, dissimilar objects farther apart

narrative: in the form of storytelling; involving, or having properties of storytelling

needs of users: requirements that people have regarding a situation, product, or service

neutral: not taking sides or trying to push participants into a certain direction

opportunistic sampling: sampling method that is based on selecting primarily on the basis of easy to realize opportunities

outsourcing: delegating work to agents outside one's own organization

package: collection of generative exercises, maybe including a workbook, camera and assignment cards, toolkits, etc.

participant: somebody participating in a study or session

GLOSSARY

path of expression: process of reasoning about a topic, moving from the present, through memories, to future dreams

pattern: regularity or structure (in theories)

persona: a fictional individual expressing properties of a target group (often built up from field research)

personalizing: adapting to an individual's needs or characteristics

perspective: viewpoint, coherent set of ideas, or way of looking at the world

phenomenon: (in DIKW) that which happens in the world and is being studied

pilot testing: short test to validate and improve the basic functioning of a (research) procedure or materials

play acting: design (research) technique in which participants (e.g., users, designers, researchers) act out a situation in order to evaluate a concept or come up with design ideas

prime: a condition or stimulus that prepares a person toward a certain condition

probe: ambiguous, creative toolkit sent to members of the target group in order to elicit feedback to inspire the designer(s)

product design: design discipline focusing on physical products

proofing: checking (a text) for correctness or for a match to the original

prototype: artifact created to explore a (design) question; also: artifact expressing a conceptual design, used in evaluating the idea with users or technologists

provoke: to evoke, by deliberate action

psychology: scientific discipline, focusing on understanding individual humans

qualitative: research aimed at in-depth understanding of human situations, behavior and motivations. Often explorative, using small samples of participants involved intensively. Often with an eye for many different facets of the specific situation of the people involved

quantitative: research aimed at numerical findings and statistical testing of theories about human situations, behavior, and motivations; often starting from and aiming for general theories at abstract levels

questionnaire: research technique in which a list of questions, open-ended or closed-form, are presented to a (large) number of respondents. These days, often conducted online

reasoning: the process of connecting ideas, often to solve a problem or create an opportunity

recruiter: agent who finds people willing to participate in a study, typically in an agency specialized for this purpose

recruiting: finding, selecting, and convincing people to participate in a research activity (here, as participants/respondents in a study)

redundancy: the quality of the same meaning being shown through multiple indicators

reflection: the process of thinking about an idea, or a part of one's life

relevance: being considered as appropriate and useful for the interests of those concerned

research: activities aimed at producing and sharing knowledge

respondent: someone who responds to questions or requests posed in a study

retrospect: in hindsight; understanding which originated looking back after the fact

rigor: adherence to the accepted rules of reasoning and research method

ritual: activity, possibly with symbolic or affective value, conducted periodically and in the same manner

sampling: method of finding and selecting participants for an experiment or study

scaffold: a framework for organizing findings and/or insights

scanning: reviewing data or text in looking for occurrences of a pattern

scenario: a story, typically of how people perform a part of their lives, or an interaction with a product or service

scope: range of a topic that fits within the aim of a study (i.e., the outer boundary of content)

screening: selecting potential candidates based on their responses to a list of specified requirements

secondary research: finding knowledge reported by others (e.g., literature search, expert opinions), as opposed to gaining insight from first-hand experience (e.g., fieldwork)

semantic: having to do with meanings

sensitizing: raising someone's awareness about factors concerning a topic

serendipity: unexpectedly finding valuable new ideas along the search for something else

service design: design discipline, focusing on services provided to customers

session: group meeting with a specific task or purpose

setup: the result of a plan or orchestration

significance: in design, a practically significant difference is one that is large enough to warrant design decisions; in statistical testing, a significant result is one that is large enough to convince the research community (in research about people, often $p < 0.05$)

similarity: likeness

snowball sampling: a form of opportunistic sampling in which participants are asked to bring along other participants from their personal network

social network kit: generative toolkit aimed at expressing relations between people

sociology: scientific discipline, focusing on people as groups

spreading activation: a model of associative thinking in which activating an idea is followed by automatic activation of related ideas

spreadsheet: computer program (such as Excel) to organize data, typically in rows and columns, supporting filtering, sorting, and numerical operations

staging an event: planning and organizing an event, e.g., a session

GLOSSARY

stakeholder: anyone who has a stake in a certain process or thing (e.g., users, family, producers, lawgivers, ...)

statement card: card used in data analysis, showing connection between a quote, its interpretation, and the person making the interpretation

stereotype: fixed idea about a person or thing, used as a model for all persons or things like them

storyboard: visual form of a scenario, often resembling a comic strip with captions

subjective: (1) related to the individual, (2) judged by an individual

survey: quantitative research technique for determining a target group's opinion or characteristics, often using a questionnaire sent to a large sample of participants from that target group

sustainable design: design which makes responsible use of (the world's) resources, through using reclaimable materials, low energy consumption, fitting the needs of people, etc.

sympathy: a positive affect towards a person or thing

tacit: silent. Knowledge that we have, but are not readily able to bring into words

target group: group of people (often a demographic segment) envisaged as end-users or consumers of the product or service being developed

technique: the way to use a tool in a study

temporal: having to do with time

theory: an explanation of phenomena (at the knowledge level in the DIKW model)

thought: an idea in the mind; see thinking, idea

timeline: horizontal line marking a stretch of time, e.g., a day, a project, or an activity

timeline toolkit: generative toolkit, giving a timeline and triggers to construct, e.g., a day in the life story

tool: instrument or product used for a specific purpose

toolkit: a generative toolkit is a set of materials to support the making of an expressive artifact

topic: area or dimensions of interest of a study

transcript(ion): a word-for-word record of everything that was said during an interview or session

transformation design: design discipline, focusing on organizations and organizational change

triangulation: in analysis: using different sources to provide more trustworthy evidence about a theme or conclusion. In data triangulation, multiple data sources (e.g., observations, quotes) are compared. In researcher triangulation the interpretations of one piece of data by different researchers are compared

trigger: something (such as an element in a toolkit) designed to evoke thoughts or associations

unambiguous: having only a single interpretation

unmet needs: people's needs which are not satisfied by their current condition

usability test: design research method, in which the ease of use and learnability of a product (or prototype) by users, typically from the target group, is evaluated.

user need: see need

validity: an aspect of trustworthiness. Internal validity: whether all steps in the study were consistent. External validity: whether the study was carried out in a way that its findings are relevant for the real-life situations they address

value: of something for someone is how good, beneficial that person holds that something to be (see also values)

values: that a person holds are the criteria he or she uses to determine if things are good, desirable, or not

variable: factor in a theory which can take on different values for different objects or people, e.g., age, location, price, motivation, ...

Velcro modeling: creating a 3D object using a toolkit that contains Velcro-covered objects and small Velcro-backed components

Velcro toolkits: generative toolkit for creating 3D artifacts, consisting of a large collection of Velcro-covered objects and small Velcro-backed components

verbal: in words (as opposed to feelings, bodily expressions, images, etc.)

vision: an idea of how the (future) world may or could be

wisdom: (in the DIKW model) level of understanding which steps above the level of knowledge

workbook: a booklet or package of evocative assignments and exercises used in sensitizing participants for a session

workplan: plan for a project or a session; typically this includes hours, materials, roles, and a precise script of the process

workshop: collaborative way of working, in which a group of people works out a sequence of assignments, typically in analysis or communication

INDEX

The index covers parts 1 and 3 of the main text. Occurrences in part 2 and the external contributions are only pointed to a few times, because the use of the entries there is sometimes different, and the cases in part 2 give examples. For each of the entries, we chose a 'most natural' form (e.g., verb, noun, or adjective), and if the same word has two very distinct meanings, the references are separated on two lines, with the differences being indicated in parentheses.

INDEX

INDEX

INDEX

INDEX

INDEX

INDEX

COLOPHON

BIS Publishers
Building Het Sieraad
Postjesweg 1
1057 DT Amsterdam
The Netherlands
T +31 (0)20 515 02 30
bis@bispublishers.com
www.bispublishers.com

ISBN 978 90 6369 284 1

Copyright © 2012 BIS Publishers,
Elizabeth B.-N. Sanders and
Pieter Jan Stappers

4th printing 2018

Design by Trapped in Suburbia

Liz Sanders joined the Design Department at The Ohio State University as an Associate Professor in 2011 after having worked as a design research consultant in industry since 1981. She has practiced participatory design research within and between all the design disciplines. Her research today focuses on generative design research, collective creativity and transdisciplinarity. Liz is also the founder of MakeTools where she works at the front end of the changes taking place today in design. Her goal is to bring participatory, human-centered design thinking and co-creation practices to the challenges we face for the future. Liz has a Ph.D. in Experimental and Quantitative Psychology and a B.A. in both Psychology and Anthropology.
liz@maketools.com sanders.82@osu.edu

Pieter Jan Stappers came to design with an MSc in Experimental Physics and a PhD on using Virtual Reality for perception studies. In 1984 he joined the Faculty of Industrial Design Engineering of Delft University of Technology, where his work focuses on developing tools and techniques to support the early phases of designing. Research emphases are context-mapping, interactive prototyping, and the role of design skills in doing research (i.e., research through design). He also teaches these elements in the BSc, MSc, and PhD design programmes in Delft, together with a team of researchers, educators and students at ID-StudioLab.
p.j.stappers@tudelft.nl

www.convivialtoolbox.com